"OTHER TONGUES—
OTHER FLESH"

GEORGE HUNT WILLIAMSON

"OTHER TONGUES—OTHER FLESH"

A STARTLING SEQUEL TO "THE SAUCERS SPEAK!"

ILLUSTRATED

BIBLIOBAZAAR

"OTHER TONGUES—
OTHER FLESH"

CONTENTS

BOOK I
GOD PROVIDED—MAN DIVIDED

BOOK II
OTHER TONGUES

BOOK III
OTHER FLESH

LIST OF ILLUSTRATIONS

ABOUT THE AUTHOR

George Hunt Williamson served with the Army Air Corps during World War II as Radio Director for the Army Air Forces Technical Training Command. He was a member of the AAFTTC Headquarters Staff. He received the Army Commendation Award from Brig. Gen. C. W. Lawrence for his outstanding record of service to the Air Force in Public Relations. He served as an instructor in Anthropology for the United States Armed Forces Institute, and was later appointed Lieutenant in the U. S. Infantry.

He attended Cornell College, Eastern New Mexico University, the University of Arizona, and took a special course at the University of Denver. He majored in anthropology with many courses in sociology, biology, philosophy and geology.

In 1948 he was awarded the coveted Gold Key for outstanding scientific research by the Illinois State Archaeological Society. He has spent a great deal of time doing field-work in Social Anthropology in the northern part of the United States, Mexico and Canada. He is an authority on Indian dances, music and ceremonial costuming. Several of his articles have appeared in scientific journals.

He is listed in the July, 1952 Supplement to "Who's Who In America", and his name appears in the latest editions of "Who Knows, And What", and "Who's Who in the West". He is included in Volume Twenty-Nine of "Who's Who In America", and also in "American. Men of Science".

He is co-author of *The Saucers Speak!* (A Documentary Report Of Interstellar Communication By Radiotelegraphy).

Mrs. Williamson, the former Betty Jane Hettler, is a chemist and an anthropologist, holding an A.S. degree from Grand Rapids Junior College; a B.S. degree from Eastern New Mexico University; and a B.A. degree from the University of Arizona. Both are members of the American Anthropological Association, and the American Association for the Advancement of Science.

FRONT FLAP TEXT

In more recent times, there has been a growing realization that on other worlds than ours, even in other universes, there are other living beings. The idea that earthbound man may someday journey into the heavens to discover other men and women, like or unlike himself, "grows by leaps and bounds. Within man's soul lies the truth—mortals exist on other spheres!

Here is a book that brings home this tremendous fact with a dynamic force and sweep that will astound the reader, and convince him beyond all doubt. Here is a *history*, a collection of *proof*, and a tremendous *theory*.

While man in his heart knows that other worlds are also inhabited, he is reluctant to admit that Earth is only one small house of the "many mansions" in the Father's house. But the truth stares him in he face, and now, having arrived at a place in his civilization where only Truth will be able to survive, it has become necessary to reaffirm

(More on inside back flap)

BACK FLAP TEXT

(Continued from front flap)

and establish three truths, namely: 1) Science and religion are one and the same thing; 2) The entire universe is magnetic in nature, and even culture is influenced by the laws of magnetism; 3) Space visitors, mentioned in the Bible and ancient mythology, have been coming to Earth throughout the ages, and are now making themselves known to aid mankind in entering a New Age.

In this book, many references and quotations are given from the latest authentic reports on Saucer phenomena. Because many believe there are contradictions in some of the reported happenings, it has been necessary to show that there is a great story and purpose behind all these experiences.

Here, in this book, is the history of *other tongues*, and of *other flesh*; calm, scientific evidence that there are brothers of ours in the skies overhead.

We are not alone in the Universe!

JACKET DESIGN BY RAY PALMER

PROLOGUE

Before the eyes of Milton's Satan peering into Chaos appeared a new expanse, another vast illimitable ocean without bounds—the distances of interstellar space; and for a moment Satan was appalled by Chaos and by space. So it is with modern man as he discovers new worlds like his own in the heavens about him . . .

The world has not let the theme of cosmic voyage willingly die, whether in poetry and fantasy, in satire or seriousness, in the pulps or in the comics. There has been the growing realization of the possibility of other universes than ours, a *plurality* of worlds, even an *infinity* of worlds. We have become more fully aware of the insignificance of both our satellite, the Moon, and this rather small planet, the Earth. Man began to think that if Life possibly did not exist on other planets in this system perhaps it would be found in other universes.

The idea that earthbound man may someday journey into the heavens to discover other men and women, like or unlike himself, seems to be a conception the world persists in entertaining. From the time of Lucian it has existed in European literature. Why the appeal of this perennial theme? Is it curiosity? Is it humility? Is it perhaps a result of the essential loneliness of man? Is it because within man's soul lies the truth—that mortals exist on other spheres?

From a fanciful vision of other worlds where all is beautiful and good and just, we come back in somber mood to Earth which seems indeed a sad and silent planet. Man on Earth knows in his heart that other worlds are also inhabited, but he is reluctant to admit even to himself that Earth is only one small house of the many mansions in the Father's House; and worse, that she is a fallen house; a disobedient house; a wayward house.

In 1867, Matthew Arnold described the Earth well when he said: ". . . a darkling plain, swept with con-fused alarms of struggle and flight, where ignorant armies clash by night."

The people of Earth today are either confused, amused, or simply terrified by the reports of Unidentified Flying Objects and various types of extraterrestrial space craft seen in the skies and detected under the seas. If they accept the theory that life exists on other worlds besides our own, they cannot believe anything but stories of monsters, robots, sinister vegetables, or armies of evil, invading, mechanical Frankensteins.

Many people today are asking: "If spacemen are here, why don't they land and contact our leaders? Why don't they explain their mission?" Did these same individuals ever stop to think that no sane Earthman would descend into a pit of crawling rattlesnakes? With all Earth's strife, with bloody wars that carry thousands of men, women and children to slaughter worse than any Circus of Nero or Medieval Inquisition, is it any wonder that spacemen have not landed here? However, these brothers from outer space *have* landed here, and they *have* contacted those whom they knew would receive them in the spirit of brotherly love and truth. It is now reliably reported that over one-hundred personal contacts have been made between Earthmen and Saucer occupants. They sought and seek those who have been looking for them. This is what they mean when they say: "We do not choose you; you choose us!"

Would these highly developed beings care to contact those who have held the people in slavery for centuries? No, because their coming to Earth will eliminate all forms of greed and selfishness. The actual "owners" of the Earth are on the side of the negative-dark forces, while the "Sons of Light" of the Space Confederation are of a *higher authority*. And being of a higher authority, they seek out those who love TRUTH and Truth alone. Like Diogenes, they search long and unceasingly, but unlike Diogenes, they find a man here and a man there; not many, but some.

The people of Earth like to picture themselves as Lords of Creation. One well-known anthropologist believes that far-off worlds may contain "gelatinous masses that control diabolic machines", but of men elsewhere, he positively states: "Never!" Those who do accept life as existing on other worlds believe this life will be much as it is on Earth: vain, full of pride, lust, greed; life that is warlike and aggressive as it is here.

While one hand turns thumbs-down on the idea of other planets being inhabited, the other hand writes on and on about the inhabitation of other worlds beyond Earth. People have been brought up on Buck Rogers, Flash Gordon, Superman, and many other fictional heroes of outer space. They have lived in a world of fantasy and make-believe for so long they don't recognize the truth when it is presented to them. Yet, our world of fantasy has its purpose.

Many gaze at the starry heavens and ask: "Is it all part of some gigantic scheme; is there really a Creator? Or have we evolved from a single cell that originally developed because of a freak accident in nature? Are we alone in the Universe?" Reason tells them that out of billions and quadrillions of worlds life must exist on many of them. And those who have complete faith in their Creator realize He wouldn't *create* Man and place him on one planet alone. They know He wouldn't create other worlds to be merely floating balls of poisonous gas or vapor. First came inhabitable worlds, then came Man!

Men on Earth are afraid that if suddenly other men on other worlds are made known to them, they will face awful retribution; that their horrible crimes against humanity and the Creator's Laws will not go unpunished. And like naughty children, they are reluctant to give up their dangerous toys and their destructive ways. So, now that their brothers from outer space are here, they are going to hide in a "closet" until these older brothers go home. Then they can come out and start their foul play all over again. One word of acceptance on the part of Earth-men and these brothers are liable to step in and teach them something, and children never like to go to school—especially if they have to be obedient and good.

Yes, there are brothers of ours in the skies over-head. They are not to be worshipped as gods; but they are to be listened to as one listens to an older brother who has traveled much and who knows the pitfalls of life and who has knowledge tempered with love of fellowman and the Creator. This brother of ours is attainable for he is here on Earth today! Will the men of Earth accept him? Whether they do or not, it is their right to decide.

Since man on Earth has arrived at a place where only Truth will be able to survive, it is necessary to reaffirm and establish three truths. Namely:

(1) Science and religion are one and the same thing. "God Provided—Man Divided". There is no religion higher than Truth and truth cannot contradict truth.
(2) The entire Omniverse is magnetic in nature and even *culture* is influenced by the laws of magnetism.
(3) Space visitors, coming to Earth in space craft, are mentioned in the Holy Bible, ancient mythology, and in other documents thousands of years old. These visitors have been coming to Earth for several million years! They are now making themselves known to the world as a whole to lead mankind thereby into a New Age as the Earth enters the more intense vibrations of Aquarius.

During the nineteenth century on Earth there was a *Great Influx* of Universal Truth. Many fine writings appeared, especially in the late 1800's. These scattered reports and ideas have a definite relationship to each other and tie into the pattern of present day happenings. Although these various writers use different terminology, they are essentially saying the same thing. They are telling Man that he is truly a god in his own right! This knowledge came to a selected few so that they could open the way for the world to awaken to a New Age—an Air Age to replace the ancient Fish or Water Age. What is the grand goal of it all? There is no goal, for we are heading for All Perfection but we will never get there. It is ever moving ahead of us as we progress. What then is the purpose of all our pleasure-pain experiences? We are to know perpetual *expanding grandeur*, thereby Spirit will come to know itself!

In this book, many references and quotations are given from the latest, authentic reports on the Saucer phenomena. Because many believe that there are contradictions in some of the reported happenings it has been necessary to show that there is a *great story* and a *purpose* behind all of these experiences. These same things have been taking place for eons! Some may wonder why I refer to the Holy Bible so often in this book. It is true that the Bible is inaccurate; but not totally so. For the most part it is the true history of a particular time and people. In order to get an accurate picture of the Saucer phenomena *every* possible avenue of investigation into the past and present must be utilized.

The author wishes to acknowledge the kind help and encouragement of others, for without them, this book would never been written.

Many thanks to Thomas M. Cornelia for suggestions pertaining to *Magnetism: The Universal 'I Am'*; to Neva Dell Hunter for ideas about *The Remnant*; to George H. Lark for library research on certain sections of the Divine Tetrad; to Lillian Laughead for her contribution of the Lemurian interpretation of the tracks on the desert; to Dr. Robert T. Lustig for ideas on the electro-chemistry of the blood; to Winchester Mac Dowell for the two illustrations of the electronic motion in the atom; to my wife, Betty J. Williamson, for research on the microcosm-macrocosm, and *Magnetism: The Universal 'I Am'*; to Frank A. Wing for his ideas about *The Prophets*; and sincere thanks to many others.

This book you are about to read is not an ultimate . . . no book is. It merely points the path, a signpost along the *Great Way* that leads to our Infinite Father. This work is dedicated to all men everywhere, with the hope that they shall know the TRUTH and the Truth shall make them free. Through *Other Tongues—Other Flesh*, may we learn to pray: "Father of us all, give us eyes to see, ears to hear, and hearts to understand!"

In brotherly love, I humbly submit this work to you.

George Hunt Williamson

BOOK I

GOD PROVIDED—MAN DIVIDED

CHAPTER 1

THE GREAT INFLUX

Space visitors put an intensification of the Cosmic program into effect in the late 1800's. The 1880's and 1890's saw the program manifest itself in strange phenomena and many books; new inventions and theories were suddenly put before the public. The Great Plan for the planet Earth moves along on levels of rises and plateaus. We are at present on a rising level. The 1890's experienced a rise, and the following fifty years was a plateau of leveling off time. The movement began before the nineteenth century, of course, but in a small way. Emanuel Swedenborg, scientist and mystic, brought great new truths to the spiritually hungry world in the 1700's . . . and there were other men, like Wesley and before him Spinoza; however the great mystic, Father Jakob Lorber, was born in 1800; Nikola Tesla, inventor, was born in 1857; Steinmetz, electrical wizard, was born in 1865; Charles Hay Fort, writer and researcher, was born in 1874; Charles Fillmore of Unity, was born in 1854; H. P. Blavatsky brought the great knowledge of Theosophy to the world in the 1800's; H. W. Percival gave the world his knowledge, and later, *Thinking And Destiny*; Dr. John B. Newbrough, in 1882, released his monumental work, *Oahspe*; Camille Flammarion, great French astronomer, was born in 1842; and among many others, P. D. Ouspensky, Lecomte du Nouy, etc.

Thus, in the last half of the nineteenth century, Universal Truth made a valiant attempt to penetrate the mind of Man before the Great Age of Materialism set in with the advent of the colossal Machine Age. Men like Brown Landone, and Flournoy, who wrote *From India To The Planet Mars*, *contributed* greatly to this expanding program under the influence of space intelligences. Even John

Jacob Astor got in the plan and wrote about the coining electrically governed world and interplanetary travel in 1897.

Besides a *Great Influx* of Universal Truth coming to the minds of Man, there was a definite pro-grain instituted on the physical plane and on the surface of Earth, itself. Space visitors were actually deposited and left on our world to mix, mate, and marry with us. The new ideas and theories first came out in book form, and this was the prelude to the appearance of spacecraft in the skies of Earth. In our present century, first came the science-fiction tales of space travel, then came the actual space visitation.

In Paris, France, in 1892, Flammarion said: "We dare to hope that the day will come when scientific methods yet unknown to us will give us direct evidence of the existence of the inhabitants of other worlds, and at the same time, also, will put us in communication with our brothers in space. What marvels does not the science of the future reserve for our successors, and who would dare to say that Martian humanity and terrestrial (Earth) humanity will not some day enter into communication with each other?" Then in 1896, Flammarion wrote *Uranie*, and in 1897 things really began to happen. Here's the report as taken directly from the old records:

Chicago Record, Friday, April 2, 1897: "*See Great Airship!* Kansas City, Missouri people excited . . . mystical black object casting before it red light startled whole city for the last two weeks! At last descended . . . ten-thousand people swear they have no hallucinations! Scoffers and disbelievers claim the people have been seeing the planet Venus or the Evening Star, even though according to the almanac this planet should have set below the horizon at least an hour before! Object appeared very swiftly, then appeared to stop and hover over the city for ten minutes at a time, then after flashing its green-blue and white lights, shot upwards into space . . . light gradually twinkling away and looking like a bright star. Time: 8:15 p. m.

"Everest, Kansas has sighted a strange airship, Competent reporters state that this must be the air-ship that was built in Oakland, California and which broke away at launching time . . . this giant air-ship hovered one half hour at a time and descended at regular intervals very close to the Earth. A giant searchlight flooded the whole city with light from this aerial monster which with the velocity of an eagle darted up and away. Power source must have been attached to the light for it dimmed as the ship went up and away. On observer states that there seemed to be a basket or car beneath a great dark object thought to be a gas *bag* overhead . . . car was shaped like a canoe and had four wings, two on each side, fore and aft . . . light was greenish or blue against the light of a locomotive in the rail yard that was yellowish. Colored lights seemed to be all around the car."

This unusual craft showed up later in Michigan, but before quoting from the record, let's analyze the above report. First of all, the authorities passed off the entire incident by calling the spacecraft the planet Venus. That same thing has happened in our present Saucer saga. They called the object Captain Mantell was chasing *Venus*, when it couldn't possibly have been that planet. This craft over Kansas City flashed blue-green lights and this color combination is now predominant in Saucer sightings of to-day. The report goes on to state that the power source must have been attached to the light for it *dimmed* as the ship went up and away. It is known today that the speed of Saucers has a great deal to do with the color changes.

Chicago Record, April 3, 1897: "*Flying Machine Now in Michigan!* People of Galesburg saw a brilliant white light approach from the SW . . . object appeared large and black with a crackling, sharp sound. It hovered close to the Earth. Reporters state that they heard *human voices* from aloft . . . from the airship! When the ship went off, it seemed to be tipped with flame. (Local comment was that the airship had caught fire!) Time: 10.00 p. m."

Chicago Record, April 6, 1897: "*Airship Now Into Illinois!* Seen first at 8:00 p. m. in NW . . . large red light. Suggestions of balloon are refuted because airship flew at tremendous speed into a high wind."

Chicago Record, April 7, 1897: "Airship seen many times last few weeks. Large numbers of people first hand witnesses. One time, a motorman of a trolley actually stopped his vehicle so he and passengers could look at the wonderful sight . . . just ahead of his trolley, the ship seemed about six-hundred feet up and about one-hundred feet long. The motorman, Mr. Newville, says it was ellipsoid with large projections fore and aft. There was a bright headlight in front and a red light in the rear."

From Hastings, Nebraska, came the report that the "airship" had been seen in Grand Island, Oxford, York and Kearney. Scoffers claimed these people had seen Venus, yet all the reporters were people of substance and not given to reporting spurious stories. This all happened in 1897, but we could date it 1956 and it would be right up to date. To-day, officialdom tries to explain much of it away as "natural" phenomena. Airplanes hadn't been invented in 1897 so they explained it away as balloons or Venus . . . today they say it's balloons, Venus, or airplanes . . . two-thousand years ago they might have called it "Apollo", or "chariots of fire", or "wheels within wheels".

Chicago Record, April 9, 1897: "*Airship Seen In Iowa!* Between West Liberty and Cedar Rapids appeared a bright light . . . giant airship . . . steel body. When leaving it appeared to be a large star weaving about and stars do not weave around the heavens!"

Chicago Record, April 10, 1897: "*Airship Sighted Over Chicago And Evanston!* People are tripping over themselves these days trying to get the best look at this green and white-lighted giant air-ship that has had the people all over the mid-west in a dither. Some people think the end of the world is near . . . Scientific minds have explained the whole thing away by now. The mystery will surely be cleared up in a few days. Mr. Carr, an aeronaut, has built an experimental balloon and is financed by a New York theatrical wig manufacturing company . . . Mr. Carr states his machine works marvelously, but *cannot go against the wind* . . . power is storage battery with propeller! Professor Hough of Northwestern University and head astronomer of the observatory stated when asked to train his telescope on the object: 'I am busy with sights on Jupiter and it would be too troublesome to change to look at this new thing.' The next day, Hough said: 'The thousands of people that are reporting this so-called strange airship are in reality looking at Alpha Orionis in the Constellation Orion!" This great scientist was too "busy with sights on Jupiter . . . it would be too troublesome . . ." Too *troublesome* to view for the first time a ship from another world! Although he refused to look at the object he seemed to know exactly what thousands of other people were seeing! How would he know since he only had the advantage of total ignorance?

Chicago Record, April 12, 1897: "*Giant Airship Continues Over Chicago And Environs!* People all over the city are in an uproar, and while everyone is viewing this grand sight on the south side, two amateur photographers who are news dealers in Rogers Park, looked out and saw the airship. Their photo shows the north Western Railway station and above it the purported airship! The photographers are Walter McCann and G. A. Overocker. This airship was seen to come in over the lake and traverse the whole city for several days."

The same report with an Omaha date line of April 11th says: "A gentleman brags he has mystery airship problem solved. He is an inventor and desires that he be allowed thirty-five acres to demonstrate his airship for the Trans-Mississippi Exposition. The gentleman didn't sign his name, but the reporter hopes the dilemma will be settled by his promises."

The same report again, with a Fort Dodge, Iowa date line of April 11th says: "Old German residents say that this very same type airship came over Germany thirty years before and the people were scared to death . . . said the devil's army was approaching and these were his vehicles!"

The same report again, with a Milwaukee, Wisconsin date line of April 11th says: "The residents of Milwaukee cannot be talked out of what they are seeing . . . thousands report the authenticity of a giant, beautiful airship with colored lights . . . the police records are full of the story for they have been called to answer what it is!"

Chicago Record, April 13, 1897: "*Airship Called A Hoax!* Several notable citizens are known to have caused airship scene . . . remains of paper and wood device in wreckage is in their yard. (No names given of the 'notables')."

The device mentioned was supposed to have been in the wreckage, but another column in the same paper said: "Airship seen in Rock Island, Illinois and Elkhart, Indiana!" How could it have been seen if it was wrecked?

Chicago Tribune, April 12, 1897: "One chap knows all about the airship. He says: 'These thousands of people didn't see a steel hull because this is the airship my friend has built in California and is on its way here to Chicago. Although, I must say, he sure has made good time for he isn't due until *next week* and the hull is *paper*, not steel. My friend, O. Chanute is on board too and I will introduce all of you to him when he arrives!' This chap is the Secretary of the Chicago Aironautical Society, Max L. Harmar."

The same strange sightings were made at Sisterville, Virginia. In 1897 and other years, there were amazing observances in Texas. The same old story, isn't it? Thousands of *people* in America observed this gigantic space ship . . . authorities called it Venus or Alpha Orionis, or a balloon. A balloon that couldn't go against the wind, yet the "airship" did just that. Notice where the report says: "Scientific minds have explained the whole thing away by now." That's exactly what they have been trying to do since 1947 in the present saga. Also, the idea that these are the "devil's" vehicles is thrown in as of the present. Not once a mention of their true nature!

The 1897 episode is very important: many space people were landed on Earth at that time. The Wright Brothers brought in the Air Age a few miles away at Kitty Hawk, North Carolina in the same era. (It is strange or is it?) that these brothers finally flew their controversial aircraft only a few years removed and a few short miles from the location where the giant, lighted "airship" of 1897 had made one of its final appearances?

After 1897 man progressed more in the coming half-century than he had in the previous ten-thousand years. Our progression is due, in part, to intellects coming here from outer space. Great men helped push men's progress ahead hundreds of years in terms of advancement. Where it had taken thousands of years to elapse between the discovery of the wheel and the bow, the greatest discoveries the world had ever seen followed each other in rapid succession. The telephone, electric lights, the radio, wireless, the automobile, the airplane, etc.

What actually took place in the 1800's was the first large public demonstration of spacecraft in the modern, industrial age. After the Industrial Revolution there had to be an influx of certain Universal truths in order to create a semblance between highly advanced technical skill and undeveloped spiritually. The space ships or "airships" of the nineteenth century were the physical manifestation of that *Great Influx!*

Communication with extraterrestrial intelligences also began at the same time. The father of wireless, Marconi, in 1921 believed he had intercepted messages from Mars or some point in outer space. The theory that the waves were produced by electrical disturbances was disproved by the regularity of the impulses.

Marconi conducted highly secret experiments before 1921 and knew beyond the shadow of a doubt that he was in direct contact with beings of other worlds! A woman in California writes: "During World War II was teaching in Scotland. In 1918, headquarters of the Y.W.C.A. in London wrote offering me the position of head of their branch office in Chelmsford near London. The main station of the Marconi World-Wide Wireless was also there. Many men from Britain died in World War I and it was my job to look out for many young girls away from home. I took room and board with a couple somewhat older than I. The husband was a very intelligent person and had a responsible position with the Marconi Wireless Company. One day, he asked me if I would like to go through the Marconi Station. I was delighted to go. During my tour through the laboratories I was startled and almost petrified when we arrived in front of a huge, ten-foot square, transparent case inside of which seemed to be a flaming mass . . . flames revolving like a wheel! I asked my friend what this was and he said that they had been receiving wireless messages somewhere outside of Earth! I asked him to be more specific. And he said: 'My dear girl, we have stations all over the Earth, but certain code is not coming from any of them! We are receiving signals from intelligent beings on other inhabited worlds!' My friend then told me that Marconi at that moment was in Australia conducting experiment and trying to discover more about this momentous happening. They believed the signals were coming from the planet Mars. I have never mentioned this experience before, and I believe Marconi kept his work secret because he knew what the world would say."

The lady who had the above experience lives in Santa Barbara, California and is a respectable citizen of that city.

Later in the 1920's and 1930's more strange messages were received throughout the world as radio was developed. And radiotelegraphic messages from Saucers are being received today! The first radio contact with space visitors was reported by our research group in Arizona in 1952, and now contact is being made in Ohio, Iowa, Canada, California, Detroit, Michigan, and other places. The contact is in both code and voice.

Space intelligences have said: "God provided—Man divided. Man has taken this true thing and added to it his own ring."

After the period of *The Great Influx*, science went a long way toward abolishing age-old theological dogma, but it went too far to the extreme and man became bathed in the new glories of the materialistic scientific world. Man on Earth had always de-lighted in dividing everything; there are continents, nations, states and commonwealths, counties and townships, cities and villages, wards and blocks, churches, cults, sects and isms, races and creeds, classes and clubs, societies and shrines, cathedrals and temples. But the Infinite Father is ONE!

Earth has been divided up so that instead of man being a brother to his fellowman, he has set up artificial lines to separate and segregate others different than himself. Man made boundaries, man made creeds and ideals, man made religious groups, man made doctrine and dogma, man made, man made. There is nothing wrong with religion, it's what man has done to and with it that's so pitiful. Science is the twin-sister *of* religion . . . truth cannot contradict truth, and there is no religion higher than Truth. The worship of the Creator and the study of His laws, causes and effects; of nature and the great powers waiting for discovery within her bosom . . . all these should be massed into ONE. Hence, science and religion are one, just as everything in the Omniverse is ONE!

When Van Tassel said: "We must present to science, the religion of science; and to religion, the science of religion," he gave the key for understanding between the two great fields of human endeavor.

To many people today, science is the modern savior or "messiah". They look to scientists and their discoveries for the answer to all of mankind's ills. Recently reports said that soon we could live forever through the latest discoveries in biological science. "What fools these mortals be", indeed! We already possess immortal life!

Thousands of spiritually hungry people have come to realize that the facts unearthed by science have not thus far been adequate to satisfy the needs of humanity, and many today are searching for something . . . orthodox theology has failed also to satisfy their deep longings, and orthodox science presents only cold, bare materialism to them. There are, of course, many scientists and theologians who are sincere, honest men, working tirelessly to aid men on this planet. But, at the same time, we must remember that all scientists are not "men of science", and all theologians are not "men of God".

Men are most reluctant to give up their secure, comfortable positions and pet theories. Desmond Leslie once said: "I'm convinced that the orthodox scientists of today are the counterpart of the orthodox theologians of the Middle Ages." Be that as it may, orthodoxy is the same thing wherever it is found, and it doesn't matter by what name you prefer to call it. Once in a great while a man comes along, or a woman, and although usually despised by their contemporaries, they manage somehow, by supreme effort, to haul all the rest of lagging humanity behind them and what we call worldly advancement or progression takes place.

In *Of Flight And Life* Charles A. Lindbergh says: "To me in youth science was more important than either man or God. I worshipped science. I was awed by its knowledge. Its advances had surpassed man's wildest dreams. In its learning seemed to lie the key to all mysteries of life.

"It took many years for me to discover that science, with all its brilliance, lights only a middle chapter of creation. I saw the science I worshipped, and the aircraft I loved, destroying the civilization I expected them to serve, and which I thought as permanent as the earth itself.

"Now I realize that to survive, one must look beyond the speed and power of aircraft, beyond the material strength of science. And, though God cannot be seen as tangibly as I had demanded as a child, His presence can be sensed in every sight and act and incident. Now I know that when man loses this sense, he misses the true quality of life, the beauty of earth, its seasons and its skies; the brotherhood of men; the joy of wife and children. He loses the infinite strength without which no people can survive, the element which war cannot defeat or peace corrupt.

"Now I understand that spiritual truth is more essential to a nation than the mortar in its cities' walls. For when the actions of a people are unguided by these truths, it is only a matter of time before the walls themselves collapse.

"The most urgent mission of our time is to understand these truths, and to apply them to our way of modern life. We must draw strength from the almost forgotten virtues of simplicity, humility, contemplation, prayer. It requires a dedication beyond science, beyond self, but the rewards are great and *it is our only hope!*"

All theology and science will not be done away with in the New Age. But under the incoming "Golden Dawn" Man will acquire a greater concept of Creation, free of ancient ritualism and the carried-over pagan ideas. Likewise, man will enjoy more radiant health due to the habit of right living and *right thinking.* Every man will be a scientist, even as space visitors are true scientists: utilizing the Forces of the Universe in the ever upward, spiraling climb toward divinity and the Father.

The Elder Brother, Jesus, said: "Know ye not that ye are Gods?" Man will wake up to this fact, and will leave the pupa of ignorance, *superstition,* dogma, orthodoxy, etc., to emerge as a "Son of God", claiming his rightful place in the divine scheme of things. Man is a co-creator with the Father, but he fails to recognize this great truth.

The great scientists of Columbus' time were no less great because they believed Columbus to be a fanatic for thinking the Earth was round. The mistakes of yesterday or today only point the way to the greater truth of tomorrow; with each new discovery we gain a greater comprehension of the whole.

Everything changes, but change itself. Let that change come; the Earth has been waiting a long, long time! Four thousand years ago, Job asked: "If a man die, shall he live again?" This question has been repeated in vain by every generation of men who have since inhabited the Earth. Now, space intelligences bring proof of life everlasting, and eternal progression.

In *Conquest Of Fear*, Basil King gives us a view of the future world when he says: "Taking Jesus as our standard we shall work out, I venture to think, to the following points of progress:

"The control of matter in furnishing ourselves with food and drink by means more direct than at present employed, as He turned water into wine and fed the multitudes with the loaves and fishes.

"The control of matter by putting away from ourselves, by methods more sure and less roundabout than those of today, sickness, blindness, infirmity and deformity.

"The control of matter by regulating our atmospheric conditions as He stilled the tempest.

"The control of matter by restoring to this phase of existence those who have passed out of it before their time, or who can ill be spared from it, as He 'raised' three young people from 'the dead' and Peter and Paul followed His example. "The control of matter in putting it off and on at will, as He in His death and resurrection.

"The control of matter in passing altogether out of it, as He in what we call His Ascension into Heaven.

Yes, it is true that "God Provided—Man Divided", but man on Earth must go back to the *whole* which the Creator made manifest unto His creation. Remember the words of Paul: "O Timothy, keep that which is committed to thy trust, avoiding profane and vain babblings, and oppositions of science falsely so called." (I Timothy 6:20).

The Truth alone shall make man free, and as Bacon said: 'Truth is the daughter of time, not of authority."

CHAPTER 2

THE GRAND MAN

In the Universe of infinite entities and infinite variety, Man is found manifesting in many degrees from Microcosm to Macrocosm. In the theory of Paracelsus, the Microcosm was man, as if combining in himself all the elements of the Macrocosm or great world. This theory in turn reminds us of Swedenborg who spoke and wrote so often about the Creator as *The Grand Man* of the Omniverse containing all the elements of the Microcosmic world. From the smallest unit of Creation to the most gigantic, there is a spiraling, circular progression. Early explorers went West to get East; and so in the Microcosmic world lies the answer to what the Macrocosmos is like.

Darwin said: "An organic being is a Microcosm, a little Universe, formed of a host of self-propagating organisms, inconceivably minute and numerous as the stars in heaven."

A. Bronson Alcott, in 1877 said: "Matter in particle and planet, mind and macrocosm, is quick with spirit."

So, we find matter manifesting and vibrating from minute to the monumental in various degrees, but SPIRIT permeates through all! In the great world of the Macrocosmos is it not logical and entirely possible that there may exist worlds so large in comparison with ours that their individual total masses may be millions upon millions of times that of Earth? And, if we grant that, is it not reasonable to say that in the small world of the Microcosmos we will find the direct opposite? In other words, atomic worlds containing real intelligent beings who live, work and love even as we?

For some time now scientists have been well aware of the fact that there is a Universal pattern of form in the minute that is duplicated exactly in the colossal of Creation!

Space visitors have said: "It is not right that man should destroy his brother by utilizing the powerful forces of atomic energy, but the destruction you witness is minor, indeed, compared to the enormity of *chaos* created in the Microcosmos by the release of such energy!" When an atomic bomb is detonated, literal Microcosmic worlds containing created life are destroyed. Of course, these worlds are in other dimensions of time and space: what we think of as a minute may be the passing of a million years to the Microcosmic citizen.

Infinity covers a lot of "territory", and we can easily have worlds and life so minute that we aver-age five-foot eighters cannot possibly see them with our organs of sight. If we accept this fact, we must also agree that there must be bigger worlds and bigger life forms. In fact, these forms could be so large that we couldn't possibly see them . . . and that brings us back to the Microcosmos.

In considering the present space visitations to Earth, we encounter Saucer occupants similar to ourselves in size and form. We do not find spacemen coming into Earth's atmosphere landing their craft on a pin head or Saucer pilots so large that they displace all the water in the Atlantic Ocean if they decide to take a dip. The reason certain space people are here and not other inhabitants of the Cosmos is because our Infinite Father has sent those brothers to us who are most nearly like ourselves in appearance and bodily size. After all, contact is difficult enough in a corporeal world without adding to the problem by sending a highly developed being who would have to announce the Universal doctrine to us from that pin-head or lovingly lead us like a Swift in *Lilliput!* The space friends here now may be far ahead of us in spiritual development, but they are probably more nearly like us than other dwellers in the Cosmos.

Before the consideration of similarities existing between matter and energy from the sub-atomic (microcosmic) through the astronomical (macro-cosmic) levels is discussed, it is important to conceive of what matter and energy are. Very recently, it was taught in our universities that most of the atom as well as most of the starry Universe was *empty* space. Now, finally, physicists are uncovering the facts that show matter and energy to be the same thing, though they cannot really understand how such a situation can exist. Their facts confuse their theories and they find themselves forced into retaining theories they now know to be inconsistent with the facts, for lack of any better theories. *Empty space* is a dead concept, for where is there no starlight? Yes, even starlight is matter and exerts pressure. Science has discovered that the famous little particle called an *electron* sometimes exhibits itself more as a particle and sometimes more as a wave. This is true also of the other so-called particles of the atom and of the Universe.

A particle can be an electron, other atomic particles, an atom, a moon, a planet, a sun, a solar system, a galaxy, a super-galaxy, and so on, ad infinitum. All creations (particles) in the Universe are similar because:

(1) All of them discharge energy. This might be considered as reference to fields of force; emission of rays; waves; frequencies; vibrations and forces. Briefly then, how can one picture something having both *particle* and *wave* properties at the same time? It is done by thinking of them as shells within shells. Some of these shells are visible to the eye as the Earth's crust, the layers of an onion, the skin of the body, or the "wheels within wheels" of Saucers. Some are visible with instruments which have determined the wave nature of electrons and other particles which emit quanta of energy. Some are detected by special photography as the four known fields of vibration around the human body and the atomic and molecular structures of various crystalline bodies as obtained by the British physicist, W. L. Bragg. The kind of motion that these shells exhibit, determines what the effect of that energy is to be. Heat, for example, is a wave pattern made up of a series of particles given off in quanta by an electron. It might be called pure energy moving with a *peculiar* kind of motion. The nature of the motion determines the effect produced, which can be any of the following: Nonvisible light; visible light measured as heat, or cold light. Remember that visibility and invisibility and the sensations of heat and cold are only sensations of the physical structure. Thus the real meaning of the term light is far beyond what is visible to the eyes. The

term light is used to designate the wave nature of all matter, its energy and its motion.

(2) In order for bodies continually to discharge energy they must continually absorb a new supply of energy. Thus the Universe consists of constant interchange of energy resulting in:

(3) A perpetual rhythmic expansion and contraction. For example, it is only possible for comets to travel at their terrific speeds for long periods of time because they are constantly replenishing their energy through their tail, and this energy is from a sun.

Now let us consider the tremendous likenesses exhibited by primary bodies beginning with the smallest we can detect, the sub-atomic:

Sub-atomic particles (and when we say particle, we must think of particle-wave for the two concepts are inseparable in speaking of basic structure) are to be considered in this discussion as particles that science can know only indirectly by their behavior Thus, heat energy given off by an electron might be comparable to satellites of the electron. Thus the electron gives off electro-magnetic radiation, which produces effects on varying portions of the spectrum depending on the kind of motion.

Perhaps these particles are those quanta of electromagnetic radiation which have been called photons and/or gamma rays. These rays, like X-rays, are without an electrical charge and are therefore not deflected in electric or magnetic fields. Gamma rays are electro-magnetic radiation of *very short* wave length, and high energy. Photons or energy vary in their velocity and thus energy according to the kind of radiation to which the matter emitting the photons is subjected.

If the radiation is in the high frequency end of the spectrum, then the photons will have a higher energy. In other words, the energy of the photons emitted by an electron subjected to electromagnetic radiation is related to the energy of the radiation, but the energy *is* emitted in distinct quanta. Photons are too small to detect experimentally in the high frequency portion of the spectrum. They are only detected in that part of the spectrum below visible light.

Photons or gamma rays by interaction with atomic nuclei have been converted into pairs of electrons and positrons (positively charged electrons). This materialization is a good example of the equivalence of matter (mass) and energy.

Scientists have divided the sub-atomic particles into two classes. The first class consists of particles which *cannot* occupy the same shell or energy level. These include the proton, electron, positron, neutron, neutrino and mu mesons. The second class consists of particles which *can* occupy the same energy level. Photons, gravitons, and pi mesons be-long to this class. The graviton is the unit of gravitational energy. According to the Unified Field Theory, gravity is just another aspect of electromagnetism like light, radio waves and other forms of electro-magnetic radiation.

Professor Vaclav Hlavaty of Indiana University Graduate Institute of Applied Mathematics recently achieved solutions to mathematical equations in Einstein's latest Unified Field Theory that revolutionize our concepts of energy, motion and matter.

Dr. Hlavaty's solutions to the Einstein equations reveal that electro-magnetism is the basis of the Universe . . . which goes beyond Einstein's attempt to unify gravitation and electro-magnetism . . . the twin forces in which he believes the Universe manifests itself. If Dr. Hlavaty's solution is correct, the basis of all cosmic forces—gravitation as well as matter and energy—is built up of an all-pervading, all-embracing mathematical field.

These theories will lead to the discovery of cosmic forces not even suspected today. *Gravitation* is not the basis of everything, but electro-magnetism is. Everything, including man, owes its existence to its electro-magnetic force field.

So-called gravity is created by the vortex of the particle itself and is related to the density and also the size of the vortex or electro-magnetic field. Thus the gravity exhibited by a sub-atomic particle may be greater than suspected at the present time. It is present as pressure toward the center of the field. Therefore, one might think of gravity as acting *inward* at right angles to the energy levels or shells. And to make a broader statement, we might say that all of the particles of the second class are acting at right angles to the spherical energy levels or shells, but the photons act *outward* and are given off as various forms of electro-magnetic energy. Both photons and gravitons modify the motion of their respective nuclear body in its role as a satellite to some larger body.

As electrons revolve about atomic nuclei in energy levels, so photons revolve around electronic nuclei, and when they are subjected to energy they are emitted as electro-magnetic energy in waves, the effect of which depends of their motion. For the possible effects glance at a chart of the electro-magnetic spectrum. The effects may be anywhere from heat on the far left, through radio waves, infrared, visible light, ultraviolet, and X-rays, to the high energy gamma rays just before the section of the spectrum designated secondary cosmic rays.

Gravitons are "particles" acting inward pulling from the center due to the pressure therein resulting from the expansion and contraction of the magnetic field which is a field of electrically charged motion. Due to the particular kind of motion of the electron in the magnetic field, no sensation of electricity is felt. The latter results when the negatively charged electrons move through the positively charged solution called *atmosphere* with a frictional motion. *Atmosphere* as used here, refers to the electro-magnetic field, not just "air".

". . . The particles that go to make up the ethers can be thought of . . . as sub-sub-atomic matter . . . and as you 'sub' lower than that we go out of existence as far as the world of matter measurable is concerned . . ." (B.S.R.A. Special Report, 10-C-53).

Now let us consider atomic structure!

Although we could probably be more nearly correct if we regarded all the so-called particles as motion rather than substance, we retain the physicists terminology in order that those who are acquainted somewhat with atomic physics can judge for themselves what is stated.

The old classical idea of an atom consisting simply of a positive nucleus with negative point-like electrons revolving rapidly around it is now found to be quite inadequate. Also, we are not so certain that there is a tremendous amount of *empty space* between these entities. For sub-sub-atomic matter would indicate satellites of satellites to a micro-infinity separated by the Infinite Light of the Creator, known to the Qabbalists as *Ain Soph Aur*, the Limitless Light.

The newer theory of wave mechanics envisions the electron as a standing wave undulating to and fro. When the electron emits energy its energy level or shell is contracted accordingly. When it absorbs energy the shell is expanded. The apparent mass depends on its speed. Since the electron rotates, we must now conceive of this undulating more or less spherical shell rotating or spinning. This rotation is brought about by the effect of flux set up by the charged solution in which the electron is found. The rotation brings about polarity, magnetism, gravity, electricity, etc.

Now, before we leave this discussion of what an electron is, let's include in our concept what would give rise to this more or less circular standing wave undulating to and fro. This can also be thought of as a manifestation of the vortex or electro-magnetic field. This effect can be pictured by imagining the wave effect of two series of vertical rows of fish passing uniformly between each other at a ninety-degree angle and then backing up. Would not this motion in rhythm give the effect of a spherical undulating wave? In the case of the atom these waves are produced by parallel lines of force passing between each other at right angles with a rhythmic "breathing" resulting from the positive-negative strain. The positive lines of force are composed of positively charged particles, and the negative lines of force of negative particles intersect them at right angles forming a flux effect. This intersection, when the lines are of equal density and vibration, forms an atom consisting of protons and electrons and an electro-magnetic field. It is because these two kinds of lines of force have different speeds that scientists have recently discovered that the speed of light is not constant at 186,000 miles per second.

Several months ago, a naval research engineer said he and four associates photographed a spot of light moving across a cathode ray tube at 202,000 miles per second, faster than the recognized speed of light.

Perpendicular to these intersecting lines of force are other parallel lines of force which extend infinitely throughout all space. These have an extremely high rate of vibration but no motion as to direction. This is what is meant by space intelligences when they say: "Light does not travel . . . light IS!" These lines of force establish polarity and the resulting effects. They are the creative causation force of the Creative Intelligence, and the insulating force between successive electron shells. They make possible creation of new particles and add to the rotation of particles already existing by spiral induction and partial penetration.

It is this force which condenses and escapes invisibly as a "neutrino" when an atom is "split". It is the part of the atom which undergoes a "resurrection." Physicists discovered the neutrino (which they believe to have a mass of less than one two-thousandth of the mass of an electron) from the fact that in the nuclear process of a neutron being converted into a proton and an electron there was some missing spin energy. The neutrino was postulated as the carrier of this energy.

It carries no electric charge, but an idea of its character might be more easily grasped by realizing that a beam of neutrinos would travel through lead of almost infinite thickness with no decrease in intensity. Indeed, the neutrino, which physicists can't see as they have seen tracks of other nuclear particles on photographic film, appears to be the creative light force of the Infinite Father. The Limitless Light . . . the *Light* that IS! It is the balancing force of the Omniverse.

In regard to the nucleus of the atom, physicists are considering various theories, trying to understand what holds its protons and neutrons together in the nucleus since electrically like forces repel. A qualitative answer is given by certain of the mesons, but quantitative measurements await further development, because the forces acting between a meson and proton or neutron are said to be approximately one thousand times stronger than the forces acting between an electron and electric field.

However, in keeping with the differences in the speed of phenomena within the atom, could we not say that the vortical currents were sufficiently strong to keep the nuclear matter concentrated in a comparatively small area regardless of its apparent mass relationships? In other words, if gravity is recognized as a force acting inward as a result of vortical currents of the atom, the weights and measures developed in the vortical currents of the Earth have no intrinsic value of themselves when referring to the atom. Information received by the B.S.R.A. states if one atom were ever truly smashed, your whole system would be turned into a super solar . . . nothing but light radiation . . . many millions of times brighter than your sun." No wonder space visitors are concerned over our atomic experiments!

Before we leave the subject of atomic structure, let's glance at the idea of the *inverted* atom. Physicists have found short-lived particles in all cases that are the electrical opposites of the prevalent particles in our atomic structure. Some of these, including the newly found anti-proton have been found in cosmic rays. These are evidently the particles that form atoms built with negative nuclei and positive satellites. Substances constructed of such atoms would be identical except that they would be *invisible* to our physical senses, which were constructed to recognize substance formed of atoms having positive nuclei and negative satellites. Physical vision is sensitive only to positive light reflecting from negative substance on a negative planet. Inner perceptions see colors resulting from negative light. Neither reflections from negative substance or reflections from positive substance *are reality*, and neither are they visions . . . they are only *reflections from reality*.

Now let us consider molecular structure:

The structure of a molecule is dependent on the structure of the atoms of which it is composed. Science has recently found that in order for two atoms of hydrogen to associate themselves as a molecule, their respective single electrons must have opposite directions of rotation or spin. Thus we see the positive-negative association into oneness reflected even in the molecule.

Like planets, some molecules possess rotational energy and others, such as the diatomic symmetrical molecules of hydrogen, nitrogen and oxygen, do not.

When atoms or molecules are arranged in perfect order, the result is known as a crystal. Irregularity of atomic or molecular order results in a fluid. A true solid state is always in a definite crystalline form. Crystals of pure metals have recently been studied and it has been found that different crystal faces of a metal behave as if they were entirely different metals. Evidently, the crystalline geometrical forms determined by the electro-magnetic field of the atoms produce a differing field on each face.

Crystals which do not have identical characteristics in all directions (not cubic) are called anisotropic crystals. When a ray of light enters an anisotropic crystal it is split into two components which travel with different velocities and follow different paths. Perhaps the crystal is here dividing the positive and negative light lines of force.

Another interesting fact of molecular structure that has recently been revealed is that the thousands of atoms in fibrous protein molecules such as those composing hair, horn, fingernail, muscle and porcupine quill, are arranged in the form of a helix. This form results when asymmetric objects (the amino acids) are joined together in such a way that each one has the same geometrical relationship to its neighbors. Some of these molecules then form a compound helix or a coil of coils, etc. Thus science is discovering the linking forms between the atom and the biological structures.

An electron micrograph of a bacterial flagellum has shown a three-strand cable which by its diameter suggests it is a seven-strand cable of seven-strand cables.

The space people have said that the forms of crystals within the blood are the source of energy for man's every motion. The crystals in the blood, by diffusing, refracting and reflecting the positive and negative light lines of force, and by opposing polarized conditions, bring about the flow of the blood by light energy and as a result, the functioning of the heart.

The fact that there are crystals within the blood stream is significant in relation to the use of the crystalline form in the Type 2 "fireball". For more information on them see *The Harvesters* in this book in the section called: *Other Flesh*.

Man, intermediate between the Microcosm and the Macrocosm, shows similarity to the atomic structure in the expansion and contraction of his muscles, in his rhythmic breathing to sustain life, and his shell-like fields of vibration surrounding the visible body.

Dr. Cecil Bowiby of Los Angeles, California, recently reported that he has succeeded in photographing four distinct fields of vibration around the human body which are in various colors invisible to the naked eye. They are, respectively, about one-half inch; six inches; three feet; and nine feet and over from the skin. He believes the fourth field is the strongest, that is, most extensive when persons radiate strong feelings, especially those of love and peace.

Now let us consider our own Solar System:

In *One Two Three . . . Infinity*, Dr. George Gamow says: "The picture of an atom began to look more like a miniature solar system with an atomic nucleus for the sun, and electrons for planets. The analogy with the planetary system can be further strengthened by these facts: the atomic nucleus contains 99.97 per cent of the total atomic mass as compared with 99.87 per cent of the solar system concentrated in the sun, and the distances between the planetary electrons exceed their diameters by about the same factor (several thousand times) which we find when comparing interplanetary distances with the diameters of the planets. The more important analogy lies, however, in the fact that the electric attraction-forces between the atomic nucleus and the electrons obey the same mathematical law of inverse square (that is, the forces are inversely proportionate to the square of the distance between two bodies) as the gravity forces acting between the sun and the planets. This makes the electrons describe the circular and elliptic trajectories around the nucleus, similar to those along which the planets and comets move in the solar system."

However, physicists have stressed the fact that "an atom differs from the solar system by the fact that it is not gravitation that makes electrons go round the nucleus, but electricity." (H. N. Russell). But what difference does it make, since gravity and electricity are both manifestations of electromagnetism! This is an example of scientists calling *effect*, cause . . . if they looked beyond gravitational and electrical phenomena they would find the *cause* of both, which is electro-magnetism.

Another difference was also discovered. An electron in an atom, on absorbing the energy of a photon (light), jumps to another orbit, and again to another when it emits light and releases the energy of a photon. Because of this phenomenon, comparison with the solar system did not seem valid. A critic said: "We do not read in the morning newspapers that Mars leaped to the orbit of Saturn, or Saturn to the orbit of Mars." This is true, we do not read it in the newspapers, but the atom with its system of electrons rotating around the central nucleus resembles the planetary system. In considering the atom, the jumping of electrons from one orbit to another, when hit by the energy of a photon, takes place many times a second, whereas in accord with the vastness of the solar system, a *similar* phenomenon occurs there once in thousands of years. Our own Solar System has experienced displacements in its planetary members over the centuries and this is similar to the "orbit jumping" of an electron.

The circular motion of an electron around the nucleus of an atom, or a planet around the sun of a solar system, gives rise to an intensive electro-magnetic radiation, and in this action they are *identical.* The circular motion referred to is an *effect* of intersecting lines of force.

Now let us consider the Galactic System:

Toward the center of the Galactic System is found the nuclear region which corresponds to the sun of a solar system and the nucleus of an atom. The many solar systems revolving about the nucleus region of a galaxy correspond to planets revolving about a sun and electrons revolving about an atomic nucleus.

At present astronomers are wondering whether magnetic fields exist in the galaxy. Cosmic radiation suggests an answer. The intensity of cosmic radiation is almost the same anywhere on the globe. This indicates that magnetic fields are bringing about a random distribution of cosmic rays in space. Cosmic ray evidence is considered the strongest argument for the existence of these fields. If an atom and a solar system operate in an electromagnetic field, we would expect to find a galaxy also operating in such a field. The rotation at the edges of a spiral galaxy is slower than near the center, just as the outer planets in the solar system travel slower than those near the sun.

The new word in astronomy is "magneto-hydrodynamics." Scientists say that interstellar space is now known to be *pervaded* by magnetic fields. Presumably they are produced by electric currents circulating in space, say the astronomers. Modern theory begins to visualize a galaxy as a tremendous electro-magnet, with currents of electrons flowing not through wires but through the viscous, turbulent eddies of gas swirling about its center. Electromagnetic forces seem competent to do what turbulence alone cannot do: they might form discrete arms and even lead to the formation of stars and clusters of stars. The modern theory of a galaxy, according to astronomers, promises to be as intricate as the now richly observed structural details. Ten years ago in their hypotheses of cosmic evolution they were thinking in terms of gravitation and light pressure. Only yesterday they realized they may contemplate a galaxy that is essentially a gravitating, turbulent electro-magnet.

Now let us consider the Supergalaxy:

Recent evidence obtained by photographic and radio astronomy indicates that our disk-shaped galaxy we call the Milky Way is itself a member of a disk-shaped galaxy or supergalaxy. The supergalaxy of which we are a member may have a population of tens of thousands of galaxies. Its nucleus is marked by the cluster of galaxies in the constellation Virgo. Radio waves are picked up from the super-galaxy just as they are picked up from near galaxies and the Milky Way. From study of the radial velocities of galaxies, the indication is that the "inner metagalaxy" (that is the nearest regions of extra-galactic space) is rotating. This rotation is believed to be a property of the local supergalaxy. Several other supergalaxies have been found indicating the possibility or rather probability of a hierarchy of systems of ever greater size *ad infinitum*. Also, scientists have come to the conclusion that the Universe has been expanding since about five billion years ago before which it was contracting. Even the Universe is "breathing" as do the lines of force that bring about the atom.

Space intelligences have said: "Progression is only recorded by change and one who understands even his present environment is indeed a master."

In 1888, S. Harris said: "Suns and planets and cosmic forces are the words in which His thoughts are written."

CHAPTER 3

MAGNETISM: THE UNIVERSAL 'I AM'

In the discussion of *The Grand Man* of the Universe, we have shown the similarity, or *oneness* of all Creation from Microcosm to Macrocosm.

When we previously mentioned an electromagnetic field or vortex, we were referring to the Fourth Great Primary Force, or the *Resonating Electromagnetic Field* (RMF) which present day science knows nothing about although they suspect its existence.

The Four Forces are: Static-Magnetic Field (SM), as in a bar magnet; Electro-Static Field (ES), as in a charged capacitor; Electro-Magnetic Wave (EM), as radio waves, light, heat, etc.; Resonating Electromagnetic Field (RMF), like that of all celestial bodies (operating in a vortex), space craft propulsion field, the basis of life, the elemental life.

Throughout space are positive and negative parallel light lines of force running between each other at right angles and consisting of charged particles vibrating at varying rates producing a rhythmic wave effect of bands. These lines of force also vary in the number of particles they contain in a given distance, that is, they vary in their density. When negative and positive lines or bands (equal to the diameter of the particle to be) with equal densities and vibrations cross, a vortex is set up which condenses the *positive* particles and these become *substance* as nuclei ... either a proton (atomic nucleus), or a comet (early evolutionary form of a planet), or a sun (nucleus of a solar system). The *negative* particles are condensed as the *Resonating Electro-magnetic Field* (*vortex*) of an atom, a planet, or a sun.

When the positive particles have condensed sufficiently, and the surrounding negative vortex has gained sufficient strength, the insulating force of pure light between and around the positive and negative forces is reduced and polarity is set up from the flux motion of the positive and negative. A strong vortex is indicated by flattened poles (oblateness) and equatorial bulging in the particle. If the vortex breaks the substance disappears as it returns into the solution of the light lines of force, known as the ether or space. (The vortex of the planet Lucifer, the planet now known as the asteroid belt, broke through hydrogen experimentation.) When the particle is sufficiently polarized, rotation results from the constant application of the positive and negative light forces to the vortex.

A comet travels in the currents of the sun's *vortex* (RMF) until its own vortex (RMF) breaks (The Andromedes, or Bielid meteors move in the path of the lost Biela's comet which disintegrated and was last seen in 1852) or it becomes sufficiently powerful to attain an orbit of its own, in which case it becomes a planet.

Now let us consider three bodies which operate in a Resonating Electro-magnetic Field of Force: (1) The Sun (acting as a nucleus): One-hundred years ago, in 1854, the eminent astronomer Sir William Herschel suggested that the Sun may be inhabited and that the inhabitants may no more suffer from intense heat than those who live in the tropical regions of Earth! He believed the Sun to be a cool body, not a hot, flaming gas ball.

Since it has been shown that the satellite planets are magnetic in nature, it is only right to assume that the governing body that rules those planets is also magnetic in nature. So, we might say that the Sun is the magnetic "brain" or ganglion of our entire Solar System. Its forces are the directing intelligence of all the functions of our System. It is from this great central, nuclear body that the planets draw their magnetic energy so that they, too, may generate forces.

The Sun's vortex is very intense as would be expected of such a huge body, and it must extend to the very outer limits of the System. Its atmosphere has three main layers: the chromosphere; the reversing layer; and the photosphere. Completely enveloping these layers is the corona. When photographed in hydrogen light the Sun displays its magnetic structure very well. Such a photograph shows a grainy effect very similar to that produced when iron filings are sprinkled in a magnetic field.

Scientists today state that the Sun is a gigantic atomic furnace radiating a tremendous amount of heat to the satellite planets each second. The temperature at its surface is said to be thousands of degrees and the internal temperature is supposedly in the millions of degrees. However, it is unexplainable how super-heated gasses can act magnetically. For, it is an elementary fact of physics that a substance loses its magnetism when heated! Since astronomers have definitely recorded magnetic effects upon the Sun, we have a direct conflict between the Sun's true nature and the suggested temperature. This conflict only indicates that the Sun is not the super-heated mass of gases that scientists think it is, but rather, a cool body as Herschel said it was.

There is much evidence to prove that the Sun it, indeed, a cool body. The process of determining the Sun's temperature is very complex and involves the radiation laws of physics. Fundamentally, here is how such temperatures are determined: the radiation of the body per square centimeter per second, times the body's effective temperature quadrupled, equals the rate of radiation quadrupled times the body's luminosity divided by its diameter squared. In solving for the Sun, one comes up with an average of 5900 absolute degrees. The mathematics involved is agreeable, but astronomers base their calculations on these two assumptions:

First, they assume the Sun is a perfect radiating body; second, and most important, they assume that the Sun is radiating heat! This is because they believe that heat on Earth, as well as heat on other planetary bodies, comes directly from the Sun. People feel the heat when they stand in sunlight, so they say the Sun must be a burning mass radiating that heat. That is like saying a radio transmitter radiates sound waves because when we turn on our radios, we hear sound. But we know that such a transmitter radiates radio waves, and that these waves are turned into sound inside the radio!

In 1543, a great comet came closer to the Sun than any previous comet had and this was repeated by another comet in 1882. They actually entered the Sun's corona which supposedly has a temperature of one-million degrees absolute. These comets traveled over one-million kilometers through this blazing corona and emerged unscathed and with no change in velocity or direction. If the Sun is radiating heat, why weren't these comets instantly disintegrated upon entering a tremendous heat of one-million absolute degrees? Surely nothing could survive such a treatment!

Astronomers have told us that the planet Mercury is devoid of life because it is only thirty-six million miles from the Sun. They have told us that if Mercury was any closer, it would have turned into "nothingness" long ago. How then did the two comets survive without at least showing some effects of their journey through the Sun's corona? We must conclude that the answer is that the Sun does not radiate heat, as such! Therefore, it cannot be any kind of a super-hot body.

The prominences supply us with some more proof of the above conclusion. These prominences are said to be hydrogen gas explosions and first appear in the Sun's photosphere. There are many theories, but as yet astronomers have been puzzled over their origin. The behavior of these so-called "hydrogen clouds of gas" contradicts one of the oldest, and supposedly, most stable law of physics . . . the law of gravity of Newton.

Some prominences travel at the unbelievable speed of 450 m.p.s. and reach an altitude of one-million miles; that's one-hundred ninety-one thousand miles more than the Sun's diameter. To add to the oddity of this phenomenon, is the fact that these prominences rise to fantastic heights, and then just "hang" in mid-air, unsupported, in complete defiance of Newton's law of gravity! Others appear to "materialize" from nowhere, and hang motionless. Surely the Sun with all its tremendous mass and "pulling" power could bring these prominences down again if they were composed of hydrogen gas. Astronomers say they are composed of such gas because the spectroscope has labeled them such. But the spectroscope is very inaccurate because between the Sun's atmosphere and this instrument, the atmosphere of the Earth intervenes, and the upper atmosphere of our planet contains almost pure hydrogen. This could be the hydrogen that astronomers say is on the Sun.

Sunspots and prominences have puzzled scientists for years, yet they are part of the same phenomenon. Sunspots and prominences are manifestations of the Sun's auroral activity as viewed from different angles. They have never photographed the solar prominences except at the edge of the Sun. Prominences take the form, or appear as sunspots when seen on the face of the Sun. The shape and particulars of the prominences cannot be observed unless the light of the Sun is blotted out. These prominences are not super-heated hydrogen gas because their very behavior proves otherwise! They behave as *forces*, not as *elements* (gas, etc.).

The prominence force of the Sun is similar to the auroral force emanating from the polar vents of the Earth. This auroral force is known as the aurora borealis in the Northern Hemisphere, and the aurora australis in the Southern Hemisphere. The names, "northern" and "southern" lights, are also given to this phenomenon. This Earth force which is continually being sent into the atmosphere, has the exact characteristics of the prominence force of the Sun. Although it is continually emanating from the Earth, it is only seen at certain times when atmospheric conditions are right.

The auroral and prominence forces are *identical*. Under the thick atmosphere of the Sun are hidden planetary bodies which are emanating aurora forces known on the Sun as prominence forces. The fact that there are planets under the Sun's photosphere is also evident from the fact that in atomic structure the electrons are balanced by an equal number of protons within the nucleus. This makes a balanced system.

The prominence forces manifest in the atmosphere of the hidden, or inner planets, pass through their electro-magnetic field, then manifest once again in the atmosphere of the Sun. Then what about the so-called "hanging prominences" which "materialize" from *nowhere* in the upper atmosphere of the Sun? The solution to this baffling question can be found easily. When the auroral forces of the outer planets (Earth, Mars, etc.) pass through their vortex or electro-magnetic field, they are ultimately drawn into the great Sun body where they manifest. At this stage, astronomers observe the "hanging prominences" which "materialize" from *nowhere*!

Another puzzle that has confronted astronomers, is that some sunspots appear to have polarity, and that some prominences are pulled mysteriously toward certain sunspots. Prominences and sunspots have already been shown to be manifestations of the auroral activity of the hidden or inner planets under the Sun's photosphere. There are twelve inner planets and twelve outer planets.

Astronomers ask why sunspots arise at the more or less irregular intervals of eleven years, and why do first spots of a new series appear in high latitudes, and why is there a slow progression of the spots toward the solar equator as the sunspot cycle advances, and why is there a change in polarity of sunspots in alternate cycles? The answers to these questions will give an accurate and complete theory of sunspots, and the answers lie in the fact that the inner or hidden planets create these conditions by their periods of rotation and revolution.

Heat and light are effects of the positive rays of the Sun. Heat is felt on the Earth because the Sun's positive rays intersect with its negative atmosphere and crust causing a friction or change in the quality of motion of the particles given off as heat radiation in consequence of this friction. The effect of the Sun's rays on the Earth's atmosphere is also responsible for the phenomenon of visible light which results from a different kind of motion of the particles.

The eyes are only sensitive to positive light rays reflected from negative substance, thus light is an interaction of negative and positive forces. The Sun does not send us heat and light, although it is responsible for its manifestation on Earth; the Sun sends only positive lines of force which interact with the negative crust and atmosphere of the Earth to produce the phenomena of the electro-magnetic spectrum which includes heat and light.

Science has explored the upper atmosphere of the Earth and found that sixty miles above the Earth artificial light is needed, and ninety miles above the Earth it is dark as "pitch". The higher we go the colder it gets, so we see even by logic that heat and light do not come from the Sun. Only lines of force come from the great sun body.

Since distance and nearness to the Sun have nothing to do with whether a planet is "boiling" or "frigid", we can immediately see that all planets in our Solar System have nearly the same climate. The Earth does not enjoy perfect climate because it is unbalanced magnetically.

What has been learned from space visitors about our Sun is not really anything new, but only a return to the ageless wisdom possessed by the Earth's most ancient races. These students of the long ago said that the true color of the Sun was blue, and it is interesting to note that the musical note of blue is Sol, a name for the Sun, itself!

(2) The planet Earth (acting as an electron): As already stated, a comet is an early evolutionary form of a planet. But the behavior of a vortex in the formation of a particle such as the Earth has already been discussed.

H. T. Statson, research associate, M.I.T., says: "The source and nature of the earth's magnetism is still one of the great mysteries of science." It is still a great mystery because the Fourth Great Primary Force (RMF) is not understood; when it is understood a key will be found to many of the present day problems of science.

We cannot think of the orbit of the Earth as being merely a circle or ellipse, because it is a *spiral* also. This is because the Sun is moving through space at many miles a second. The Earth's orbit could only be an ellipse or circle if the Sun were standing still. Remember, the Earth is carried along within the solar vortex (RMF), in addition to following its own orbit.

The Earth's auroral force emanates from the polar vents at both north and south poles. The positive light lines of force leave at the north polar vent, and the negative light lines of force leave at the south polar vent. The bending of these light lines of force when they leave the polar vents manifests as the aurora under proper atmospheric conditions, and they follow the general form of the RMF.

Reports state that recent polar expeditions have discovered the actual vents or openings that lead into the interior of the Earth at the North and South Poles. Ancient tradition asserts the existence of a fountain of life in the bowels of the Earth and in the North Pole. It is the "blood" of the Earth, the electro-magnetic current, which circulates through all the arteries; and which is said to be found stored in the "navel" of the Earth.

Tschermak noted the resemblance of structure between meteorites and volcanic products. This is because both meteorites and matter or "bombs" ejected by volcanoes are created in a vortex. The "bombs" ejected from volcanoes do not come from the bowels of the Earth, but are actually created within the volcanic vortex which is a sub-vortex of the Earth's RMF.

Hurricanes, known also as cyclones and typhoons, are the most dangerous storms on Earth. Their vortex may cover half a million square miles. Sometimes a hurricane generates a number of tornadoes on its fringes. Hurricanes sometimes spend energy *equivalent* to that of several thousand atomic bombs per second. Therefore, we can see the tremendous power of a vortex. The heavy rains carried by a hurricane are concentrated in great spiraling lines which run inward, showing again the Universal spiral form. Tornadoes, whirlpools, etc., are sub-vortices within the Earth's vortex.

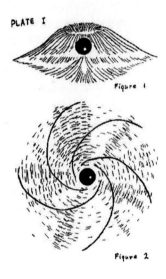

PLATE I

Plate I shows two views of the RMF of a nuclear particle. Fig. 1 shows a side view of the RMF surrounding a nuclear particle. Fig. 2 shows the same RMF viewed from above, and looking down toward the polar vent area.

In these illustrations the nuclear particle is shown as a black sphere. This sphere can represent an electron, an atomic nucleus, a Saucer, a moon, a planet, a sun, the nuclear area of a galaxy, or the nuclear area of a supergalaxy, in their respective Resonating Electro-magnetic Fields.

The shape of galaxies (spiral nebulae) as observed through the telescope is the perfect shape of an RMF. This shape is seen throughout the Creation from Microcosm to Macrocosm, and the form is Universal. Other examples would be the form of Saturn with its rings; and the shape of several types of spacecraft (Saucers). Celestial bodies and Saucers take the shape of their respective RMF, that's why there is so much similarity.

Spiral nebulae when appearing edgewise look like Fig. 1, and when they appear more nearly circular, because their equatorial planes are perpendicular to the line of sight, they look like Fig. 2.

(3) A Saucer (acting in an artificial and controlled RMF): The statement has been made that a Saucer can enter the Earth's vortex (RMF) because it has an RMF itself, therefore, a rocket ship cannot penetrate the cleavage layer of the Earth's RMF and is disintegrated because it does not operate in such an RMF. The rocket craft has a magnetic field to be sure, or else if couldn't exist, but it does not have a resonating force field about it.

Since Resonating Electro-magnetic Fields are found throughout the Omniverse, they are interacting and only a Saucer or spacecraft with an *artificial* and *controlled* RMF can travel in an interstellar manner.

Meteorites do not have RMF, and therefore, some will say they cannot penetrate the Earth's field or vortex. First of all, many meteorites and tektites are formed *within* the RMF of the Earth itself by a process of gathering together at a vortex center of primal matter present everywhere in so-called space. When these meteorites and tektites get large enough, like raindrops, they fall by the inward force of the vortex (scientists would say "gravity" and Einstein in his Unified Field Theory says "magnetism").

The Earth was originally created in this manner, and cosmic debris was gathered toward its vortex center until it was big enough and had a field intensive enough to go from the comet to the orbiting planet phase. The Earth is still gathering material daily and adding to its mass by the formation of meteorites within its own RMF. These meteorites drop to the surface of the planet.

The stone meteorites are created within the Earth's vortex, as are the tektites. These tektites do not come from the Moon as has been suggested. The iron meteorites are created by vortical action within the solar vortex (RMF).

An object that doesn't have an RMF will be disintegrated when it enters a vortex in proportion not only to the intensity of the RMF, but also in proportion to its energy which depends on mass and velocity. Thus, a dense, fast-moving object would not be disintegrated to pure energy, while a less dense, slow body would be if given the same expo-sure time in the same field.

For example, Capt. Mantell's plane was torn to pieces when it came in contact with the RMF of the Saucer, whereas it would have disintegrated into pure energy if it had attempted to enter the Earth's RMF.

Another example is found when we consider the asteroid belt between Mars and Jupiter. These asteroids are fragments of a planet once known as Lucifer. The question arises: "How could the fragments from this destroyed planet have entered the Earth's vortex since they did not have an RMF themselves?" The reason is that the asteroid fragments, or any other fragments beyond our planet's RMF, *can* enter the Earth's field . . . but they disintegrate by so doing. The law is NOT: "*Nothing* can enter the field unless it also has an RMF" . . . but the law IS: "*Anything* can enter the field, but it will be disintegrated in proportion to its energy (mass times velocity squared) and the intensity of the field (RMF) it is entering.

First, a fine dust came from exploded Lucifer and struck the Earth turning everything red, then a fine sand came, then coarser sand, then gravel, then meteorites destroyed villages. When Lucifer was destroyed, and its vortex broke, the smallest particles had the greatest velocity, therefore, the larger fragments came last. For more information on Lucifer-Maldek see *Maldek and Malona* in this book in the section called: *Other Tongues*.

Some researchers say that Saucers operate in a *static field*, but this is not the case. No interplanetary craft could travel as it does in a static field. Only utilization of the Fourth Force, or RMF will enable any kind of a craft to go from one world to another.

Saucers and all spacecraft contain their own atmosphere around them like a celestial body. They can go under water and the RMF will keep the liquid from touching the craft. Refer once again to *Plate I*: In Fig. 1, the black sphere can represent a Saucer in its RMF. The perfect shape of a spaceship is a globe or ball, and planets that have only recently succeeded in developing interplanetary craft use such devices. Celestial bodies are round and globe-like for the same reason. As a planet advances scientifically its technicians are able to intensify the RMF, and the Saucer takes

But thought is a perfect STATIC! ?

on the shape of its on field. That is why very flat, discus-shaped Saucers have been seen and also, globes have been observed. The more highly advanced the world, the flatter the craft. Eventually, no craft is needed to travel the interstellar distances, and beings are projected" to other worlds by thought alone! The reason Saucers sometimes have blinking lights on the top and bottom of their craft is because these are the polar vent areas of the ship, just like the polar vent area of Earth which emit the auroral force. Crossed lines of force exist at the vents, therefore observers see blinking of pulsating lights of various colors. North-South and East-West propulsion operates on different force. Also, a different force is used if the Saucer goes up or down.

The human being has a very complex field with a maze of vortices. Therefore a Saucer pilot can leave the RMF of his craft by two methods. First of all, as the Saucer lowers Earthward, its RMF is reduced and drawn into the rim of the craft. Otherwise, its own field would keep it off the ground. If the ship is to be lowered all the way to Earth, then the RMF must be completely drawn into the rim area. This action enables any occupant of the Saucer to emerge unharmed. Secondly, if advanced enough, a Saucer pilot can control his own field composed of numerous vortices and thereby go through another RMF of low intensity. When Christ walked on the water and performed other so-called miracles, he utilized such knowledge.

If the reader will refer to photographs of the crescent-shaped arrow-craft or mastercraft in *The Coming Of The Saucers*, by Arnold and Palmer, the craft's flowing center can be observed. This center is the polar vent area where lines of force are crossing. In the same book, mention was made of the Saucer that exploded over Maury Island. Sometimes the craft are not constructed perfectly, and their own RMF begins to tear them apart. The angle of incidence of a Saucer determines whether it has a high or low intensity field. Likewise, the more the poles are flattened on a planet, the more intense is its RMF.

From the Delawarr Laboratories, Oxford, England, comes the following information: "We have been able to materialize energy particles in a controlled magnetic field and would agree that the materialization of 'saucers' at certain positions in the earth's magnetic field is entirely possible." (B.S.R.A., CQC-B-7, April 1, 1954).

Many ask: "How are Saucers constructed? They don't exhibit rivets, bolts, screws . . . their surfaces are extraordinarily smooth and their openings don't show when closed!" Needless to say, a Saucer is not "built" as we on Earth construct anything. First of all, an electro-magnetic field is set up, and within this field, a technician constructs sections of a Saucer by his own powers of thought! This is similar to the vortex within the volcano creating the ejected "bombs"; or the Earth's vortex, itself, originally creating the Earth. After the various small sections are completed, they are joined by pins that are hidden from view. Therefore, no obvious joining-together shows from the exterior of the craft. People of other planets do not hammer and pound, cut and saw; they utilize their own creative abilities (such as we all possess) to construct their craft and many other objects. Their clothes have no seams, and this is also because they are "woven" in an entirely different manner than ours! In *The Secret Of The Ages*, Robert Collier says: "All about you is energy . . . electronic energy . . . exactly like that which makes up the solid objects you possess. The only difference is that the loose energy round about is unappropriated. It is still virgin gold . . . undiscovered, unclaimed. *You can think it into anything you wish* . . . into gold or dross, into health or sickness, into strength or weakness, into success or failure. Which shall it be? 'There is nothing either good or bad,' said Shakespeare, 'but *thinking* makes it so.' The understanding of that law will enable you to control every other law that exists. In it is to be found the panacea for all ills, the satisfaction of all want, all desire. It is Creative Mind's own provision for man's freedom. And now man is beginning to get a glimpse of the final freedom that shall be his from all material causes when he shall acquire the complete understanding that mind is the only *cause* and that *effects* are what he sees. There is no intelligence in matter . . . whether it be stone or iron, wood or flesh. Matter is Vital Force crystallized into the pattern we have given it. Mind is the only intelligence . . . it alone is eternal . . . it alone is supreme in the Universe. Therefore, all Vital Force is good. It is only our patterns that are at fault."

Before leaving *Magnetism: The Universal 'I Am'* it is only proper to discuss what I believe to be the greatest discovery pertaining to the field of anthropological science. Scientists have long pondered the question of what is culture? What constitutes culture? Why culture?

Cosmetology is called the science dealing with the effect of cosmic phenomena on life. If we consider it from the standpoint of magnetism and its effects on humanity and culture, it becomes sort of a science of *cultural magnetism.*

In *The Saucers Speak!* a space intelligence said: "On your Earth there are magnetic anomalies. Your scientists wonder why meteorites fall in a pattern in certain locations over the world. They also wonder why great civilizations are found where meteorites are found. The answer is simple. The anomalies attract the meteorites, and these same anomalies amplify Universal influx from outer space. Therefore, you will find better living conditions, finer art and music and so on in the same place you find the meteorites."

In geology, anomaly is a departure from the normal pull of "gravity" as calculated for any particular place on the Earth's surface. Scientists say that when positive, the anomaly indicates very heavy material beneath the surface; when negative, very light material. Examples of such magnetic anomalies are the Oregon Vortex; Mystery Spots at Santa Cruz, San Jose, Guerneville, and Los Gatos, California; Mystery spot at St. Augustine, Florida; and other locations are known to exist in several places in the United States. There are a number of vortices in the Ojai Valley, others in Canada, others in Mexico, etc. Scientists who have investigated the strange anomalies have only concluded that they know absolutely nothing about the causes for strange visual effects and other distortions in the various anomalies.

An anomaly has its own vortex which is a sub-vortex of the Earth's RMF. The anomaly acts as a Universal radio because it amplifies everything coming in from outer space. Highly sensitive individuals have strange experiences when they enter an anomaly area. Their ability at reception is increased to a fantastic degree. If man on Earth wants to communicate with other planets he should set-up his equipment in one of these vortices!

One of the interesting phases of the study of meteorites is their distribution over the surface of the Earth. If one would look at a world map that shows the distribution of the *iron* meteorites, it would be immediately seen that where the meteorites fall there is great civilization or highly civilized peoples. This, as stated before, is because meteorites are attracted to the anomalies, and the anomalies are amplifiers of Universal knowledge constantly permeating all space as the "music of the spheres." Great cultural centers are found over and near such anomalies! The individuals living in such areas are receivers of this Universal knowledge and it manifests itself in great works of art, music, literature, scientific achievement, architecture, philosophy, etc. Depending on what vibration an individual is operating in, he will create in one of these fields.

Here at last is the answer to: Why culture? Careful studies of geological maps in connection with the

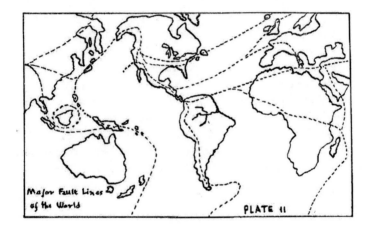

PLATE II. MAJOR FAULT LINES OF THE WORLD

number of cancer cases in different areas showed Brunler that the radiation (vortical action?) of the Earth must have an important bearing on this disease. Therefore everything man does, thinks, says, creates, etc. is *magnetic* in nature! Magnetism is truly the Universal '*I Am*'.

A study of the major fault lines of Earth also shows that culture follows these lines because magnetic anomalies are found along them as well as volcanoes. Trace the fault lines on the world map of *Plate II* and see where they cross areas of great cultural advancement. Remember, this does not necessarily mean civilized centers. Native peoples have created many wonderful cultural items that have never been equalled in modern civilization.

The many complex questions arising when origin of certain cultural traits are discussed can be answered by investigation of anomaly areas as they follow the fault zones of Earth. It is interesting to note here that the Seven Shangri-Las or Seven Great Hidden cities mentioned by Brown Landone are found directly over major fault lines of Earth! Any center of cosmic truth preserving the ancient wisdom would have to be located in such an area. Its inhabitants would require the amplifying qualities of the anomaly in order to continue their higher metaphysical research as masters.

Truly, *God Provided—Man Divided!* For all is magnetic, all is one, all is God!

Spinoza said: "The Universe is ONE. There is no supernatural: all is related, cause and sequence. Nothing exists but substance and its modes of motion."

BOOK II

OTHER TONGUES

ISHTAL—MAXIN

In the Solex-Mal, this is the symbol for the "All-Seeing Eye," the "Light of Creation," the four-pointed star stands for the Four Great Primary Forces of Creation, the flower of twelve petals represents the twelve planets.

CHAPTER 1

THE SOLEX-MAL

This is the symbol of the Solex-Mal, the Solar or Mother Tongue, the universal language of all mankind. This language was the original tongue once spoken on Earth by all people and is still used by the inhabitants of other worlds in outer space. It is a symbolic, pictographic language.

Solex means Solar, and Mal means Tongue. In Spanish, the word Mal means bad, sin, evil, hurt, injury, illness. In the drawing heading this chapter, we see the Solar Disc or Circle on the left. Extending out from this disc, to the right, is a curved or curled tongue. Therefore, it is literally a tongue as well as a language referring to a tongue.

How did the word Mal meaning tongue come to signify evil and other negative conditions? James 3:5-8 says: "Even so the *tongue* is a little member, and boasteth great things. Behold, how great a matter a little fire kindleth! And the tongue is a fire, a world of iniquity: so is the tongue among our members, that it defileth the whole body, and setteth on fire the course of nature; and it is set on fire of hell. For every kind of beasts, and of birds, and of serpents, and of things in the sea, is tamed, and hath been tamed of mankind: But the tongue can no man tame; it is an unruly evil, full of deadly poison.

Job 5:21: "Thou shalt be hid from the scourge of the tongue: neither shalt thou be afraid of destruction when it cometh."

I Peter 3:10: "For he that will love life, and see good days, let him refrain his tongue from evil, and his lips that they speak no guile."

Proverbs 10:20: "The tongue of the just is as choice silver: the heart of the wicked is little worth."

Proverbs 12:18: "There is that speaketh like the piercings of a sword: but the tongue of the wise is health."

Proverbs 12:19: "The lip of truth shall be established for ever: but a lying tongue is but for a moment."

Proverbs 15:4: "A wholesome tongue is a tree of life: but perverseness therein is a breach in the spirit."

Proverbs 18:21: "Death and life are in the power of the tongue: and they that love it shall eat the fruit thereof."

Proverbs 21:23: "Whoso keepeth his mouth and his tongue keepeth his soul from troubles."

Jeremiah 9:5: "And they will deceive every one his neighbor, and will not speak the truth: they have taught their tongue to speak lies, and weary themselves to commit iniquity." Jeremiah 3:18: "My little children, let us not love in word, neither in tongue; but in deed and in truth."

Again in James, 1:26: "If any man among you seem to be religious, and bridleth not his tongue, but deceiveth his own heart, this man's religion is vain."

In a Psalm of David, Psalm 39:1, we find: "I said, I will take heed to my ways, that I sin not with my tongue: I will keep my mouth with a bridle, while the wicked is before me."

There are many other references to the tongue of man in the Bible, but those referred to will be sufficient to show how the word for tongue in the original Mother Language came to be used in later languages and meant bad or evil.

St. Matthew 15:11: "Not that which goeth into the mouth defileth a man; but that which cometh out of the mouth, this defileth a man."

And in St. Matthew 15:17-20, Jesus said: "Do not ye yet understand, that whatsoever entereth in at the mouth goeth into the belly, and is cast out into the draught? But those things which proceed out of the mouth come forth from the heart; and they defile the man. For out of the heart proceed evil thoughts, murders, adulteries, fornications, thefts, false witness, blasphemies: These are the things which defile a man: but to eat with unwashen hands defileth not a man."

Therefore, evil comes from the heart of man and the tongue is the conveyor of that evil to other men. We must not translate Solex-Mal to mean Solar Bad or Solar Evil. For originally there wasn't any evil in our Solar System. Therefore, Solex-Mal means, simply, Solar Tongue. The word Mal has come down to us from the dim past and is still used in certain languages of our Earth.

The inhabitants of the Earth at one time spoke and used the Solar Tongue. All anthropologists and linguists agree that at one time there was only one language, and that from that one language all those existing today came into being. The countless languages of Earth are likened unto a tree with many branches. As we go from the top of the tree we see the branches thinning out; suddenly there are only two or three large branches; then we arrive at the single trunk. Science knows what languages are represented by the two or three large branches, but they have never yet discovered the original, parent language of Earth. All languages of today are related to it.

Our Holy Bible wholly agrees with this theory, and tells us how many languages came out of one. In Genesis 11:1-9, we read: "And the whole earth was of one language, and of one speech. And it came to pass, as they journeyed from the east, that they found a plain in the land of Shinar; and they dwelt there. And they said one to another, Go to, let us make brick, and burn them thoroughly. And they had brick for stone, and slime had they for mortar. And they said, Go to, let us build us a city and a tower, whose top may reach unto heaven; and let us make us a name, lest we be scattered abroad upon the face of the whole earth. And the Lord came down to see the city and the tower, which the children of men builded. And the Lord said, Behold, the people is one, and they have all one language; and this they begin to do: and now nothing will be restrained from them, which they have imagined to do. Go to, let us go down, and there confound their language, that they may not understand one another's speech. So the Lord scattered them abroad from thence upon the face of all the earth: and they left off to build the city. Therefore is the name of it called Babel; because the Lord did there confound the language of all the earth: and from thence did the Lord scatter them abroad upon the face of all the earth."

The Tower of Babel was built by Nimrod and intended to reach to heaven. Nimrod, king of Babylon, wished for greater power and decided to war on God. His tower of bricks in Shinar was built by six-hundred-thousand men and was so tall that it took a year to reach the top. From it some men shot arrows at the sky, and they came back bloodied. When the tower was not quite finished, God sent seventy angels to confuse the tongues of the workmen. One did not understand the next; they fought, some were transformed into apes and demons, and the survivors were scattered as the seventy nations on the face of the earth. One third of the tower sank into the earth, one third was burned, one third remained. Whoever passes the place where the tower stood loses his memory completely. Tradition names the tower of Birs-Nimrud at Borsippa as the original. The story may have been inspired in the nomadic people by the ziggurats and the swarming cosmopolitan life of the large Babylonian cities. Somewhat similar legends accounting for the diversity of languages are found in Africa, eastern Asia, and Mexico.

Ancient manuscripts tell us that at one time man on Earth lived in a Golden Age and "spoke with angels." This simply means that in Atlantis and Lemuria and before, Earth people were in constant contact with beings from outer space or "angels." Through evil and greed and lust, the Golden Age passed from the Earth and with it went the ability to speak the Solex-Mal. We will again speak this "language of angels," in the New Age now dawning.

Already we can see the evidence mounting that man needs a common, universal language. The new language of science is "Interlingua". A grammar and a dictionary of Interlingua has been published. This publication climaxed twenty-five years of work by expert linguists who developed the new language. It comes from some of the languages of the western world and in its written form more closely resembles Spanish than any other, although it also has French, Italian and English words. It has a twenty-seven thousand word vocabulary, including seventeen thousand scientific and technical terms which already have wide international usage. The grammar is simpler than that of any of the national languages and can be learned in a short time.

The following is written in Interlingua: "Energia es necessari pro toto que occure in le mundo. In temporas passate le plus grande parge del energia applicate esseva fornite per le fortia muscular del homies e del animales domestic." The English translation of the above is: "Energy is necessary for all that occurs in the world. In past times the greatest part of the applied energy was furnished by the muscular strength of men and domestic animals."

Interlingua is now a scientific language, but it could become a means of international communication in other fields. For the greatest possible progress in science it is essential that research workers know the results of work along similar lines by investigators in other countries. There should be a continual exchange of ideas and results. Wouldn't it be wonderful if any person could travel through the world and converse understandably with any literate person in any nation?

The new world interlanguage is Esperanto. It is steadily growing in practical use in every civilized land. The pronunciation is simple, there are no irregular verbs, and there are no exceptions to the few grammatical rules. It is so constructed that a vocabulary is quickly acquired. Esperanto short-wave broadcasts average one-hundred fifty-five a month and it is taught in five-hundred and fifty schools and colleges, some in the United States. It is being increasingly used by business, and particularly by travel organizations to solve language barriers.

The following is written in Esperanto, see how easy it really is: "Inteligenta persono lernas la interlingvon Esperanto rapide kaj facile. Esperonto estas la moderna, kultura lingvo por la internacia monda. Simpla, fleksebla, praktika solvo de la problemo de generala interkompreno, Esperanto meritas seriozan konsideron."

Bill Cunningham, in "The Boston Herald," said: "There can never really be one world until there's one language . . . one working language that the people running that world can speak, write and understand . . ."

Undoubtedly we need some sort of international language to surmount the barriers that diverse languages have created ever since the building of the Tower of Babel. The difficulty lies in getting people to learn a tongue different from their own. Why learn an artificial language, say the English-speaking nations, when English is so eminently suitable? On the other hand, the French and the Germans and the Italians stubbornly insist that French or German or Italian is the best means of communication. However illogical such a position might appear, one really can't blame them. So we need an international language.

The meetings of the United Nations Security Council bear out this need. Everything the Russian delegate says has to be translated into English and French. Not only is this a waste of precious time, but it is also a burden on those who understand Russian and French as well as English. They have to listen to the delegate's words three times running. If the delegate could speak in some international language, much time would be saved and his speeches would have to be heard only once.

Many of the old ways will be eliminated in the New Age. Even now we can see the trend. We are now in a transitional stage to the Golden Dawn just ahead of us. We will again "speak with angels," for we will understand and speak the Solex-Mal, the original, and Universal Mother Tongue of Creation.

The inhabitants of other worlds call our Earth Saras or Saros. Saros is a Babylonian numeral representing sixty sixties or three-thousand six hundred. It is also the Chaldean cycle of years, and in ancient Chaldean it meant "repetition", or "repetition of cataclysms". A fitting word for the Earth planet! Our world is also called Chan or Shan. This word also describes our Earth very well, indeed! Our world has been termed the "sorrowful planet". Perhaps the word *sorrow* came from *saros*; at least, it sounds like it could have.

Eventually, dictionaries will not even be used, for the Solex-Mal is a symbolic, pictographic language. When reading it in written form, one interprets symbols instead of reading words. Therefore, a symbol will be understood by all whether they have ever seen the particular symbol before or not.

The following symbolic writing was received by our research group in northern Arizona in 1952. It is believed to be written in Solex-Mal. It has not been translated as yet. Some of it is Atlantean in character and the signatures of prominent personages are in evidence. It is evidently a complete message in itself.

TAUMA

RAU

MAMMAU

RAMDA

LENN-YAH

MU-NATAI

KAAR-MU-DUM

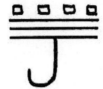

MEXEL-TAUX-MANILIL

MASU-RA

MEXEL-MANU-VEC

RAGDA-MUNLIL

JOSH-TAU-MAXIM

MESMAI

LENNA (PROTRUDING TONGUE SYMBOLS).

LENISH

LENMAL

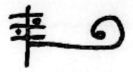

LENVA

SHOSH (SNAKE-FORM SYMBOLS).

SHAP

SHOP'H

SHEN'LIL

FAMMA (ARMS-FORWARD SYMBOLS).

FAMMIL

FAMMNAL

FAMMOSH

ASAP'H (CIVILIZATION ON WORLD SPHERE).

ASAP'H-UN (CIVILIZATION UNDER WORLD SPHERE).

SART-MUNDAI

EDEN-MAI (THIS COULD BE THE SYMBOL FOR THE
DIVISION IN THE GARDEN OF EDEN).

XEN'PH-MAU

MAX-MAL-KISH-ROK TAU-MUN

(SIGNATURE OF A PERSON).

AGASSI-PAN-AGASSI-MALDEC-TOM-MU (THERE IS
REFERENCE HERE TO THE PLANET MALDEK (C) AND
TO THE MOTHERLAND OF LEMURIA. (MU).

EXTEL-HAI

UR

EIL

MUS

NA'SHI

SHUK-TUM-MU (LEMURIA, MU, MENTIONED AGAIN).

(SIGNATURE OF A PERSON).

RAGIF-KONT-VA

MEGAL-MEX-MAL

UDAI-HUN-DALAI

ENLIL

KAL-MU-KAL

ISO-TOK-MAL

LESH-TAL

PITASH-ROK (EVIDENTLY IDENTICAL WITH PITACH-
RHOK, MOUNTAINS OF POSEID OR ATLANTIS.

IMELEX

UR-MUN ZELPH

SHAM-TOK-MARU (THE EIGHT-POINTED STAR IS THE "STAR OF BAPTISM" OR "REGENERATION.")

MEP'TH-MAU

MEP

MEP'TH

NAAG

TESH

ELHIM-NAZ

RAGGA-DAHL

REG-MAHL (THE FOUR GREAT PRIMARY FORCES
CONTAINED WITHIN THE UNIVERSE, WHICH, IN
TURN, IS WITHIN THE HAND OF GOD).

VIZ

MARN

MARF

MAR-TOK-MARU

MAR-TOK-KAL

MAR-TOK (THE "SHADOWED" LEFT EYE SHOWS
THAT THIS INDIVIDUAL DOES NOT HAVE SPIRITUAL
PERCEPTION).

TEC-LACMAL

RAP'H

ERMON

PHAMMON (A HIGHLY DEVELOPED INDIVIDUAL
DISPLAYING MANY ACCOMPLISHMENTS. THE
"SHADOWED" MOUTH SHOWS THAT HIS TONGUE
SPEAKS NO EVIL).

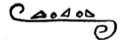

PHLIL

PHLAN

URNA ("U" OR URN-SHAPED SYMBOLS).

URNAS

URNAN

URNEP'H

SHEO-SHEOI (TO THE APPLES WE SALT
WE RETURN).

AKASH (MEMORY OF OTHER LIVES. SIMILAR TO
AKASA IN THE SANSKRIT, ONE OF THE FIVE
ELEMENTS OF THE SANKHYA PHILOSOPHY,
IDENTIFIED AS SPACE, ETHER, OR SKY. DEVOTEES
WHO GAZE UPWARD UNTIL STIFFENING MUSCLES
PREVENT CHANGE OF FACIAL POSITION ARE
TERMED AKAS-MUKHI, OR "SKY-FACERS").

PLAMMA (PAST LIVES REMEMBERED BY MEMORY
STIRRED THROUGH DREAMS).

PLAMMA (NEW EXPERIENCES DISCOVERED
IN DREAMS. "PLAMMA" MEANS FORCES ACTIVE
AT NIGHT).

ARAMMA (FORCE OR FORCES AIDING
PROGRESSION UPWARD; THE ROAD TO
EVER-EXPANDING GRANDEUR).

Much of the foregoing symbolism is similar to the ancient scroll writing of the Atlanteans. Every written thought in Atlantis was a challenge to the reader's mental development and a great variety of translations could be given to the same scrolled copy. The scroll form was used because it is symbolic of evolution, it is ever expanding.

Atlantis, however, used a modified form of the original Solex-Mal. So we would expect to find great similarities if not exact duplications in some cases.

Actually, there is nothing new under the sun; the New Age will not really be "new" at all—we are only returning to that status which we lost millennia ago.

In St. James 3:10, we find: "Out of the same mouth proceedeth blessing and cursing. My brethren, these things ought not so to be."

Poisonous insects were often used in ancient times to symbolize the deadly power of the human tongue—and it was an accurate portrayal. But in the near future blessing and cursing will not proceed out of the same mouth; the mouth that insists on cursing will be sealed up, but the mouth which blesses will be the mouth that tastes of the fruit of things promised.

Aphorismic statement was one of the favorite methods of instruction used in the Pythagorean university of Crotona. One aphorism says: "Govern your tongue before all other things, following the gods." Just as science and religion will be one, so will all language be *one language*: the evil tongue will be silent and the wise tongue will rejoice; we shall "follow the gods", for this is the promise of OTHER TONGUES!

CHAPTER 2

TRACKS ON THE DESERT

A man from another world stepped onto the planet Earth on November 20, 1952. My wife and I and our friends witnessed this happening which took place 10.2 miles from Desert Center, California on the highway toward Parker, Arizona. The full account is given in *Flying Saucers Have Landed* by Leslie and Adamski.

I was the first one to arrive at the footprints after the contact had been made. I could see where the spaceman had deliberately scraped away the top soil in order to get down to a more moist sand that would take the impressions from carvings on the bottom of his shoes. I got down on the ground in order to get a close observation of the symbols. The carvings on the shoes must have been finely done for the impressions left in the sand were clear-cut, well-defined and evidently of a high order of workmanship.

The footprint symbols tell why men from outer space have come to earth and what might happen if men on Earth refuse to live the Universal Laws of the Infinite Father. There are many, many meanings to the various symbols, and only a partial interpretation can be given here. We must bear in mind that these are "out of this world" symbols; however, since the planet Earth is a part of the Great Totality, we can expect certain facts to remain

ABOUT ELEVEN MILES FROM
DESERT CENTER, CALIF. TOWARD PARKER,
ARIZ. L. MCGINNIS, L., GEO. ADAMSKI, R.

constant throughout that Totality. Furthermore, in ancient times there was communication between the Earth and other worlds. The ancient symbols of Earth are the symbols of space beings, also.

Many people have asked: "If the space people are so intelligent why didn't they just type out a message in English and hand it to you? That would be so much more simple than all this footprint riddle business!" These people forget that a typed sheet of words wouldn't be proof of any such contact and besides, people like their "riddles", it makes them think—and that's just what the space friends want. They made those footprints in order to arouse curiosity,

GEO. ADAMSKI STANDING WHERE SAUCER HAD
HOVERED. ONLY A FEW FEET FROM FOOTPRINTS.

and through people's desire to know what the symbols mean will
come realization. They will get "in tune" so to speak with the entire
idea of visitors from space.

Briefly, a breakdown of symbols shows the following:

1. Use Of Simplified Pictography: Pictographic representation
   would almost be the same no matter where or by whom used.
   The forms used are definitely limited.
2. Use Of Simple Dots And Lines: These would necessarily be the
   same no matter what world they were used in. For example:

   (a). Use of numeral 3 to represent Triune God-head; Body,
        Soul and Spirit, etc.
   (b). Use of dots, smaller or larger as the case may be, to
        indicate planets and respective satellites.

THE AUTHOR (FAR RIGHT) MAKING THE PLASTER
CASTS. MRS. WILLIAMSON, BAILEY, MCGINNIS, WELLS
(L TO R).

LEFT FOOTPRINT. ARROW POINTS TO TOE OF
TRACK. (COMPARE WITH PLATE IV.)

How else could it be done?

3. Use Of A Footprint To Convey Desired Message:

    (a). After all, this would be a most simple way because the marks left by the foot are ample proof of a contact and these same marks can be studied; casts can be made of them; and photographs can be taken, etc.

    (b). Also, the foot-shape itself gives us a clue as to how to read the message. We know that in walking we step on the heel and end of the toe. Therefore, in reading the symbols, we start with the symbols on the heel, proceed from there to the arch, and then to the toe symbols.

    (c). Also, each footprint, left and right, is to be taken as a unit in itself. So, each one has a separate message to convey; yet, both are related in an overall message.

    (d). We must also take into consideration the fact that the symbols that were observed on the ground are exactly the reverse (direction) of the

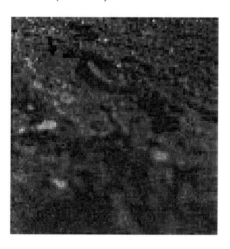

RIGHT FOOTPRINT. ARROW POINTS TO TOE OF
TRACK. (COMPARE WITH PLATE VI.)

symbols on the sole of the shoes making the impression of the prints. A mold is always the opposite of the original, etc.

However, our visitor from Venus drew attention to the footprints themselves; not to the soles of his shoes. So, the spaceman must have taken this fact into consideration when planning the message and corresponding symbols. We are not to read the symbols on the plaster casts, for as stated above, they are the reverse of what should be read. In interpreting these symbols then, we must keep all these facts in mind, remembering them as they appeared on the ground originally.

4. Use Of The So-Called Swastika And Other Symbols: The true clock of the universe is in the form of a Swastika. It is the Big Dipper revolving about the North Star. Some of the other symbols represent the form of the star-grouping in certain constellations. How else would you show these heavenly bodies and their arrangements except by drawings of what they look like? These would, of course, be true universal symbols. Certainly the spacemen wouldn't give us symbols we couldn't understand. What good is a message if we don't know the meaning of it? The form of certain constellations would be different as viewed from other worlds, but space people would know what the form was that appeared to men on Earth.

I made the plaster casts of the left and right footprint. From a preliminary study of the casts (and drawings that had been made prior to the pouring of the plaster) a partial reconstruction of the original

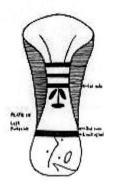

PLATE IV. LEFT FOOTPRINT

marks was made. Therefore, the drawings of the footprints as reproduced in the Phoenix *Gazette* of November 24, 1952 were not completely accurate. I had made hurried drawings from my field-notes for immediate publication in the paper. Later, I did considerable work on the casts and during certain tests many of the smaller symbols came to light. Anyone, searching through the world's oldest records would come to the same conclusions as I have.

I took several photographs of the events on November 20, 1952. Five of these photographs are re-produced in this book. (See Plate III, Fig. 1-5, pp. *96*).

From the impression left by the LEFT FOOT, we get the following interpretation:

A. The LEFT footprint (See *Plate IV*), taken as a total, represents things Spiritual and Cause.
B. In reading the footprint, we read from *heel* to *toe*; for when stepping we begin on the heel and end on the toe. Therefore. the footprint message should be read from bottom to top.
C. That which is represented on the *arch* is chief, principle or prime. The Sign of the Archer is also on the *arch*.
D. On the *heel* we see a simple pictographic story. The "7"-shaped figures appear to be like simple bird forms denoting flight. We see a tilted Saucer in the shape of an open mouth (oval) symbolizing the fact that spacemen have a message to give to their brothers on the Earth. There seems to be a system of 3's represented:

   (1) Saucer oval
   (2) "7"-shaped figures (also made up of two lines each)
   (3) Three circles or dots

There is clockwise motion here as in swastika symbols on the right footprint. This shows that the planetary bodies represented are in constant motion. The planets in what we call the first, second, and third orbits are shown:

   (1) Mercury
   (2) Venus

(3) Earth

Also, the two "7"-shaped figures seem to form an enclosure around two of the planet symbols and the oval Saucer figure. This shows that these two planets are connected with the landing contact and personal interview, but Mercury is not. In other words, a space craft has come from Venus and made contact with Earth. The three circles or dots used to represent these three planets are drawn roughly to scale. Therefore, one can immediately see what circle represents what planet, etc.

E. On the arch we see nine separate lines drawn and used to construct the symbols here. The numeral 9 was assigned as the symbol of Life Force by the ancients. The esoteric meaning is: "to revolve in circles or orbits". Here too, is undoubtedly the secret of Saucer propulsion. The utilization of universal or cosmic energy. No fuel is needed, except the ideal "fuel" of the Universe itself in the form of some type or adaptation of electro-magnetism. The three lines, above the arrow-like figure, represent the equation: one plus one equals three. In otherwords, by adding the laws of attraction and repulsion we get manifestation or propulsion. The two upper vertical, curved lines represent the forward motion of the space craft, and since they do not meet, and can never meet, they curve away and outward from each other. This shows that the propulsion force is to be found throughout the Universe. We also find a more spiritual message in the symbols on the arch. The arrow-like figure represents one whose faith is low. One whose spirit acknowledgeth the gift of spirits, but not the All person. The three horizontal lines directly above indicates that the spacemen have found three different types of people on Earth. One type believes only in earthly or material things; another believes in things spiritual; and the third has faith and believes in the All Creator. Unless a man puts away the materialism that is in him, he cannot rise to the emancipated heavens of the Creator. Also, the two lines extending upward represent the upraised arms of a man seeking. The Universal prayer of mankind. The Creator has sent people from outer space to guide Earthmen as they free themselves from darkness and bondage. These spacemen, in the name of the Infinite Father, will raise up men with eyes to see and ears to hear.

This message is therefore proclaimed to all the inhabitants of the Earth.

Therefore, the LEFT footprint shows that our brothers from outer space have come to the Earth

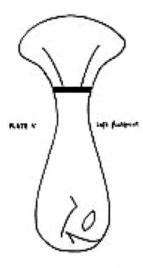

PLATE V. LEFT FOOTPRINT

to let us know our own spiritual condition at this time and to show us how this condition can be improved. It also shows by what method they arrived here.

The symbols in both footprints bear a strong resemblance to a crude drawing of a fish. We must also take into consideration the fact that a built-up layer was superimposed on the flat sole of the original shoe. Since this section was added to the bottom of the shoe it must mean that we are only to consider that part and omit the general outline and shape of the foot itself. When we do this we immediately recognize the outline of a fish. (See *Plate V*).

In the LEFT footprint, that which appears to be the eye of a fish, is also a geometrical figure known as *Vesica Piscis*. It is a rough outline of a fish itself, formed by two curves joined at extremities. It was held in high veneration in ancient times. In pictorial art, the Vesica Piscis is the oval aureole or glory within which the early painters depicted figures of Christ, the Virgin, or an apostle. It is an emblem that replaced the earlier figure, the fish or Ichthus, and is found on the sarcophagi of the catacombs, in medieval symbolism, seals, etc. The broad arrow found here was also in use since earliest times, and was found on all ancient buildings.

The fish was frequently associated with world saviors. Vishnu was expelled from the mouth of a fish. The Egyptian Isis is often shown with a fish on her headdress. Oannes, the Chaldean savior, is depicted with the head and body of a fish from which his own form protrudes at various points. Christ was symbolized by a fish. The mysterious Greek name of Jesus means a fish. *Ichthus*—used in early Christian art as a symbol, because the letters of this word are the initials of the Greek words: Jesous CHristos THeou Uios Soter (Jesus Christ, Son of God. Savior). Therefore, the first monogram of the Christians was a fish. Oannes came out of the sea, was amphibious. He brought to the Chaldeans their culture, showed them how to build cities, and retired again to the sea. Quetzalcoatl, the Mexican Toltec hero-god, is represented by a whale which rose out of the sea; the old serpent covered with feathers who lies in the ocean. He, too, was amphibious and was known as "the Heart of the Sea". And he, too, reputedly brought to his people their culture.

In some ancient records, the planet Venus is symbolized by a fish. In connection with the fish symbol we should consult the Holy Bible. In St. Matthew 12:38-41, we read: "Then certain of the scribes and of the Pharisees answered, saying, Master, we would see a sign from thee. But he answered and said unto them, An evil and adulterous generation seeketh after a sign; and there shall no sign be given to it, but the sign of the prophet Jonas: for as Jonas was three days and three nights in the whale's belly; so shall the Son of man be three days and three nights in the heart of the earth. The men of Nineveh shall rise in judgment with this generation, and shall condemn it: because they repented at the preaching of Jonas; and, behold, a greater than Jonas is here."

Again, in St. Matthew 16:3-4, we read: "And in the morning, It will be foul weather to-day: for the sky is red and lowering. O ye hypocrites, ye can discern the face of the sky; but can ye not discern the signs of the times? A wicked and adulterous generation seeketh after a sign; and there shall no sign be given unto it, but the sign of the prophet Jonas."

As we continue to study the symbols of the LEFT footprint, we see 3 bars above an arrow-like figure. If we consider the fish symbol here, it is interesting to read, Jonah 2:6: "I went down to the bottoms of the mountains; the earth with her bars was about me for ever; yet hast thou brought up my life from corruption, O Lord my God."

Here we find reference to the "earth with her bars". We consider the Earth to be in the third orbit, so the three bars could stand for that fact. Also in Jonah we find reference to "the earth with her bars was about me for ever; yet hast thou brought up my life from corruption". So, too, we find the two expanding lines above the third bar going upward or outward, away from the head of the fish symbol. Also, remember, Jonah was in the belly of the fish three days and three nights.

Feet themselves, represent the natural, external plane of life in contact with the world; and the feet of the spaceman represent the contact and presence of space beings with Earthmen and the Earth planet.

Swedenborg says that a fish symbolizes sensual affections which are the ultimate affections of the natural man. Also, those who are in common truths, which are also ultimates of the natural man. Also, those who are in external falses.

Their likeness to birds (swimming of fishes; flying of birds) suggests that fishes correspond to affections for intellectual activity. And what does the fact that they live in the water instead of the air show in regard to the kind of thoughts to which they have relation? Plainly the fishes of the mind enjoy a lower, less spiritual kind of thought than the birds. The water, which is their home, corresponds to truth of a natural kind—truth of natural science, of worldly industries, of the letter of the Word, and of practical right and wrong.

An interest in gathering facts of science is a hungry fish swimming in the water and devouring all the little creatures which come within his reach. And presently some larger fish swallows up our little fish with many others like him. So stronger, broader, scientific minds absorb the observations of smaller minds and deduce from them the great principles of science. There is in ourselves an enjoyment in grasping the broader principles of knowledge, which feeds upon our special interests in particular subjects. This is a larger fish feeding upon the little ones.

The interest in knowledge of worldly affairs is also a spiritual fish, which feeds with eager appetite upon our observations of the world, and may in turn contribute to a noble interest in tracing the Creator's providence in worldly affairs. So too, an absorbing interest in the external forms of worship, are fishes which may easily become food for more spiritual affections. But these same fishes-affections for gathering natural knowledge, are bad when they refuse to minister to the spiritual life, and at-tending only to the evidences of the senses, fall into many errors which they eagerly confirm.

In Genesis 1:20-21, 26 and Psalm 8:6-8, we see that man on Earth is supposed to have dominion over the *fish* of the sea. These can be the spiritual fish (affections) and man is told he must have control over them.

In St. Matthew 13:47-49, we find: "Again, the kingdom of heaven is like unto a net, that was cast into the sea, and gathered of every kind: Which, when it was full, they drew to shore, and sat down, and gathered the good into vessels, but cast the bad away. So shall it be at the end of the world: the angels shall come forth, and sever the wicked from among the just."

In St. Matthew 4:18-19, St. Luke 5:3-11, St. John 21:1-13, we see the disciples as fishers of men. They would also be fishers in the sense that it would be their duty and privilege to lift men up from the sea of atmosphere of natural worldly life into the air and sunshine of true spiritual life.

Therefore, we see that the space people are now present with us on Earth and are attempting to lift us up out of our present stricken condition into a fuller, more satisfying existence, by their guidance and aid. At one time the world was in the Age of Taurus, The Bull. The Egyptians worshiped Apis or Hap, a sacred bull. And a calf was worshipped by the Israelites in the desert during the exodus from Egypt. Then came the Age of Aries, The Ram. The men of David's time were shepherds—shepherds in the Age of the Ram. King David, Jacob, Moses, Cyrus the Mede, all these had been shepherds, and the Psalms speak of God leading the multitudes as if they were his precious sheep-fold. Then came the age we are just now leaving—Pisces, the Age of the Fishes.

Each of these ages lasts approximately two thousand years. However, each one is usually about two thousand, one hundred and fifty years long, and the passing from one such age into another is always accompanied by both external and internal storm and stress such as the world is now going through. The last change took place about two thousand years ago when Jesus came on the earthly scene as the Great Piscean Avatar or Teacher—and the new world that formed itself from that turbulent era and area was the western Christian civilization that we know today. Since this great enterprise has worked itself out and fulfilled its mission, it is now drawn to a close, and the New Age of the Water-Bearing Aquarius is upon us.

As a Piscean Master, Jesus fed the multitude with fish; he walked on the water; his followers were fishermen, and as we said above, he made them fishers of men. Clement of Alexandria enumerates the fish, the anchor, the ship and fisherman as fitting objects to be employed by the Christians on their seals and lamps. These are all Water-Fish-Age symbols. An early Christian drawing shows the Church, in the form of a ship, borne by Christ amidst the storm and stress of life. Pisces is a rainy constellation, bringer of storms, and controls the fate of sailors. Since the time of Christ the world has progressed along avenues that dealt almost entirely with water. For several hundred years all of man's ambitions were wrapped up in the seas and oceans. He traveled by sails to the far corners of the world; he became a great explorer using the waterways of the world to serve him in his quest. The result was the discovery of new lands in the West, and new frontiers promised new life and new hope for mankind. The darkness and brutality of the Middle Ages was forgotten in these new-found lands, and man as a spiritual being leaped to the challenge of development.

Until very recently, our great sources of power were nothing but waterpower. We had steam engines for this and that; we built great dams to conserve this power. Only a few years ago man took to the air; but he had always longed to fly. Primitive man had watched the eagle with envy.

Man graduated as a shepherd (Aries), and as a Fisherman (Pisces), and now he becomes a Gardener in Aquarius the New Air Age. This title expresses the kind of work that he has to do in his new role. Psychologists insist that the conscious and the subconscious minds stand almost exactly in the relationship of *gardener* and *garden*. The gardener sows his seed in the soil that he has prepared; he waters the ground, and selects a site upon which the sun will shine—but he does not try to make the seed grow. He leaves that to Nature. Therefore, we speak the Word but we leave it to Divine Power to make the demonstration. The dominant note of the New Age then is Spiritual development and Spiritual demonstration.

It takes mankind about twenty-six thousand years to go through the class of twelve lessons about the Creator, which we call the Zodiac. We have gone through these lessons many times before, and we will have to repeat them in the future, but each time we go through the same lessons at a much higher level with a different quality of knowledge, for it is not an endless circle, but an upward reaching spiral. The change we are now experiencing is not a change brought about by merely passing from one Sign or Age to another, such as happened in passing from Taurus into Aries, or Aries into Pisces; our present change is not one brought about by a two-thousand year plus cycle, but brought about by the ending of a Solar Year, or twenty-six thousand years. That is why we are now going through a great upheaval; physically, mentally and spiritually.

The LEFT footprint therefore, taken as a whole, can signify the Piscean Age; and that Age has ended, for the fish is trampled underfoot!

From the impression left by the RIGHT FOOT, we get the following interpretation:

A. The RIGHT *footprint* (See *Plate VI*), taken as a total represents things Material and Effect.
B. In reading the footprint, we read from *heel* to *toe*; for when stepping we begin on the heel and end on the toe. Therefore, the footprint message should be read from bottom to top.
C. That which is represented on the *arch* is chief, principle or prime. (The symbol here of three dots can mean: Since; Because; Equals; Result In; For The Reason Of).
D. On the *heel* we see the Clock of the Universe going in a clockwise direction. In the center we see one circle (dot). This represents or symbolizes the Creator, the Infinite; the curved arms symbolize the Four Great Primary Forces; the arms

project from the circle in the center, and being joined to the circle, they are coming from it. That is, these forces emanate from the Creator. The swastika, popularly called a "good luck symbol" and one of the many symbols of the Four Great Primary Forces, was a favorite among the ancients throughout the world and still clings to the hearts of present (Masonic, etc.) humanity. Pythagoras on his return from Egypt taught that the numeral 4 referred to the Great Creative Forces of the Universe. The legend is that: "At the command of the Creator the Four Great Primary Forces built the universe and all therein. They . . . the Four Great Builders, the

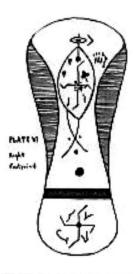

PLACE VI
Right
Footprint

PLATE VI. RIGHT FOOTPRINT

Heavenly Architects and Geometricians, the Four Great Strong Ones . . . built the earth and formed its life." The swastika symbol evolved from the simple cross symbol, and both are among the most ancient symbols of Earth. The swastika is the Key to Universal Movements. Since Four Great Primary Forces were used in Creation, and are now governing the movements of all bodies throughout the Universe, these forces are working from West to East, and carry all celestial bodies in the direction of West to East. These forces by their actions cause the revolving bodies to continue their force, so

103

that apparently the force comes from the movements of the body. The atomic element is simply a collector, carrier, and distributor of the portions of primary forces that have been handed to it; atomic force does not obtain its energy from elements of the atom. By smashing the atom the flow of forces through it is destroyed. The ancients used the flow, they did not destroy it. This power is the Will and Command of the Infinite. The esoteric or hidden meaning of the swastika was known by the priesthood and this meaning was not communicated to the layman. (See Plate XVII" *p. 253*). The swastika is an ancient sign in India and is sacred for it was one of the body marks of the Lord Buddha and has a solemn meaning among both Brahmans and Buddhists. The swastika has been said to resemble the apparatus used prehistorically to make fire and thus represents sacred fire, living flame. Milani thought it was a symbol of the sun and "seems to denote its daily rotation". Or it may be lightning, the storm, the Aryan pantheon; benediction, good omen. The swastika is very ancient and widespread for it was used in Crete, in ancient Rome, on Celtic rocks in Scotland, rock carvings in Sweden and throughout the Orient. The wheel cross, which is thought for Stone Age man to have symbolized the sun, is displaced in the Bronze Age by the swastika. American Indians of the pre-Columbian period used this cross for a number of purposes. The most frequently mentioned is as a symbol of the four directions which were important in Indian ritual. It has also been identified as a wind symbol, storm symbol, and phallic meanings have been attributed to it. If the cross pieces point to the right, it is a lucky sign; if they point to the left it is an unlucky sign. In China the swastika was the symbol of a benevolent society. The word swastika comes from the Sanscrit and in Northern Europe it was called Fylfot. In China it is known as Wan. This is especially interesting because in "The Saucers Speak!" Wan-4 was a representative of the Safanian Solar System. And Wan is the Chinese word for swastika. Also notice the use of the numeral 4. Apparently, from the beginning the Four Great Primary Forces, called in the most ancient writings the Sacred Four, have played a cardinal part in man's religion. It would appear that most of the ancient theology was based on their workings, and many theological lines and divergences sprang from them. Another ex-ample of "God Provided—Man Divided". The Sacred Four are still very much with us. But just *what are* these four?

Since the arrival of friends from outer space it is possible to know the true meaning of this sacred number. The Four Great Primary Forces are: Static Magnetic Field; Electro-Static Field; Electro-Magnetic Wave; Resonating Electro-Magnetic Field. Ancient temples were dedicated to these Sacred Four as representative and symbolic of the almighty power of the Creator. Ancient man at one time on Earth understood the true meaning of the Sacred Four, but later this meaning was lost to him; however, it continued to be used in rituals and thus was handed down from generation to generation. These Sacred Four were the Executors of the Seven Great Commands of Creation. The ancient conception was: "In the beginning chaos reigned throughout the universe, which was in darkness and without sound. Then the Creator, desiring to create worlds, commanded His Four Great Forces to establish law and order in the universe so that creations might commence. When law and order became established the Creations were carried out by the Sacred Four according to His desires and commands." Apparently all ancient peoples had their special names for the Sacred Four according to their language; some had scores of names for them. They were designated as: The Sacred Four, the Four Great Ones, the Four Powerful Ones, the Four Strong Ones, the Four Great Kings, the Four Great Maharajas, the Four Great Builders, the Four Great Architects, the Four Great Geometricians, the Four Great Pillars of the Universe, the Four Genii, the Amshaspands by the Mazdeans, the Elohim and Seraphs by the Hebrews, the Rabiri and Titons in Hesiod's theogony, etc. Not only did the Sacred Four get sundry names bestowed upon them by various people; but symbols in the form of crosses were designated to emphasize the names. The swastika, itself, always retained a warm corner in the people's hearts. As said before, this symbol is found throughout the world in all ages from ancient Mexico to early American Mound Builder to Egyptian, etc. Therefore, in the heel, we see the Four Great Forces emanating from Deity, and traveling from West to East around a center. Why do we look to the most ancient symbols for interpretive material? This is because "We have found in the most ancient records of the Aryan language proof that the indications of religious thought are higher, simpler, and purer as we go back in time, until at last, in the very oldest compositions of human speech which has come down to us, we find the Divine

Being spoken of in the sublime language which forms the opening of the Lord's Prayer." (Duke of Argyll). Remember, the swastika was primarily a sun symbol and was associated with Apollo. It has always been associated with those who apparently came to Earth to teach men better ways of living; of governing themselves; agricultural methods; and greater appreciation of the physical form in beauty and perfection. Therefore, the swastika is not indigenous to Earth. It is certain that this ancient symbol came to the people on Earth from a source in outer space and was then incorporated into religious beliefs on this planet. So, it is not too difficult to see that it would be very useful and would find its way into a universal symbol. All men everywhere would understand the significance of the Sacred Four and the Creator. In the book, "Astronomy" by Arthur M. Harding, Ph.D., in the section entitled "The Clock In The Northern Sky" we find: "The Great Bear is the oldest of the constellations. It moves slowly around the pole star, making one complete circuit in twenty-four hours. Here is a Celestial Clock that never runs down, requires no attention and is always absolutely accurate. From this natural clock the expert astronomer can get his time with an error of only a few minutes if he knows the day of the month. When the Dipper is below the pole star it is in its natural position. Six hours later it will be standing on the end of its handle on the East side of the pole. At the end of twelve hours it will be upside down and over the pole and at the end of eighteen hours it will be found West of the pole and standing on its bowl. The Dipper is directly over the pole in May, West of the pole in August, directly beneath the pole in December and East of the pole in late February." Taking this description of the Great Bear Constellation into consideration we find we have a definite swastika design that is, by drawing, a clockwise swastika. However, it moves counter-clockwise around the pole star. (See *Plate VII*, Fig. 1). So it

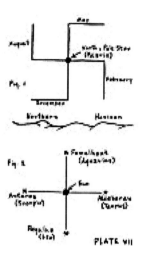

PLATE VII

is easy to see why the space people might very well use the swastika as a universal symbol or emblem.

Now we will interpret the four symbols that are drawn between the four arms of the swastika in the *Right Heel*. The early writings of the Persians and the Chinese tell us that there were Four Bright Stars in the sky that protected and watched over the others. Notice the use of the Sacred Four again. These stars were said to be in the West, the North and the South. These positions evidently corresponded to the Vernal Equinox, the Autumnal Equinox, the Winter Solstice and the Summer Solstice—the Four Cardinal points of the sky. If we turn the Zodiac back to where it was five-thousand years ago we find four bright stars in the Four Cardinal points of the heavens. (See, Fig. 2). If we look into the sky in the vicinity of these four points we can find no stars of any considerable brightness and we perhaps may be inclined to doubt the accuracy of this ancient literature or to wonder whether the four bright stars have faded considerably during the intervening years. However, we must recall that, because of the westward precession of the equinoxes, the Four Cardinal points do not have the same location with reference to the stars as they had ages ago for the constellations of the Zodiac are continually slipping in an easterly direction with reference to the Vernal Equinox. Therefore, we must study the Zodiac as the Persians and other ancients saw it! Suppose we turn the Zodiac back (westward) through sixty degrees (60°). Imagine our surprise at finding four bright stars: Aldebaran, Antares, Regulus, and Fomalhaut—almost exactly in the places assigned to them by the Persians. Since the Zodiac has slipped through sixty degrees in about five-thousand years we can tell approximately when the observations of these ancient peoples were made. Of the four bright stars that the Persians and Chinese said were in the Four Cardinal points of the Zodiac, Aldebaran is in the constellation Taurus (the Bull), Antares is in Scorpio (which Abraham and his followers called the Eagle), Regulus is in Leo (the Lion), and Fomalhaut is in the outskirts of the constellation Aquarius (which was usually represented by a man pouring water out of a vessel). It was, therefore, natural for early peoples to think of four living creatures—the Bull, the Eagle, the Lion, and the Man—as being situated in the four principle points of the Zodiac—the Vernal Equinox, the Autumnal Equinox, the Winter Solstice and the Summer Solstice. Although the Persians and Chinese seem to have been more interested in the four stars than in the constellations with which they were associated, the early Hebrew writer called special attention to the Four Living Creatures. An interesting bit of evidence that the constellations of the Zodiac have been slipping around the Celestial Sphere since the very dawn of history is to be found in the Book of Ezekiel and in Revelation. It is obvious from the descriptions of the "wheels" made by the Prophet Ezekiel that here was a landing of four Saucers and their respective pilots or occupants. However, this is discussed in detail in this book under *The Prophets* in the section called: *Other Flesh*. We see in Ezekiel 1:10: "As for the likeness of their faces, the *cherubim*, they had the face of a man; and they four had the face of a lion on the right side; and they four had also the face of an ox (bull) on the left side; they four also had the face of an eagle." In Revelation 4:6-7, we read: "And round about the throne, four living creatures full of eyes before and behind. And the first creature was like a lion, and the second creature like a calf (bull), and the third creature had the face of a man, and the fourth creature was like a flying eagle." It is obvious that the writers of the above passages were referring to the symbols of the constellations or four bright stars as they appeared in the Zodiac about five thousand years ago. The four bright stars associated with the Bull, the Eagle, the Lion, and the Man were situated at the Vernal Equinox, the Autumnal Equinox, the Winter Solstice and the Summer Solstice, and, according to Chinese legends, kept watch over *all the others*. Therefore, we can get a fairly accurate interpretation of the four symbols drawn between the four arms of the swastika in the Right *heel*. First of all, for simplicity, let us look at the symbol drawn in the upper right hand section of the swastika. It looks like: This symbol is V-shaped and very closely resembles the V-shaped constellation or star group known as Taurus (the Bull).

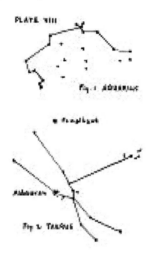

PLATE VIII. FIG. 1: AQUARIUS. FIG. 2: TAURUS

(See *Plate VIII*, Fig. 2). In the lower right hand section we see: This symbol closely resembles the star grouping in the constellation of Leo (the Lion). (See *Plate IX*, Fig. 1). In the lower left hand section we see: This symbol closely resembles the fishhook-shape of the star group in Scorpio (the Eagle). (See *Plate IX*, Fig. 2). In the upper left hand section we see: This symbol resembles the main star grouping in Aquarius (the Man). (See *Plate VIII*, Fig. 1). Therefore, we can see why the four symbols have been drawn between the four arms of the swastika instead of at the four points. It is because now these four constellations of the Zodiac have slipped into a more Easterly direction. So, the swastika in the *heel* is definitely the Universal Time Piece or Clock. Its position indicates where those constellations are *today*. The diagram on *Plate X*, Fig. 1 shows the four symbols from the heel representing the four constellations and their relative positions five-thousand years ago. The drawing on the *heel* itself shows their relative positions today. (See *Plate X*, Fig. 2). We can see that the four arms of the swastika have moved clockwise

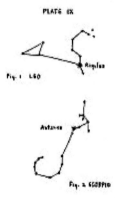

PLATE IX. FIG. 1. LEO. FIG. 2. SCORPIO

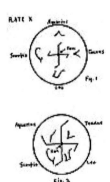

PLATE X.

in an Easterly direction. When thinking of the swastika as the Universal Clock, the center of it represents the pole star Polaris; when thinking of it as pointing to the four constellations and showing their present position, the center represents the Sun. By looking at *Plate XI*, and moving the swastika arms sixty degrees to the East (Right) one can readily see the meaning of *Plate X*. Therefore, our space

PLATE XI

brothers are showing us the position of the four constellations as they are in the heavens at this time. Here they have given us the key to Universal Movement—from West to East and *constant*.

The use of the sacred four numeral is world-wide and very ancient. It has been claimed by the ancients that there are Four Ages of Man through which this Earth has already passed. Each of the Ages ended in catastrophe. We are said to be now living in the Fifth Great Age of the planet Earth. In the center of the Aztec calendar stone the Sun-God Tonatiuh is depicted and the Aztec history of the world divides Earth events into Five Suns or Ages. The first four Ages were ended successively by a jaguar, a hurricane, a fire and a flood. Our present Sun or Age is supposed to be destroyed by an earthquake. Amazing new interpretations of the Aztec calendar stone are now being made by research scientists. Evidently the stone tells the same prophetic story that can be found in the interpretation of the Great Pyramid of Gizeh. It says that there are pyramids in North America and that they were somehow hidden when the white man began his march on America from Mexico. From the idea of a clock we immediately think of the passage of time or of past events or cataclysms that have transpired on Earth. So, the four could also stand for these past Ages. The fact that they are passed Ages is shown by the arms of the swastika being moved in a Easterly direction. It *also* seems that the symbols of the Bull, Eagle, Lion and Man were used (or drawn) on the sides of the four Saucers seen by the Prophet Ezekiel to show that man as Man is to be found everywhere in the Creation, throughout the Omniverse. The Universe extends out from small Earth in all Cardinal directions of North, East, South and West. And, as the ancients believed, these four "royal" stars (or suns of other inhabited worlds) were watching over *all* the rest! There is little doubt that Ezekiel saw four Saucers—complete with portholes, a type of landing-gear, pilots and emblems. As for the difference in the angles of the bent arms of the swastika in the *heel*, is seems this could represent the unbalance in this section of the Universe at the present time, and it might also indicate the change that will automatically take place in the Big Dipper star grouping as time goes on. But, since it represents a clock, why shouldn't it show past, present, and future? The four points of the swastika also mean many more things. (See Plate XVII).

E. On the *arch* we see the symbol of three dots. This means: Because of. Therefore, this could stand for future catastrophe. *Because of* what has happened to four Ages of Earth represented in the *heel*. Three stars or dots always represented a Triune God in ancient times. And when you have the Triune God or Creator you have effect and result. The sacred three is exclusively ascribed to the Supreme Deity and means a "work of perfection". So we can see why three dots represent: *Because of*. For example: Because of the Creator worlds were formed, etc. These three small dots represent Body (Mortal); Soul (Mind); and Spirit (Immortal). We can see that Body is below. Above, and more closely together and associated are Soul and Spirit. Man's soul knows truth of the spirit; body is farther removed and is shown as a larger dot because physical manifestation is of such importance to Earth. These three dots form an inverted or upside-down triangle. The crossed lines between Soul and Spirit show that this is the meeting place (origin) where the Mortal Body below, of a lower vibratory rate, obtains Universal Truth. One line, which separates Soul (Mind) from Spirit leads directly into the joined lines forming the oval. The other line separating Spirit from Soul (Mind) does not connect directly with the oval but seems to be trying to penetrate the edges, not yet having gained entrance but attempting it. This is similar to the sperm entering the egg to fertilize it. In other words, things of the Soul (Mind) have entered into this section of the Universe and Man has received it. But things of the Spirit (Immortal) have not entered this section of the Universe except to a limited degree to the other planets. This can be seen as a club-like figure in the section of the planet Mars to be extending itself into the edge-line of the oval and is directly beneath the meeting place of the line from things of Spirit (Immortal) with the edge-line of the oval. The two crossed lines are not entering this section of the Universe equally, therefore there is a definite state of unbalance here.

F. The swastika within the oval figure again represents the Sacred Four. The oval itself is once again the Vesica Piscis and many of the symbols are contained within this oval. It is similar to the aureole of sacred art. This is a radiance enveloping the whole figure of Christ, or any sanctified being. Sometimes it is an oval and sometimes it is nearly circular in form. The swastika here divides the oval into four sections. These can represent four separate "rooms" or "houses" in this part of the Universe. The two horizontal arms are composed of spear or arrow-like heads. The head or point of an arrow, spear or javelin are ancient symbols showing the *Forces are active*. First of all, we have the planet Mercury represented in the upper right hand section. The trefoil, or three-leaved flower design with stern represents this planet as being in the State of the Flowering of Perfection. A trefoil is an ornamental foliation of three divisions or foils. What more perfect symbol to show the Triune Godhead! The symbol representative of All Perfection here represents "flowering" of this Complete Perfection itself. Here, also, could be perfect harmony of Body, Soul and Spirit.

Going to the upper left hand section we find the planet Venus. We see no moons here and there were none for Mercury, either. Here are two wedge-shaped figures symbolic of "Builders of Foundation for Universal Truth". A wedge is a piece tapering to a thin edge and used in raising heavy bodies. This means the raising of the Mortal to unite or meet the Immortal in Man. Cuneiform characters have a wedge-shaped stroke. These characters were used anciently in writing in Persia, Assyria, etc. So, we can see why these figures symbolize constructiveness or "building"—in the spiritual, not the material sense.

Going to the lower left section we find the planet Mars. Only one satellite is shown here, although Mars has two artificial moons. Possibly two satellites were originally shown, but because of inaccurate drawing and casting one has been lost. There have been many strange tales told about these satellites in past history. Ancient poets knew of these two moons before their discovery by Asaph Hall in 1877. Ancient astrological works mention them. For more information on them see *Maldek and Malona* in this book in the section called: *Other Tongues*. Below Mars in this section of the drawing we see a strange, club-like figure running into the outer edge-line of the oval. This represents the fact that the people of Mars have more revelation of Universal Truth coming from the Triune Creator below. However, it is not a complete revelation symbolized by the fact that the line from things of Spirit does not join the club-like figure, but instead, rests just above it. Still, there is a connection and therefore an influx from the sources below. It will be noticed that there are no lines coming into the top half of the oval as they are below. There have been more complete revelations in these sections of Mercury and Venus. Each small dot that represents a planet is in relative size to the other dots. Going to the lower right hand section we find the planet Earth. Here we see the known Moon of Earth and the "Dark Moon" or second Moon of Earth. The "Dark Moon" is mentioned in records of great antiquity throughout the world. We see a thin, vertical line almost extending to the outer edge-line of the oval. Therefore, there is a seeking on Earth; a desire in Earthmen's hearts and soul to reach the Infinite Source of All Wisdom and Knowledge of Universal Truth. These truths are, in turn, embodied in Soul and Spirit represented below. But this line has not made a direct connection as yet. Compare it with the parallel line in the Mars section. It only lacks the club-like appendage, and it too, will make a connection.

Now let us look at the two horizontal arms again. We see that the arrow-like head on the left is pointing downward. This indicates clearly that Mars is directly beneath or behind Venus in State of Progression. The one on the right is pointing upward, showing that Mercury and Venus both are above Mars and the Earth in State of Progression. You will notice there is nothing beneath the Earth. Therefore, this planet is in the lowest State of Progression in this section of the Universe, and especially in this Solar System.

Now we go to the dark oval on top of the vertical, open oval. The material meaning here is that the oval stands for the planet Saturn. This dark oval appears to be a sort of balance on top of the entire *toe* symbol. Saturn knows Mind of Total Universe. Here is found the greatest mechanical advancement in our Solar System. Saturn is the Balancer of the System pointing out wrongs from rights. It enforces the law of compensation: "As ye sow, so shall ye reap." This is in line with Divine Will. We can see Saturn here with its rings in the oval form. The oval is an ancient symbol of the mouth. Saturn, as dispenser of Justice throughout this System is the "mouth" that conveys the Knowledge of Justice. This oval is not contained within the larger one because the Knowledge Saturn conveys to her brothers in this System is not from this System alone, but is from the Creator—and therefore it is not limited. A line extends from Saturn, and through Saturn, and enters the joining part of oval and continues down to the top arm of the swastika where it meets in another circle or dot. This dot represents the planet Jupiter.

Jupiter is the Creator's Interpreter of Law. Knowledge and Wisdom flowing from His throne. This planet gives to those who desire it: "Ask and ye shall receive; seek and ye shall find; knock and it shall be opened unto you." Jupiter is in a progressed state of mental and spiritual advancement over the four planets around the swastika in the oval. The spiritual meaning here is that the dark oval represents the "All-Seeing Eye". For we see, extending to the right, another arrow-like head representing active forces emanating from the "All-Seeing Eye". The oval is also an ancient symbol for the eye. The fact that Saturn is shown above Jupiter means that Saturn is the seat of the Universal Tribunal, but these two planets are closely associated in state of progression as shown by the direct line from one to the other.

Now we come to the skeleton-like hand on the right side of the vertical oval. Five fingers and a thumb are shown of a left hand, palm away. Five is the numeral symbol of the Full Godhead—the Four Great Primary Forces, plus the Creator. It also stands for the Four Senses and the Cardinal Sense of Feeling. This hand is away from the oval, and not contained within it. Therefore, it is not limited by the oval which encloses and designates only a very small portion of this section of the Universe. The active-force arrow-head points directly to this hand. Also notice that the arrow-like heads on the horizontal arm of the swastika keep the movement going clockwise just as the bent angles of the vertical arm do. The hand is the most ancient symbol of the First Person in the Godhead. It represents the creative power of God. In Proverbs 1:24, we read: "Because I have called, and ye refused; I have stretched out my hand, and no man regarded." And in Ecclesiastes 9:1, we see: "For all this I considered in my heart even to declare all this, that the righteous, and the wise, and their works, are in the hand of God: no man knoweth either love or hatred by all that is before them . . ." The Greek Christians represent the souls of the just by showing little naked human beings, praying with joined hands in the great hand of God. This hand issues from the clouds, whence it appears to have descended to Earth to take the souls of the righteous, and return with them to heaven and paradise. The hand also symbolizes ability, power, and thence confidence. To lay the hand upon anyone is to inspire him with life. Hands mean power, arms mean still greater power, and shoulders mean all power. Communication is produced by the touch of the hand, inasmuch as the life of the mind, and thence of the body, exerts itself in the arms, and by them in the hands. To hold up the hands means faith looking toward the Creator. When hands and feet are mentioned together, the former symbolizes the interiors of man; and the latter his exteriors; or both, whatever is spiritual and natural in man. Hands show the faculty of receiving. The feet are in contact with the dust of the world; they are less responsive to the guidance of the will and thought; they are not so directly concerned in doing for others, but serve rather in bringing us where we can be of use, and holding us firmly while the hands do the work. When contrasted with the hands the feet represent rather the effort to determine the course of life toward good or evil, while the hands represent the more particular thought in regard to the service to be done to others. The hands are obedient to inner desires and thoughts. So, we can see why space people have used the symbol of a foot to convey their message to us; why they have used the hand symbol inside of the fish symbol; and why they have used the symbol of the Great Fish, itself. In this RIGHT footprint we see the time element in the head of the fish, and this is represented by the swastika. There is no eye represented here because the fish is more or less blind to certain time conditions. See St. Matthew 24:36: "But of that day and hour knoweth no man, no, not the angels of heaven, but my Father only." And again in Mark 13:32: "But of that day and that hour knoweth no man, no, not the angels which are in heaven, neither the Son, but the Father."

The RIGHT footprint therefore, taken as a whole, can signify the Aquarian Age; and that Age is now manifesting, for the RIGHT footprint itself is not a fish symbol, but the fish is shown *inside* the total footprint, therefore it is *swallowed up* by the New Age. The RIGHT footprint shows something of the past of the planet Earth; something of the present; and something of the future in that certain events will take place if Universal Law is not learned or practiced here. It shows that space people have been to Earth before in remote times of antiquity and it shows our neighboring planets of this System and what their relative positions are in regard to States of Progression. In this footprint, we also see the Germ of Man's Life encased within the darkness of the interior of the Great Fish. Man's life on Earth can open into glorious fulfillment never before realized. The active force from the oval of Saturn pointing to the symbolic left hand with palm away, shows that Man can progress or rise through the hand being offered by our brothers from outer space at this time.

It is, of course, impossible to come to any kind of a *conclusion* in such a short analysis of *the tracks on the desert*. Much of the material used here first appeared in my: "A Preliminary Report On Analysis Of Symbols From Footprints Left By A Man From Outer Space—November 20, 1952." Everyone who diligently studies the footprint symbols comes up with a new interpretation and sheds new light on the meaning of it all. The people of outer space have given these symbols in the way they have so that man will *think!* It is evident that the symbols in both the LEFT and RIGHT footprints have many, many meanings and a great message for the people of Earth.

To show that a great deal of research is still needed before we can get anywhere near a complete interpretation, suppose we thought of the oval and crossed lines in the RIGHT footprint as representing a man form. Each planetary body would therefore represent a certain part of Total Body Form in the Grand Man or the Creator. If this is so, then we must go into the meaning of various parts of the body. For example, the hands mean spiritually all the desire and thought which we put into the deeds we do. In a word, the hands are the deeds, which, regarded spiritually, consist of the desire and thought which prompt them. The hands are extremes of the body, and obedient to inner desires and thoughts. Love of doing or service and knowledge of how to do. The right hand represents love and the left hand represents thoughts we put into our work. Those on the *left hand* are those who learn but do not do. In St. Matthew 6:3, we read: "But when thou doest alms, let not thy left hand know what they right hand doeth . . ." And in Psalm 31:5: "Into thine hand I commit my spirit: thou has redeemed me, O Lord God of truth." And again in Psalm 31:15: "My times are in thy hand: deliver me from the hand of mine enemies, and from them that persecute me."

For a more complete footprint interpretation we will have to study the symbolism and meaning of numbers as well as symbolic anatomy. Also, more research will have to be conducted along the lines of the world's most ancient symbolism. For instance, the emblematic *hand of the mysteries* was a carved hand covered with numerous symbols and this was extended to the neophytes when they entered into the Temple of Wisdom. An understanding of the symbols embossed upon the surface of the hand brought with it Divine power and regeneration. Therefore, by means of these symbolic hands the candidate was said to be *raised from the dead*. The hand of the mysteries is also known as the hand of the philosopher. When the disciple of the Great Art first beholds this hand, it is closed, and he must discover a method of opening it before the mystery contained therein may be revealed. In alchemy the hand signifies the formula for the preparation of the tincture physicorum. The four fingers represent four Divine Agents through the combined operations of which the Great Work is accomplished. The wise take their oath by the hand that they will not teach the Art without parables. To the Qabbalist the hand signifies the operation of the One Power (The crowned thumb) in the four worlds (the fingers with their emblems). Besides its alchemical and Qabbalistic meanings, the hand symbolizes the hand of a Master Mason with which he "raises" the martyred Builder of the Divine House. The crowned thumb is Absolute Light, unknown and unrevealed, whose power shines through all the lesser lights that are but sparks of this Eternal Effulgence. The Creator's works are all contained within the "hollow of His hand". A man's physical body has five distinct and important extremities: two legs, two arms, and a head, of which the last governs the first four. The number *five* has been accepted as the *symbol of man*. By its four corners the pyramid symbolizes the arms and legs, and by its apex the head, thus indicating that one rational power controls four irrational corners. The hands and feet are used to represent the four elements, of which the two feet are earth and water, and the two hands fire and air. The brain then symbolizes the sacred fifth element, aether, which controls and unites the other four. It is easy to see why the space intelligences have used the symbol of a hand with its corresponding number five. I am certain that the readers of this book will have much more to offer toward a more complete understanding of the *tracks on the desert*. Mr. George H. Lark, librarian of the Philosophical Research Society, Inc. in Los Angeles, California sent drawings of the RIGHT and LEFT footprints to Florence Sternfels, a psychic of New Jersey. She has worked with Dr. Rhine at Duke University on different phenomena in the parapsychology field. Mr. Lark did not mention Saucers, etc. when writing to her and he did not explain the drawings in any way. After meditating on the footprints she wrote: "It seems the owner of the feet is very odd, and it could be a woman because of the long hair. This person seems to be in another world or on another planet and talks in a strange language and has an unusual sounding voice. This person also dresses very strangely. Whatever the mystery is everyone will know in a short time. People like the one the footprints belong to certainly appear to come from another planet." This is very interesting information considering the fact that this woman had no knowledge of what these prints were or from where they might have come!

Of our space friend who placed his tracks in desert sand, we might say: "How beautiful upon the mountains are the *feet* of him who brings glad tidings . . ."

The Lemurian interpretation of the *tracks on the desert*, is given here by itself since placing it with the preceding material would have only confused both interpretations.

The LEFT footprint stands for the *old continent* of Mu. Mu, Empire of the Sun, Motherland of the human race on the planet Earth, lies beneath the waters. She is also called Kui, Pan, or Lemuria. (See *Plate IV*).

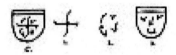

A. Closed lotus means Mu no longer exists. The fish represents sunken Mu and is, as mentioned before, the symbol of the Piscean Age. Mu will remain submerged until all influences of the Piscean Age are removed for she will emerge from Pisces to Aquarius.

1. Mu lies beneath waves.
2. The invisible Trinity of Father, Son, and Holy Ghost, pervades all, even the waters. The Empire of the Sun shines no more for she has set. Since a triangle represents heaven we see that inhabitants of Mu are in their heavens.
3. The closed eye—Mu sleeps. The third eye, or the spiritual eye of the Piscean is closed. This also represents a Cosmic Egg.
4. Arabic numeral (1) meaning the Infinite *One*, the Creator. Since this symbol forms the fish it means Mu is swallowed up. All life returns to the *One*.
5. Mu lies in an abyss at a great depth.

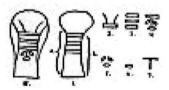

B. The lotus flower, the floral symbol of Mu. The lotus was the first flower to appear on Earth.

1. A water jug, (a) with or (b) without the top portion of the lotus. The water jug is the Aquarian Age. The new continent of Mu will emerge from the water during the Aquarian Age on Earth.
2. This symbol represents colonists who went out from Mu, the Motherland. The left line represents those who went West, and the right line represents those who went East.
3. The three bars represent Mu because she emerged originally in three stages. The rectangle is a Hieratic symbol for Mu.
4. Mu is submerged; upside down.
5. Lemuria, or Mu, was divided into three parts and water separated the land.
6. She was a tableland.
7. The "T" represents Tau—resurrection or emersion, also the Crux or Southern Cross in the heavens. Mu will be resurrected (the new heavens, new Earth, New Age will emerge) in the region of the Southern Cross.

The RIGHT footprint stands for the *new continent* of Mu. The New Heavens and the New Earth, the New Golden Dawn or Age, the Aquarian or Air Age; the New Mu will emerge from the Pacific Ocean. (See *Plate VI*).

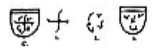

C. The Four Great Primary Forces of Infinite Spirit are continually active in the Universe.

1. The Four Forces are revolving in vortices—the Central Sun or Creator, the Initiator.
2. These could possibly be the symbols of the different activity of each Force. The Four Great Primary Forces are: Static Magnetic Field; Electro Static Field; Electro-Magnetic Wave; Resonating Electro-Magnetic Field.
3. Life takes form through the activity of the Four Forces. The face tells us that the human form is a Universal form. Because we are made "in the image of God", whose countenance is as

the Sun, full of beauty and "too pure to behold iniquity", we too should reflect that loveliness with a smiling face; and this face is smiling. Remember in "The Saucers Speak!" where we mentioned the experiment of Dr. David Todd in 1924? Contact was attempted in Washington with the planet Mars. Several of the messages received took the form of a crudely drawn *human face*!

D. The new, resurrected continent of Mu, brought up through cataclysmic changes in the *Pacific*.

1. All comes from the Great Totality, the One. All in the New Age will be according to the Divine Will. (This large dot appears as the first symbol above the heel on the RIGHT footprint and was not interpreted in the previous section).
2. Lemurian colonists (reincarnated) will return from East and West and merge into a new race. This will take place through the coming of positive (male) and negative (female) lines of force.
3. (a) The One Spirit; (b) Symbol of the Sun, the male principle of the One; (c) Symbol of the Moon, the female principle of the One. Therefore, from the One androgynous Spirit springs male and female.
4. The Cosmic Egg, having been resurrected from the water, brings forth new life. This could also be a sperm and would mean the same thing. (This symbol as a black oval was seen on the side of the large mother-ship that appeared on the desert, November 20, 1952. However, it was on its side thus:).
5. Life takes place through the action of the Four Great Primary Forces within the One.

6. The Seven Planets of Ancient Wisdom will again be at the heart of the new race and they will be guided by the planetary forces.

7. This is a symbol of emersion of New Mu. She will emerge as a unit; the three lands will be one. 8. Here is another symbol of the Four Forces radiating from the One; Infinite Spirit shown by the thumb. All forces will be understood and utilized for good in the New Age. The hand is the hand of God and will rule supreme. The hand is a universal form just as the face is.

9. Through purity of living, purity of thought, meditating on the One, the Central Sun, and through prayer the spiritual third eye will be pierced and opened in the new race. All will experience telepathy, clairvoyance, etc. The activating force will be the Fourth Primary Force or the Resonating Electro-Magnetic Field (RMF). The symbol of an arrow means the force is active. There is a connection here with sound and may be the means of rediscovering the lost Sacred Word.

10. These are geometric patterns. God geometrizes, for everything has mathematical pattern.

11. This is a musical note, symbol of the "Music of the Spheres". This sound, or vibration, in the fourth dimension of motion, together with geometric patterns in the fifth dimension of motionlessness, is the cosmic glue which holds the Universe together.

In Job 13:27, we read: "Thou settest a print upon the heels of my feet." And it has been truly written: "There shall be signs in the heavens above and *signs in the earth beneath.*" The *tracks on the desert* fulfill ancient prophecy, brought to us by OTHER TONGUES!

CHAPTER 3

MALDEK AND MALONA

How art thou fallen from heaven, O Lucifer (O day star), son of the morning! How art thou cut down to the ground, which didst weaken the nations! For thou hast said in thine heart, I will ascend into heaven, I will exalt my throne above the stars of God: I will sit also upon the mount of the congregation, in the sides of the north: I will ascend above the heights of the clouds; I will be like the most High. Yet thou shalt be brought down to hell, to the sides of the pit. They that see thee shall narrowly look upon thee, and consider thee, saying, Is this the man that made the earth to tremble, that did shake kingdoms; that made the world as a wilderness, and destroyed the cities thereof; that opened not the house of his prisoners? All the kings of the nations, even all of them, lie in glory, everyone in his own house. But thou art cast out of thy grave like an abominable branch, and as the raiment of those that are slain, thrust through with a sword, that go down to the stones of the pit; as a carcass trodden under feet. Thou shalt not be joined with them in burial because thou hast destroyed thy land, and slain thy people: the seed of evil-doers shall never be renowned. Prepare slaughter for his children for the iniquity of their fathers; that they do not rise, nor possess the land, nor fill the face of the world with cities. For I will rise up against them, saith the Lord of hosts, and cut off from Babylon the name, and remnant, and son, and nephew, saith the Lord." (Isaiah 14:12-22).

The word Lucifer comes from a Latin word meaning, "Light-bringing", a name sometimes given by poets to the Moon, or to the planet Venus when it appears as the morning star and to the day. In ancient times, this word was wrongly interpreted to mean Satan.

The Hebrew meaning of the word seems to be "brilliant", "splendid", "illustrious", or as in the Septuagint, Vulgate, the Rabbinical commentators, Luther, and others, "brilliant star!" and in this sense was the proper name among the Hebrews of the morning star. Tertullian and Gregory the Great understood this passage of Isaiah in reference to the fall of Satan; in consequence of which the name Lucifer has since been applied to Satan; and this is now the usual acceptation of the word.

Dr. Henderson in his *Isaiah* renders the line: "How art thou fallen from heaven, O illustrious son of the morning!" Dr. Henderson says: "The application of this passage to Satan, and to the fall of the apostate angels, is one of those gross perversions of Sacred Writ which so extensively obtain, and which are to be traced to a proneness to seek for more in any given passage than it really contains."

The only place in the Holy Bible where the word Lucifer is found is in Isaiah. The early church fathers were under the impression that, the passage could only refer to Satan, the prince of darkness. However, Satan in the Bible has no connection with the Lucifer of Isaiah.

Isaiah was figuratively speaking of the king of Babylon in reference to his glory and pomp, but he was actually referring to the destruction of a planet known to the ancient world as the "shining one". Lucifer and its remains are now to be observed in the telescope as the Asteroid Belt.

By a curious chain of reference the passage in Luke 10:18 once was thought to refer to Isaiah 14:12, but this passage says: "I beheld Satan as Lightning fall from heaven." Even though this passage speaks of Satan, Lucifer became the chief of the fallen angels, the name borne by Satan before his rebellion. However, it must be stated again that Satan is in no way connected with Lucifer.

In *"The Saucers Speak!"* Zo said: "Your so-called Hydrogen Bomb could make an asteroid belt out of you. This happened many years ago to the planet of what you would call the fifth orbit. We knew what they were doing but we didn't interfere. We cannot stand by and see another waste. After their destruction there were terrible disasters on Masar (Mars). Great volcanic eruptions took place. Many of our people perished. We would have been thrown out of this Solar System and lost if we had not quickly constructed two artificial satellites. Some of you scientists have noticed that our so-called moons Phobos and Deimos reflect too much light to be made of earthy substance. They are right. They are metallic in nature. They readjusted our unstable condition and saved a planet."

It is true that the ancient poets knew of the satellites of Mars before their discovery and ancient astrological works mention them. Jonathon Swift in "Gulliver's Travels", 1726, wrote that Mars had two satellites and his complete description of them was most accurate. They were actually discovered as late as 1877 by Asaph Hall of the Naval Observatory in Washington, D. C. How did Swift and all these other individuals know that Mars had two moons?

If the Prophet Isaiah was actually referring to a "fallen star" or a destroyed planet let us see if his description as found in the fourteenth chapter fits such a happening.

To begin with he wonders how Lucifer, then a morning star, fell from heaven. A morning star now can be Jupiter, Mars, Saturn or Venus when rising shortly before the sun, and forming a conspicuous object in the sky just before dawn; hence, figuratively, a forerunner, or one who announces and guides. For a planet to be called the morning star it must be West of the sun and visible before sunrise. When bright planets are East of the sun and therefore visible in the early evening they are called evening stars. The ancients not realizing they were the same stars in different roles, called Venus when the evening star, Hesperus or Vesper and when it was the morning star, Phosphorus. Mercury was called Mercury when it was the evening star, but it was called Apollo when it was a morning star:

When we think of morning star now we immediately associate it with the planet Venus. Therefore, we think the ancient word Lucifer also applied to Venus. However, this is not the case. Venus and Mercury were known primarily as evening stars, but when Venus was a morning star it was called Phosphorus. (This word comes from the Greek, phos, light; and phero, bear). The Asteroid Belt, then the planet Lucifer, was also known as *the* morning star.

Did the destruction of Lucifer take place in Isaiah's time? This is not likely, for history tells us that there were great catastrophes on Earth as early as the 13th century B.C. And remember, space intelligences refer to our Earth as Saros (Saras) "the sorrowful planet", or the "planet of much cataclysm".

The Old Testament is literally full of references to the end of the planet known to the ancients of Earth as Lucifer, and to outer space intelligences as Maldek, the "silver-tongued". The first three letters of the planet's name (Mal) mean: *tongue*. For a moment, let us refer once again to James 3:5-10. There is a double meaning to be found here, for James is not only talking about the literal tongue of man, but he is speaking metaphorically of Maldek (Lucifer).

James 3:5: "Even so the tongue is a little member, and boasteth great things. Behold, how great a matter a little fire kindleth!"

In reference to Maldek, this could be translated: "Even so the *planet Maldek* (tongue) is a little *world* (member), and boasteth great things. Behold, how great a destruction (matter) a little explosion (fire) causes (kindleth!)."

James 3:6: "And the tongue is a fire, a world of iniquity: so is the tongue among our members, that it defileth the whole body, and setteth on fire the course of nature; and it is set on fire of hell."

This verse can also be translated: "And the tongue is a fire, that world of iniquity: the tongue is among our members that which defileth the whole body, and setteth on fire the wheel of nature (or birth), and is set on fire by hell (Gehenna)."

Referring again to Maldek, James 3:6 could read: "And *Maldek* (the tongue) is *aflame* (a fire), that would of iniquity: *Maldek* (the tongue) is among our *planets* (members) that which defileth the whole *solar system* (body), and setteth on fire the *vortex* (wheel) of nature (or birth), and is set on fire by *the unseen state* (hell)."

In Greek, *hell* is here translated as Gehenna (Hebrew, Gehinnom). Gehinnom was the valley of Hinnom, near Jerusalem, where the city's refuse was thrown and burned; hence, hell-fire and hell itself; the place of future torment of the wicked.

The last part of James 3:6 can also be translated: ". . . and it is set on fire of hell."

In referring to Maldek, this would give us: ". . . and *Maldek* (it) is set on fire of *the unseen state* (hell)."

This means that Maldek was a world of iniquity that exploded and burned and was a planet in our solar system that defiled all the other planets because of its evil, and Maldek (the tongue) set on fire its vortex, the power of its birth and being, and therefore was set on fire of the unseen state . . . because Maldek released the terrible hydrogen power she broke her vortex and was thereby reduced to an unseen state.

James 3:7: "For every kind of beast, and of birds, and of serpents, and of things in the sea, is tamed, and hath been tamed of mankind (nature of man)."

We see here that man in this solar system had tamed everything, for all things of nature were under his control.

James 3:8: "But the tongue can no man tame; it is an unruly evil full of deadly poison."

Man could not tame Maldek (the tongue) for it was an undisciplined child of the solar system, it wished to have power over all other planets and desired the authority of the Creator himself. Maldek was therefore "full of deadly poison".

James 3:9: "Therewith bless we God, even the Father; and therewith curse we men, which are made after the similitude of God."

Maldek (the tongue) praised the Father, but cursed all men who are in the likeness of God.

James 3:10: "Out of the same mouth proceedeth blessing and cursing. My brethern, these things ought not so to be."

Maldek blessed and cursed at the same time, but this is not living true Universal Law of the Infinite Father. These things should not exist side by side.

I mentioned before, that the Old Testament has many references to the destruction of Lucifer or Maldek. Maldek, as a world, came to an abrupt end during the Exodus from Egypt in the days of Moses (13th century before Christ). The Exodus took place amid a great natural upheaval that terminated the period of Egyptian history known as the Middle Kingdom. Contemporary Egyptian documents describe the same disaster accompanied by "the plagues of Egypt".

One of the first visible signs on Earth of the destruction of Maldek was the reddening of the earth's surface by a fine dust of rusty pigment. Ipuwer, an Egyptian eyewitness of the catastrophe, wrote his description on papyrus: "The river is blood. Plague is throughout the land. Blood is everywhere."

The Papyrus Ipuwer corresponds very well with the Book of Exodus 7:20: "All the waters that were in the river were turned to blood." And in Exodus 7:21: "There was blood throughout all the land of Egypt."

The presence of the red dust in the rivers caused the fish to die and there was decomposition and foul odor. Exodus 7:21: "And the river stank." Exodus 7:24: "And all the Egyptians digged round about the river for water to drink; for they could not drink of the water of the river." The Papyrus Ipuwer says: "Men shrink from tasting; human beings thirst after water. That is our water! That is our happiness! What shall we do in respect thereof? All is ruin."

Men had boils and sickness; cattle died from the irritating red dust. Exodus 93: "Behold, the hand of the Lord is upon thy cattle which is in the field, upon the horses, upon the asses, upon the camels, upon the oxen, and upon the sheep: there shall be a very grievous murrain (pestilence or plague)."

After the coming of the red dust, another strange phenomenon took place. Exodus 9:8: "And the Lord said unto Moses and unto Aaron, Take to you handfuls of ashes of the furnace, and let Moses sprinkle it toward the heaven in the sight of Pharaoh." Exodus 9:9: "And it shall become small dust in all the land of Egypt, and shall be a boil breaking forth with blains upon man, and upon beast, throughout all the land of Egypt."

This "small dust", like "ashes of the furnace", sounds identically the same as the radioactive ash that fell on men and animals in the Pacific Ocean after atomic tests there recently. Even some of the fish were contaminated. It is possible that this "small dust" or "ash" was the radioactive material sent out after the explosion of Maldek and entered the Earth's atmosphere before the next happening . . . the shower of meteorites that struck Earth.

Exodus 9:18: "Behold, to-morrow about this time I will cause it to rain a very grievous hail, such as hath not been in Egypt since the foundation thereof even until now." Stones of "barad" are translated here as "hail". However, "barad" is the term for meteorites. Midrashic sources and the Babylonian Talmud tell us that the stones which fell on Egypt were hot. Therefore, the "hail" could not have been ice, for this description fits only meteorites. The ancient Egyptian word for "hail" was *ar*, and means a driving shower of sand and stones. Also, in the Book of Joshua it is said that "great stones" fell from the sky, and they are called: "stones of barad".

Exodus 9:24: "So there was hail, and fire mingled with the hail, very grievous, such as there was none like it in all the land of Egypt since it became a nation." Exodus 9:25: "And the hail smote throughout all the land of Egypt all that was in the field, both man and beast; and the hail smote every herb of the field, and brake every tree of the field."

Exodus 9:28: "Entreat the Lord (for it is enough) that there be no mighty thunderings (voices of God) and hail; and I will let you go, and ye shall stay no longer."

The fall of meteorites is accompanied by explosion-like noises and in this case the crashes were "mighty".

The Papyrus Ipuwer says: "Trees are destroyed, no fruits, no herbs are found, grain has perished on every side, that has perished which yesterday was seen. The land is left to its weariness like the cutting of flax."

In the *Visuddhi-Magga*, a Buddhist text on world cycles, we find: "When a world cycle is destroyed by wind, there arises in the beginning a cycle-destroying great cloud. There arises a wind to destroy the world cycle, and first it raises a fine dust, and then coarse dust, and then fine sand, and then coarse sand, and then grit, stones, up to boulders as large as mighty trees on the hilltop."

So, Maldek came to an end with the coming of the red dust in the time of Moses and the Exodus from Egypt. As time went on the Earth was engulfed in more dense matter from the fallen planet.

Exodus 10:22-23: "And there was a thick darkness in all the land of Egypt three days: They saw not one another, neither rose any from his place for three days."

Maldek caused terrible destruction on Earth and darkness was over the entire world. Mars was also greatly damaged by this catastrophe and that will be taken up later on.

The Papyrus Ipuwer speaks of a great earthquake: "The towns are destroyed. Upper Egypt has become waste. All is ruin. The residence is overturned in a minute."

Exodus 12:30: "And Pharaoh rose up in the night, he, and all his servants, and all the Egyptians; and there was not a house where there was not one dead."

It should be stated here that the word Marduk may have come from Maldek. Marduk was the chief god of the Babylonian pantheon . . . from his mouth issued flame. In the battle of Marduk with Tiamat, "he (Marduk) created the evil wind, and the tempest, and the hurricane, and the fourfold wind, and the sevenfold wind, and the whirlwind, and the wind which had no equal."

This description fits Maldek who created chaos with hydrogen devices or "the evil wind". Maldek, therefore, created "the wind which had no equal". Hydrogen detonations are without equal because they will completely destroy a planet if used. I must pause here for awhile in order to say that *no true hydrogen bomb, as such, has ever been detonated on Earth!*

Van Tassel has shown us that space intelligences are not particularly concerned with the explosion of plutonium and U325, the Uranium mother element, because this atom is an *inert* element. But they are concerned with the attempt to explode an actual hydrogen bomb. If we had set-off such a bomb we would now be nothing but a bunch of floating cinders . . . we would be as Maldek, an asteroid belt. Space friends vowed that they would never again allow a planet in this Solar System to destroy itself; therefore, no government on Earth will explode true hydrogen . . . it will not be allowed.

The element hydrogen is life-giving along with five other elements in the air we breathe, in the water we drink, and in the composition of our physical self. Explode a true H-bomb and all life on Earth will be extinguished. Van Tassel told us months and months ago that our scientists were "tinkering" with a formula they did not understand. The explosion of an atom of *inert* substance and that of a *living* substance are two different things.

Hydrogen "devices" have utilized deuterium and tritium, not hydrogen, as such. The elements exist in simplest form as atoms, and these atoms are composed of a nucleus about which electrons revolve. Elements are distinguished from each other by the number of electrons revolving about the central nucleus. Each electron carries a negative electrical charge which is off-set by a positively charged particle in the nucleus known as a proton. Elements may contain additional particles in the nucleus, which carry no electrical charge and are known as neutrons.

All of this basic explanation is to show why no true hydrogen bomb has been detonated. The simplest element is hydrogen which in its most common form consists of one electron and thus one proton in each atom. Two other forms of hydrogen are known which, in addition to the one electron and one proton also have respectively one and two neutrons in their atomic structure. These two rare forms of hydrogen are known as deuterium and tritium. Deuterium exists in the proportion of one atom of deuterium to every sixty-four hundred atoms of ordinary hydrogen, in nature. Tritium is an artificial radioactive element. Because their masses are so greatly different in proportion to ordinary hydrogen, the differences in properties are quite marked.

Deuterium and tritium then, are isotopes of hydrogen, and because of their extreme rarity it is possible that they would not have the dangerous "chain-reaction" results that common or ordinary hydrogen would . . . for hydrogen of the common type is found in all living things on Earth. To create and detonate a true H-bomb would be to announce to the rest of the Universe that the planet Earth had suddenly come to an end like a flaming, exploding star in the corner of the Milky Way Galaxy. The history of Maldek would repeat itself: "How art thou fallen from heaven, O Earth . . ."

In getting back to Marduk, we find that in his battle with Tiamat, mother of the gods, he killed her and when he became the most powerful of all things he set about to create order in the universe. He then split Tiamat's body in two. This sounds like Maldek battling the elements of nature and finally subduing the atomic power (mother of the gods or forces). Maldek became powerful because of this mastery and attempted to rule all other planets. Maldek split this hydrogen force of nature (Tiamat).

After the Exodus from Egypt, the Wandering in the Desert lasted for forty years according to the Holy Bible. Then for a number of years the conquest of Palestine went on. Between the time when the Israelites left the desert and started the difficult task of the conquest, and the time of the battle at Beth-horon, twelve years may easily have passed. According to rabbinical sources the war of conquest in Palestine lasted fourteen years. During the fifty-two years between the catastrophe of the Exodus and the time of Joshua commanding the Sun to stand still at the battle of Beth-horon, the Earth was shrouded in dense clouds and the observation of the stars was difficult.

The Book of Joshua was compiled from the more ancient Book of Jasher.

Joshua 10:11-13: "And it came to pass, as they fled from before Israel, and were in the going down to Beth-boron, that the Lord cast down great stones from heaven upon them unto Azekah, and they died: they were more which died with hailstones than they whom the children of Israel slew with the sword. Then spake Joshua to the Lord in the day when the Lord delivered up the Amorites before the children of Israel, and he said in the sight of Israel, Sun, stand thou still upon Gibeon; and thou, Moon, in the valley of Ajalon. And the sun stood still, and the moon stayed, until the people had avenged themselves upon their enemies. Is not this written in the book of Jasher? So the sun stood still in the midst of heaven, and hasted not to go down about a whole day."

Therefore, about fifty-two years passed after the Exodus before the Earth encountered another swarm of meteorites from the destroyed Lucifer-Maldek. At least, there wasn't any major catastrophe until the time of Joshua.

It should be mentioned that the Book of Jasher is one of the long-lost, and long-sought for sacred books, which should have been included among the other books of the Bible but which was not because the original manuscript could not be located. In Joshua 10:13, it says: "Is not this written in the book of Jasher?" And the account is to be found in the Book of Jasher 30:11.

In reference to the fifty-two year period, it is interesting to note that the natives of pre-Columbian Mexico expected a new catastrophe at the end of every period of fifty-two years. Fernando de Alva Ixtlilxochitl (circa 1568-1648) was a great early Mexican scholar. He claimed that only fifty-two years elapsed between two great world catastrophes, and each of these catastrophes terminated a world age.

Because of the memory of the catastrophe, the people of the Earth feared it would occur again, but not much happened until the eighth century before Christ, in the days of Uzziah, king of Jerusalem. At this time there occurred a devastating catastrophe called *raash* or "commotion". *Raash* is translated "earthquake". Amos lived at this time and predicted some sort of great cosmic upheaval before the *raash* took place. Later, Isaiah, Joel, Hosea, and Micah all declared that the Earth would encounter more of the same in the future. Many generations later it was remembered how the people "fled from before the earthquake (raash) in the days of Uzziah king of Judah". (Zechariah 14:5). Uzziah reigned from about 189 to about 740, and since a new calendar was introduced in the Middle East in the year 747 B.C., the great upheaval or "commotion" must have taken place in that year of 747.

Hebrew sources say that the Prophet Isaiah began to prophesy immediately after the "commotion" of the days of king Uzziah. He said:

Isaiah 1:7: "Your country is desolate, your cities are burned with fire: your land, strangers devour it in your presence, and it is desolate, as overthrown by strangers."

Isaiah prophesied in "the days of Uzziah, Jotham, Ahaz, and Hezekiah, kings of Judah". Somehow, Isaiah knew that at intervals of fifteen years a catastrophe occurred. The "commotion" of the days of Uzziah was only the beginning of sorrows and more destruction caused by Lucifer-Maldek.

I believe that Isaiah was visited by space intelligences who told him that catastrophe would come to Earth caused by the great fragments of Maldek. The space friends would have been able to calculate the time that the destruction would return. Proof of this is found in Isaiah 6:1-3: "In the year that king Uzziah died I saw also the Lord sitting upon a throne, high and lifted up, and his train filled the temple. Above it stood the seraphim: each one had six wings; with twain he covered his face, and with twain he covered his feet, and with twain he did fly. And one cried unto another, and said, Holy, holy, holy, is the Lord of hosts: the whole earth is full of his glory."

Isaiah 6:-12: "Then flew one of the seraphim unto me, having a live coal in his hand, which he had taken with the tongs from off the altar: And he laid it upon my mouth, and said, Lo, this hath touched thy lips: and thine iniquity is taken away, and thy sin purged. Also I heard the voice of the Lord, saying, Whom shall I send, and who will go for us? Then said I, Here am I; send me. And he said, Go, and tell this people, Hear ye indeed, but understand not; and see ye indeed, but perceive not. Make the heart of this people fat, and make their ears heavy, and shut their eyes; lest they see with their eyes, and hear with their ears, and understand with their heart, and convert, and be healed. Then said I, Lord, how long? And he answered, Until the cities be wasted without inhabitant, and the houses without man, and the land be utterly desolate. And the Lord have removed men far away, and there be a great forsaking in the midst of the land."

The space visitors told Isaiah to go and tell the people until "the cities be wasted without inhabitant", "And the Lord have removed men far away". This sounds as though some people were taken by space craft to a safer place.

In reflecting on the terror that Lucifer-Maldek had caused for many centuries since the Exodus, Isaiah was inspired to write: "How art thou fallen from heaven, O Lucifer, son of the morning!" Then the prophet asks how Lucifer was "cut down to the ground, which didst weaken the nations!" Therefore, Lucifer's destruction along with the Earth receiving a pounding over many years by meteor showers, caused the nations to be weakened. Many people will ask: "We have meteor showers now, why don't we have great catastrophe like they had in the time of Moses, Joshua or Isaiah?" It is true that we do have meteor showers in this day and age, but they are nothing compared to what the Lucifer-Maldek showers were, for these showers were much more dense.

Somehow Isaiah knew that the planet Lucifer had tried to become the ruling world of the Universe, for he says: "For thou hast said in thine heart, I will ascend into heaven, I will exalt my throne above the stars of God." Lucifer intended to rule all the worlds (stars).

Then Isaiah says: "Yet thou shalt be brought down to hell, to the sides of the pit." In Hebrew and Greek, the literal meaning of hell is "the unseen state", and the meaning of hades is "the unseen world". Therefore, Isaiah, meant that Lucifer was brought down to an unseen state . . . after the destruction it was an unseen world.

Isaiah said, "They that see thee shall narrowly look upon thee, and consider thee." Did he mean that observation would be difficult? The largest of the asteroids is Ceres, and it is only 480 miles in diameter. Ceres along with the brightest asteroids is said to be sometimes visible to the naked eye, when nearest to our Earth and under exceptionally favorable conditions, but the rest are, naturally, telescopic, as their size is too small in relation to their distance. Is this what Isaiah meant when he said: "They that see thee shall *narrowly* look upon thee?"

The prophet said that those who looked on Lucifer later would say: "Is this the *man* that made the earth to tremble, that did shake kingdoms; that made the world as a wilderness and destroyed the cities thereof; that opened not the house of his prisoners? (or, did not let his prisoners loose home-wards)."

In calling Lucifer a *man* it would seem that the prophet was referring to an actual person, perhaps the king of Babylon. But this is not the case. In Hebrew, there are four words that can mean *man*. One of these words means: a man, human being; another means: a man, a mortal; and another means: a male. But the word *man* used in Isaiah 14:16 means: a husband, individual.

Therefore, Isaiah is saying: "Is this the *individual* that made the earth to tremble . . ." Or, he is saying: "Is this the *husband* that made the earth to tremble . . ."? In neither case does it imply that Lucifer was an actual *man!* Lucifer could represent a husband very well, because the planet Maldek had a moon. This moon was known as Lilith. A moon is often feminine and the moon deity is usually a goddess. The Greek goddesses Selene, Artemis, and Hecate were all identified with the moon. According to Moslem tradition Lilith cohabited with the Devil (from Lucifer?) and was even his wife.

In our contacts with space intelligences in Northern Arizona, the planet Lucifer was always referred to as Maldek (Maldec) and its moon was called Malona. Father Lorber also mentions Malona in his work. He is discussed in this book under *The Great Influx* in the section called: *God Provided—Man Divided.*

Isaiah says that Lucifer shook kingdoms, made the world a wilderness, and destroyed her cities. This is certainly true as we can see from the references already given. Cities and fields were pelted with meteoric fragments, the earth was shaken with earthquakes.

Lucifer did not open "the house of his prisoners" and he "did not let his prisoners loose homewards". Those responsible for the destruction of Lucifer-Maldek were "prisoners" of their own making. They were not allowed to leave the doomed planet and suffered the same fate as their world. They were "freed" when the planet was destroyed because they lost their physical equipment and were known as spirits again.

Isaiah says: "But thou art cast out of thy grave like an abominable branch." All other worlds go through space in majesty, but Lucifer didn't even have a final resting place. The blasted fragments of a once beautiful and proud planet were left to float endlessly in space that others might know what Lucifer had done. It would be a warning to all others that this should not be. It is interesting to note here that in May, 1854, Leverrier read a paper before the French Academy upon the asteroids, their eccentric orbits and irregularities. He said that the hypothesis stated by Dr. Olbers that the asteroids were derived from the wreck of a larger planet that had exploded, is incompatible with the real truth, inasmuch as the forces necessary to launch the fragments of a given body in such different routes would be of such *improbable intensity* as to render it mathematically absurd! Leverrier didn't know what a hydrogen detonation could do!

The prophet then tells us: "Thou shalt not be joined with them in burial, because thou hast destroyed thy land, and slain thy people." Lucifer was not to end its days as other worlds which had completed their usefulness. Because of the evil of this planet, its land and people were destroyed in a horrible holocaust. "The seed of evil-doers shall never be renowned."

Because of Lucifer's self-destruction, his children or people would "not rise, nor possess the land, nor fill the face of the world with cities". The spirits from Lucifer were not to reincarnate on Earth to the extent that they would hold dominion over it in "cities".

"For I will rise up against them, saith the Lord of hosts, and cut off from Babylon the name, and remnant, and son, and nephew, saith the Lord."

Swedenborg, in his Science of Correspondences tells us that *Babel*, or *Babylon* represents those whose externals appear holy, while their internals are profane. In the prophets of the Old Testament, *Babylon* means the profanation of good, and Chaldea means the profanation of truth. According to Swedenborg, Lucifer signifies self-love, the profaning of holy things. Lucifer means the same as Babel. It is from the self-love of Lucifer that we get the modern phrase: "Proud as Lucifer".

This again applies to the reincarnational cycle of Luciferians. They were to be completely cut off from "the profanation of good". Never again would such a destruction take place in our Solar System. They would not be allowed to encourage the internal profanity of those on Earth.

In Isaiah 14:29, we read: "Rejoice not thou, whole Palestina, because the rod of him that smote thee is broken: for out of the serpent's root shall come forth a cockatrice, and his fruit shall be a fiery flying serpent."

This could be translated: "Rejoice not all you who conceive false principles, because the vortex of Lucifer who struck you with force is broken: for out of the center of the coiled, spiral vortex shall come forth a venomous serpent that will corrupt and tread, and the fruit of this will be a fiery flying serpent."

A cockatrice was a fabulous serpent with deadly glance, reputed to be hatched by a serpent from a cock's egg, and commonly represented with the head, legs, and wings of a cock and the body and tail of a serpent. The word cockatrices comes from the word *cocatris* (corrupt), and *calcare* (to tread). When cockatrice is used in the Bible it means an *unidentified* venomous serpent.

Swedenborg tells us that Palestina (Philisthea) means those who conceive false principles and reason thence concerning spiritual things which overflow man. All those who conceive falsely are told not to rejoice just because Lucifer was destroyed by having its vortex shattered, because out of the center (root) of the coiled, spiral vortex (serpent) would come an unidentified destructive object that would corrupt and tread the land, and the result or product (fruit) of this would be a fiery, flying object.

Here we see that the people are warned that the catastrophe is not over yet because a large meteoric fragment will head for the Earth and it will divide into smaller fragments like "fiery flying serpents" and when it strikes the Earth it will "corrupt and tread the land". One object, perhaps larger than the rest, is mentioned specifically.

The Great Meteor Crater near Canyon Diablo in Arizona, about six miles south of the Sunshine Station of the Santa Fe Railroad, was evidently caused by one of the "fiery serpents". These meteors were thus described by the ancients because as they headed for Earth they did, indeed, look like flaming dragons or snakes. It is important to note in this connection that the morning star of the Toltecs, Quetzal-cohuatl, is represented as a great dragon or serpent: "cothuatl" in Nahuatl is "serpent", and the name means "a feathered serpent". The morning star of the Chichimec Indian tribe in Mexico is called "serpent cloud".

The ancestors of the present day Navajo Indians are said to have seen one of their gods come down from the sky in a cloud of fire and bury himself in the ground at the spot where the Great Meteor Crater exists in Arizona. A cedar tree on the rim of the crater grew to be over seven hundred years old. Some scientists think that the meteor that caused this tremendous crater may have been a small comet. And what better description would fit a comet than a "feathered serpent"?

Of course, Meteor Crater was not formed by a "true" comet, but the meteor itself was of such tremendous size, it would seem more like a comet than a meteor, which we associate with little "shooting stars". The meteorite weighs somewhere between a million and ten million tons. It threw out between three and four hundred million tons of rock when it hit the earth. The crater is about 4,100 feet wide, about 570 feet deep, and about three miles around. The outside rim is over one hundred feet high. The time when it fell is unknown. Scientists say probably more than one thousand years ago and maybe as much as fifty thousand years ago.

However, the fall of this gigantic meteorite is found in the legends of the Navajo Indians, and this tribe hasn't been in the Southwestern area very long. They came from Canada "hundreds", not "thousands" of years ago. Therefore, it is believed that this great meteor was a part of the "fiery flying serpent" that headed for Earth in the time of Isaiah the prophet.

Isaiah 24:17-19: "Fear and the pit, and the snare are upon thee, O inhabitant of the earth . . . for the windows from on high are open, and the foundations of the earth do shake. The earth is utterly broken down, the earth is clean dissolved, the earth is moved exceedingly."

When did the catastrophe come? Isaiah 14:28: "In the year that King Ahaz died was this burden." Ahaz was the son of Jotham, King of Judah, and father of Hezekiah. Ahaz succeeded his father as eleventh King of Judah, and reigned sixteen years. (740-724 B.C.). Therefore, the catastrophe came on the day on which King Ahaz was buried, some-time in 724 B.C.

Isaiah 24:1: "Behold, the Lord maketh the earth empty, and maketh it waste, and turneth it upside down, and scattereth abroad the inhabitants thereof."

Isaiah continued his ministry until about 690 B.C. His name means: "helper". And he did everything he could to help and warn the people of the impending catastrophes. After the death of King Ahaz, Hezekiah was King of Judah and during his fourteenth year another catastrophe was expected.

Isaiah 28:2: "Behold, the Lord hath a mighty and strong one, which as a tempest of hail and a destroying storm, as a flood of mighty waters overflowing, shall cast down to the earth with the hand."

A "mighty and strong" heavenly body was to be cast down to Earth. Isaiah 29:5-6: "Moreover the multitude of thy strangers shall be like small dust, and the multitude of the terrible ones shall be as chaff that passeth away: yea, it shall be at an instant suddenly. Thou shalt be visited of the Lord of hosts with thunder, and with earthquake, and great noise, with storm and tempest, and the flame of devouring fire."

Isaiah 28:21: "For the Lord . . . shall be wroth as in the valley of Gibeon, that he may do his work, his strange work; and bring to pass his act, his strange act."

This refers to the "strange act" in the valley of Gibeon when Joshua witnessed a meteoric shower and commanded the sun to stand still. Isaiah knew of this happening and says the new catastrophe will be similar to it.

The prophet referred his readers to the "Book of the Lord". Isaiah 34:16: "Seek ye out the book of the Lord, and read: no one of these shall fail." Evidently this book belonged to the same series as the Book of Jasher, in which the records of the days of Joshua at Gibeon were preserved. Other ancient records must have been in the "Book of the Lord". The Book of Jasher is once more available, but the other book is still lost.

There were more catastrophes in the years ahead, but there is not sufficient room here to list all of them.

Planets of our Solar System were greatly disturbed by the destruction of Lucifer-Maldek, and its moon Lilith-Malona. The Chinese say: "In the tenth year of the Emperor Kwei, the eighteenth monarch since Yahou, the five planets went out of their courses. In the night stars fell like rain. The earth shook."

Mars and the Earth suffered more from Lucifer than any of the other worlds. The two moons of Mars have already been mentioned, however, other facts must be added. How could Jonathan Swift have guessed not only their number (two), but their size and their short revolutions? Homer knew about the "two steeds of Mars" and Virgil wrote about them. Asaph Hall gave the names of Phobos (Fear) and Deimos (Panic) to these two moons. These names were suggested by Mr. Madan of Eton, England because the ancients said Mars had two steeds and gave them these names. It should also be mentioned that Voltaire told of these moons in the story of Micromegas more than a hundred years before their discovery!

Phobos, the inner satellite, revolves at the distance of 5800 miles from the center of Mars, and 3700 miles from the surface; it completes a sidereal revolution in only 7h 39m, a period less than one third that of the planet's rotation. As viewed from the planet, therefore, it rises in the west and sets in the east. *No other known satellite in the solar system revolves in a shorter interval than the rotation period of its primary.*

The distance of Deimos from the center of Mars is 14,600 miles, and its period of revolution is 30h-18m. It is smaller than the inner satellite (5 miles?), and only one third as bright. The size (diameter) of these satellites is not exactly known. Phobos is about ten miles in diameter and Deimos is about five miles in diameter.

In mythology, the two steeds were yoked when the Greek god of war, Ares (Mars) prepared to descend to the earth on a punitive expedition. This sounds like the two artificial satellites (steeds) of Mars were used together for launching plateforms before Mars sent spaceships to the undisciplined Earth in ancient times. To "yoke" animals, means to join the heads or necks of animals for working together.

In the eighth century before Christ, Mars suddenly became a great and feared god. In Babylon and other ancient centers, prayers were composed and invocations and hymns were sung, many magic formulae were used in incantations. These prayers with lifted hands were addressed directly to the planet Nergal (Mars). Like the Greek Ares, Nergal is called "king of battle". Mars became the great sword god, because in one of its conjunctions, its atmosphere was stretched so that it appeared like a sword.

The Chaldean Nergal is called "Sword-god", and the Roman god Mars was depicted with a sword. In Babylonian inscriptions of the seventh century, Mars was called "the most violent among the gods". Great good Mars became the frightful god of war.

> *"Shine of horror, god Nergal, prince of battle,*
> *Thy face is glare, thy mouth is fire,*
> *Raging Flame-god, god Nergal.* p. 181
> *Thou art Anguish and Terror,*
> *Great Sword-god,*
> *Lord who wanderest in the night,*
> *Horrible, raging Flame-god . . .*
> *Whose storming is a storm flood."*

Remember what Zo told us: "After their (Luciferians) destruction there were terrible disasters on Masar (Mars). Great volcanic eruptions took place. Many of our people perished." Mars literally then, became a "horrible, raging Flame-god . . ."

Evidently the people of Mars knew what was coming so they constructed the two artificial satellites known as Phobos and Deimos. These two objects were well named (Fear and Panic) for they were created during a time of great fear, not only on Mars but on Earth as well. And there certainly was panic as Isaiah has shown us.

Although Lucifer actually came to an end in the time of the Exodus, it is believed that Mars did not receive as much of the destructive force of the blast as Earth did. This was due to its orbital position at the time. Mars took the main shock in the time of Isaiah.

Nergal (Mars) was the war god of the men of Cuth whom Shalmaneser placed in the cities of Israel in place of the ten tribes. II Kings 17:30: "And the men of Babylon made Succoth-benoth, and the men of Cuth made Nergal, and the men of Hamath made Ashima."

The two "moons" of Mars readjusted the unstable condition caused by Lucifer-Maldek and balanced the Resonating Electro-Magnetic Field of the Plan-et. Moons are "balancers" of planets with which they are connected.

The people of Maldek who had been tampering with the force of "the terrible wind that has no equal", were warned by members of the Universal Tribunal on Saturn that their doom was certain if they carried out their plans to detonate actual hydrogen. But they would not listen; therefore, the children of Maldek and the innocent were removed to other worlds. The "black magicians" and "scientists of the left hand path" were left on Maldek to greet chaos of their own making. They believed that if by some chance the hydrogen would not do what was expected of it they would have control of the greatest power in Creation. They could then exalt their "throne above the stars of God".

They would "be like the most High". But since evil destroys evil, the proud Lucifer was "brought down to hell (the unseen state)". What was to come of the spirits of those who perished in the fall of this world?

The allegory of the Fall of Man and the fire of Prometheus is also another version of the myth of the rebellion of the proud Lucifer, hurled down to the bottomless pit, Orcus. In the religion of the Brahmans, Maha-sura, the Hindu Lucifer, becomes envious of the Creator's resplendent light, and at the head of a legion of inferior spirits rebels against Brahma, and declares war against him. Siva, the third person of the Hindu trinity, hurls them all from the celestial abode into Honderah, the region of eternal darkness. But here the fallen angels are made to repent of their evil deed, and in the Hindu doctrine they are all afforded the opportunity to progress.

Therefore, the souls of those responsible for the fate of Lucifer-Maldek were sent to some far off world or worlds in interstellar space, a "region of eternal darkness". Through countless lives they will be made aware of the enormity of their crime to their fellow man. And they will be able to progress once more "up the worlds". They will eventually find the "Great Path". All are on the road to All Perfection . . . none are lost!

That last day of days on Maldek must have been one of unbelievable madness and terror. The sacred "White Light" known as Ishtal-Maxin went out in their Temple of Temples; the sky was dark, ominous, foreboding; even the stars refused to shed their light.

In the Book of Job we find reference to the "wicked" and this may be a description of Lucifer.

Job 18:4-21: "He teareth himself (his soul) in his anger: shall the earth be forsaken for thee? and shall the rock be removed out of his place? Yea (Nevertheless), the light of the wicked shall be put out, and the spark of his fire shall not shine. The light shall be dark in his tabernacle, and his candle (lamp) shall be put out with him. The steps of his strength shall be straitened, and his own counsel shall cast him down. For he is cast into a net by his own feet, and he walketh upon a snare. The gin shall take him by the heel, and the robber shall prevail against him. The snare is laid (hidden) for him in the ground, and a trap for him in the way. Terrors shall make him afraid on every side, and shall drive him (scatter him) to his feet. His strength shall be hunger-bitten, and destruction shall be ready at his side. It shall devour the strength (bars) of his skin: even the firstborn of death shall devour his strength. His confidence shall be rooted out of his tabernacle, and it shall bring him to the king of terrors. It shall dwell in his tabernacle, because it is none of his: brimstone shall be scattered upon his habitation. His roots shall be dried up beneath, and above shall his branch be cut off. His remembrance shall perish from the earth, and he shall have no name in the street. He shall be driven (They shall drive him) from light into darkness, and chased out of the world. He shall neither have son nor nephew among his people, nor any remaining in his dwellings. They that come after him shall be astonied at his day, as they that went before (lived with him) were affrighted (laid hold on horror). Surely such are the dwellings of the wicked, and this is the place of him that knoweth not God."

If this excerpt from the Book of Job is read substituting Lucifer for "wicked" a startling similarity is at once noted between the description of "wicked" and the last days of Lucifer. "The light of the wicked (Lucifer) shall be put out. The light shall be dark in his tabernacle; destruction shall be ready at his side." Then it says: "It shall bring him to the king of terrors." What is the "king of terrors" but the "wind that has no equal": hydrogen devastation! "His remembrance shall perish from the earth", and indeed it has. Knowledge of the destruction of Lucifer has been a closely guarded secret of the Mystery Schools for centuries.

"They that come after him shall be astonied (dazed or dismayed) at his day, as they that lived with him laid hold on horror."

"Such are the dwellings of *Lucifer*, and this the place of him that knoweth not God."

Space intelligences say: "You can never use your great atomic power for peace or peaceful pursuits because the very nature of atomic power is destruction not construction. How can you attain peace by that which is itself essentially unpeaceful? We do not 'split atoms' for that destroys the flow of force through them. Instead, we use that flow of forces. Your people say that 'peace is for the strong' but this is not true. You will never attain your long-sought for world peace through armed might or military strength. You can't force other men to your will in order to assure peace 'at any cost'. What kind of a 'peace' is it that is attained by pointing a gun in another man's back? Therefore, can you make certain undeveloped souls desire peace? No, a thousand times no! They must progress to the place where they realize that death and destruction through war is senseless; they must actually learn to want peace. "Do you know that you destroy untold, literal worlds when you perform your so-called 'atom-splitting' process? All is the same in the Omniverse, from microcosm to macrocosm. Why is it that man of Earth has heard yet understands not? Peace is not for the strong for it has been truly written that 'the meek shall inherit the earth'. And you will never use atomic power for peace in your Golden Age now dawning."

The Earth is now on the same path that Lucifer-Maldek took. Atomic power on that planet ended in destruction to end all destruction. But it will not happen on the Earth; our brothers in outer space will not allow the Earth to end as Maldek did. There will be catastrophes, yes, but greet them with a prayer on your lips and joy in your heart for it is a sign unto you that your deliverance is nigh.

Maldek was the "silver-tongued", or simply, "the tongue". Before the planet was eliminated from the family of our Solar System there were altogether thirteen planets. Perhaps in the end of Maldek we have the origin of the unlucky number thirteen! Since there are two planets between Mercury and the Sun and one yet beyond Pluto, Maldek was in the seventh orbit. This is a very significant fact, not only because of the symbolic meaning of the numeral seven, but because of the fact that the tongue is situated in the middle or center of the head and face. Since Maldek was number seven among the planets it was situated in the center of the solar family, with six other worlds on each side. (See *Plate XII*).

PLATE XII

There has been great meaning attached to the numbers seven, twelve and thirteen for generations. Christ had twelve Apostles, and eventually there were thirteen (St. Matthias or St. Paul can be the thirteenth); one of the thirteen, Judas, destroyed himself. Originally, there were thirteen planets with a Sun (Christ) and one (Lucifer-Maldek) destroyed itself. St. Matthias shouldn't be considered the thirteenth because he took Judas' place in the original twelve. St. Paul is therefore really the thirteenth through his astounding conversion.

Jeremiah 9:3: "And they bend their tongues like their bow for lies: but they are not valiant for the truth upon the earth; for they proceed from evil to evil, and they know not me, saith the Lord."

Lucifer-Maldek may be gone forever, but "tongues like bows" still bend for lies; the spirit of Lucifer lives on; "They profess that they know God; but in works they deny him, being abominable, and disobedient, and unto every good work repro-bate." (Titus 1:16).

From all space . . . from all space! We cry for thee, Maldek, Maldek . . . thy fate is sealed in eternity . . . thou art lost to us forever . . . Ishtal-Maxin, Aramma? Maru, Maldek . . . Maldek . . . Maldek . . . Ishtai.

It is finished, O Father of us all!

So, we come to the end of the section called, *Other Tongues*. Much research and work is still needed before the information that was presented here will be anywhere near complete. Tape recordings of the Solex-Mal were played for Japanese and Oriental students at two different universities. They unanimously agreed that there were some words that were identical with their own language, but that the strange, sing-song language most nearly resembled Ainu. The Ainu are perhaps the strangest people on Earth. They are an indigenous race of Japan having light-colored skin and features of a European cast. Ainu could very well be the Earth language closest to the Solar Tongue, the Mother of all languages.

In 1900, a book was published that demands serious attention. It is called, *From India To The Planet Mars*, (A study of a case of somnambulism), by Th. Flourney, Professor of Psychology at the University of Geneva. Many remarks on the Martian language are to be found and there is a plate showing the Martian alphabet. The Martian characters are similar to those of the Solex-Mal.

Previously, the theory was held that Lucifer collided with another celestial body, or that Lucifer was in reality two separate planets, and these collided. However, new discoveries show that Lucifer and its single satellite Lilith were destroyed by a "thermal" catastrophe, and what would hydrogen destruction be but "thermal"? Much research needs to be done along these lines, also, but the following is quoted from *The Astronomical Validation of the Correlation Between Electro-Magnetism and Gravitation*, a progress report of the Educational Research Laboratories, Valley of the Pines, Montague, Michigan.

"It is generally considered that since there is no accepted reason to believe otherwise, all the asteroids came from a single parent body that was less than the Earth in mass and size. From this view the problem of origin becomes a problem of the means of disruption. The several possible modes of disruption resolve themselves into two main types: The one of a catastrophic nature which might have produced jagged fragments and splinters of irregular shape such as it is presumed some of the asteroids possess; the second of a thermal, radioactive or stellar nature, which might have produced molten or gaseous fragments that would eventually solidify into nearly spherical shapes. The density of the asteroids is not known, but the 'EMG' formulae indicate that it ranges from 2.5 to 3.5. They could be mountainous 'rocks'; but are they the jagged fragments of a 'cold' collision, or the cooled, originally molten and now nearly spherical fragments of a 'thermal' catastrophe? The implications of the 'EMG' formula favor the latter assumption, by suggesting a satisfactory solution to the problem of the variable asteroids."

The problem of the asteroids is nothing new, it all started when Dr. Olbers suggested that the four planetoids known in his time had been formed by the explosion of a single planet. Soon, scientists began to disagree with this conclusion. The main reason why may have been that this hypothesis brought on the inevitable counter-question of *what* had caused the original planet to explode. And that question would have been very hard to answer. H. J. Jeffreys and Prof. K. Hirayama agree with the explosion theory.

Today, more than a thousand planetoids are known compared to Obler's four, and scientists say the estimated total mass of Lucifer is anything but impressive. They say if they gathered all the fragments together they would make a planet far smaller than our Moon. Dr. H. H. Nininger has shown, by his research on the great meteor crater near Winslow, Arizona, that much of the original meteor that hit that area was "vaporized" and turned into fine cosmic dust on impact. This is what happened to Lucifer also. Therefore, not even half of Maldek can be accounted for by asteroid observation.

Much will be learned in the New Age about *Other Tongues!*

Through the Solar Tongue: the Tracks On The Desert; and through Maldek, "The Tongue", itself, we have glimpsed *other worlds!*

BOOK III

OTHER FLESH

HOPI CEREMONIAL DANCERS

CHAPTER 1

THE MIGRANTS

"In the beginning God created the heaven and the earth. And the earth was without form, and void; and darkness was upon the face of the deep. And the Spirit of God moved upon the face of the waters." (Genesis 1:1-2).

In the beginning, the Earth was a comet. After it had gathered enough cosmic debris it became a planet, a new world. For untold ages this satellite of the Sun was a molten mass of fire. Meteorites from outer space bombarded the whirling sphere, great clouds arose. Finally, the great blanket of clouds condensed and it rained incessantly; the "cooling off" process had begun. Life first appeared on Earth when it was still boiling and seething with chemical turbulence in the air and in the hot seas. Some time during this period a synthesis occurred, and there was the first movement of life in some unknown spot of the Earth's vast seas. A microscopic glob of transparent jelly, flagellate. These multiplied and spread through the seas, where evolution was to start and eventually produce the indigenous life forms of the planet Earth. New types of half-plant, half-animal creatures began to inhabit the waters of the Earth. Hard parts, protective shells, plates and skins appeared and the continuous fossil record began.

The Earth planet, now cooled and teeming with mineral, vegetable, and animal life, was ready at last to receive *human life*. On another planetary system spiritual life migrated through interstellar space and began to struggle independently with the problems of Earth planet environment. At that moment the Word was made Flesh and Man in his present form . . . WAS!

"And it came to pass, when men began to multiply on the face of the earth, and daughters were born unto them, that the sons of God saw the daughters of men that they were fair; and they took them wives of all which they chose. And the Lord said, My spirit shall not always strive with man, for that he also is flesh: yet his days shall be a hundred and twenty years. There were giants in the earth in those days; and also after that, when the sons of God came in unto the daughters of men, and they bare children to them, the same became mighty men which were of old, men of renown. And God saw that the wickedness of man was great in the earth, and that every imagination of the thoughts of his heart was only evil continually. And it repented the Lord that he had made man on the earth, and it grieved him at his heart. And the Lord said, I will destroy man whom I have created from the face of the earth; both man, and beast, and the creeping thing, and the fowls of the air; for it repenteth me that I have made them." (Genesis 6:1-7).

So we come to the place where man appears on the planet Earth. The human race in its present pattern has been upon this planet anywhere between seventeen million and ten million years. For centuries scientists have pondered the question: "How did life in the human form make its advent upon Earth?" The famous Missing Link between the Anthropoid Apes and Man will never be found because the link is a *spiritual* and not an *organic* link. A great migration of souls known as the "Sons of God" arrived on Earth when the evolution of its indigenous life was progressing and incarnated in certain animal forms. This caused the basic difference between the human and other mammal forms. The primate species went on living and breeding as a true species, giving us the monkeys, apes, and gorillas of today. But the ape-forms that were borrowed for incarnation by the spirit-souls arriving from outer space, apparently supplied the original expressions of the human. These forms continued to breed and develop, and gradually sublimated the ape-forms into the races of man as society now recognizes them.

The scientist of today can be an atheist or a devout man, for he can fit the evolutionary theory into his own concepts nicely. He can either believe that God brought certain chemical substances together when the first single-celled life appeared in our warm seas, or he can believe that the happening was purely accidental.

Evolution is a fact, but does not, however, as so many assume, teach that man is descended from an ape or monkey. Modern evolutionists teach only that man and the apes had a common ancestor of whose characteristics they know little, and who may have approached in structure and appearance the modern man more than the modern ape. Neither does evolution pretend to explain the origin of life, or to prove that the development of man has been entirely mechanical or accidental. Evolution is simply a theory that every known plant or animal, whether living of extinct, developed out of a previous form. This theory is now accepted universally by all scientists in every country of the world, and only the reasons for, and the methods of transmission of the successive modifications are questioned.

Science has proven by the Earth's record, written undisputedly in her rock formations, that the evolution of indigenous earth-life is a true fact. Fossil bearing formations literally tell the Earth's auto-biography. This *indigenous* earth-life, developed from the single-celled organisms into a highly evolved ape-form over millions of years. The "Sons of God" made wives of the ape creatures and the progeny was antediluvian man, or prehistoric-primitive man. The physical attributes belonged to the anthropoid apes and the spiritual attributes belonged to the migration which came from the planets of the star-sun Sirius. Science is only wrong when it takes certain fossil remains and tries to fit them into the category of the "missing link." As said before, this link is a *spiritual* link, not an *organic* link.

The Migrants arrived on Earth during the middle division of the Tertiary Period. This is known as the Miocene Epoch. In the strata of this epoch are found "Eoliths" or "Dawn Stones" (flints). They are roughly shaped, and some authorities claim they were fashioned by primitive human beings. Others say that the Miocene flints are of natural origin. The "Dawn Stones" were undoubtedly used by the offspring of the "Sons of God" and the "daughters of men".

The Migrants made the Earth planet their abode in order to gain experience on the physical plane. The Sirian planets centralized Thought Incarnate so to speak and man was sent to Earth, a prisoner of pain for education. Man's heart was heavenly in divine creation, his body was physically handicapped by weight, but he acquired proficiency in altering his body. Man could create by thought and he created monsters and abominations.

Man, therefore, came from races of angels mixed with beasts, and he is now engaged in separating the brute from the angel. He has a mission on Earth for he is this planet's keeper and essentially has lessons in flesh to learn. Man must know pain, suffering, and sorrow so he can become a fit subject for higher planes.

Man finally put thought into practice, and created abominations. When he first arrived on Earth he had no body as we think of a body, so he looked upon beast and bird and chose the physical vehicle most likely to give him attributes producing qualities of spirit. The various cat forms were attractive to *The Migrants*, but the ape form was the form most suitable for their Earth environment and experience. The ape form gave them a more flexible and better controlled hand with the all important opposable thumb. Without the thumb man couldn't have produced a civilization. The cat form was discarded.

In "Star Guests" the Elder Brother tells us: "Mankind was not always as ye see him walking the earth at present; mankind was possessed of physical features making him hideous unto God. Mankind had queer members, too potent of evil to be long tolerated. Mankind had features of the Beast. He was of eagle-head and lion body. Great was his brutishness." This reminds us of the griffin, a mythical creature, half animal (lion) and half bird (eagle). It was used to represent the two natures in Christ, divine and human. But its earlier meaning symbolized the period of the Great Abomination when man was literally half eagle and half lion. There are countless references in mythology and history to this abomination period and some of these will be mentioned later.

The Elder Brother continues: "From the evil which he did when he had come to earth and found earth-forms upon it, was man cleansed by fire and flood. He came through vast ordeals which shaped his physiognomy as ye do see it now. He had strange claws and stranger tissues. He was of the Brute and yet not of it. From the depths of degradation to which he had sunk he arose with skull of ape; he walked upright on two legs; he became the prey of beasts instead of hunter. He made for himself habitations in trees and prowled by night seeking food. Deep, deep was his ignorance. Little more than beast was he indeed, with almost no spark of divinity left to him."

The abomination was so vast that forms were fusing together into monsters having no purpose but self-destruction. Men and animals were growing interchangeable of spirit and structure. Man was beastly and beast was manlike. Spirit knew not itself, whether it were divine or whether it were experiment of Thought Incarnate. They had so interchanged that they could no longer be accepted by the Host on the Sirian planets as divine. All physical forms had to be cleansed. "Pure beast must be preserved as beast; pure angel-man must be preserved as angel-man. Therefore, a vast catastrophe was decided upon. Ice from polar seas was melted and released upon continents of monsters." The Elder Brother tells us: "No longer could life make physical vehicles by thought. Forms existing in purity were preserved. Monsters and anomalies were destroyed. No longer could they propagate. Pure species were saved and pronounced sterile unto all but themselves."

By being pronounced "sterile unto all but themselves" means, of course, that they could only breed their own species and kind. That is why today man can only mate with other human beings. No longer can the half-man and half-animal creatures be produced. The only reference to them today is in ancient legends. The griffin has already been mentioned. It was the Gryps or Gryphus of Greek mythology. A monster with the head and wings of an eagle, the body of a lion, and sometimes the tail of a serpent. The most familiar and least complicated of the composite beings known as bird-man creatures are the medieval angels and demons, the fairies, the Greek Keres (represented as tiny human figures with butterfly wings).

Many representations of Egyptian gods embody combinations of human and bird anatomy, for they say the gods were first birds and animals and only gradually evolved into men. Perhaps the most complicated and fearsome of these creatures is the Gorgon, which had serpent hair, the hideous face of a woman, the wings of a bird, and the body of a lioness with bronze claws. The most frightful of these was Medusa.

The important feature of the Hindu Garuda bird is that it is one of the few combinations with the head of a bird. Other features vary considerably with locale (it is known in India, Indochina, China, Japan, and many other places).

The Egyptian soul was sometimes depicted as a bird with a human head, as was also the Greek Harpy, which befouled everything it touched. The Sirens were similar in form, but had beautiful voices and lured men to their downfall. The Welsh Washer of the Ford is a spectral female in black with the wings of a bat. The Furies are another of these combinations. The Sphinx is a combination of man-bird-beast, that is, the head and chest of a man, wings of a bird, and the body of an animal. In Egypt sphinxes were always male, and had the body of a lion. The Greek female sphinx also had a lioness' body. The Babylonian shedu, the Hebrew shedim, and the Sumerian clad were similar to the Egyptian, and male. They had the bodies of bulls, neatly curled beards, and often wore hats. The female counter-part of the sedu was called lamina or lamassu and could fly. The Syrian female sphinx had wings and resembled the Egyptian.

The sacred bull-men of Babylonia are extraordinary beings. They were first seen only on rock drawings, and small seals, but later they were used for imposing statuary like the winged bull with a human face from Sargon's palace in Khorsabad.

The so-called "dragon" of Babylon was found on the walls of the Ishtar Gate. It was called the "mighty snake". It had the head and scales of a snake, but the body of an unidentified monster. This creature had lion's paws and eagle's claws.

The Centaurs in Greek mythology were a race of monsters, half man and half horse. The Greeks also had legends of Cercopes: a race of ape-like but human pigmies. The ancient Arcadian Pan was a goat from the waist down, and a man with goat ears and goat horns from the waist up.

References to the strange bird cult of Easter Island are numerous in the native art. A remarkable example is the following representation of the bird man holding an egg in his hand. The original was carved upon a block of stone, itself egg-shaped. The egg in the birdman's hand symbolizes the creative

THE BIRD MAN

power of thought once enjoyed by man; but since the Great Catastrophe, man no longer can create by thought alone. Those who perished physically in this catastrophe were not dead spiritually but they sloughed off their monstrous features and were known en masse for spirits again, but without physical equipment.

An entire book or books could be written on the subject of man-bird-beast creatures. *The Migrants* or "Sons of God" arriving from the Sirian planets mated with the "daughters of men" who were the indigenous bestial female earth-forms that were coming to high evolutionary development on this planet. The account of that mating still exists in the so-call myths, legends and folk tales of the people of the world. After the Great Catastrophe the Son of Thought Incarnate entered upon the Earth scene. In "Star Guests", he says: "Came I to this planet at the Father's behest. Man was pure ape or pure spirit. He had escaped the Great Catastrophy in areas where his species was clean. He was beastly but cleanly beastly and he knew not the scheme of creating by thought that which pleased his whim. Came I first to earth on a mission. The Father desired that knowledge of good and evil be restrained. Man was to suffer and die as beast, returning to the planets of the star-sun Sirius on physical death of beastly body. But came I to the Father with better plan. The world of men could be cleansed of the beast by my instruction. Over countless generations could man be lifted back slowly to his lost angelic status. Life upon life he could live and perish, and live again. Slowly he could come up through new forms of ape-men until he was indeed a god restored to the Godhead! Not through varied forms but through manifestations of the same form, could he regain unto ennoblement. And the same form meant the ape-form. Thus was reincarnation born as men of earth understand reincarnation today. So man came to remain in possession of ape-body. Man had used the ape-form for thousands of generations, finding it more efficient for his caprice than lion-form. Thus was he manifesting when catastrophe overtook all creation. Therefore, know ye, that ape-forms are pure forms of species but man hath appropriated ape-forms and improved upon them until ye do be angel apes yourselves. Man as spirit hath no form that is constant. Man as spirit hath any form which serveth constructive purpose in making Love externalize. But man on the physical plane maintaineth the Ape Form of the Great Catastrophe."

The book, "*Star Guests*" is published by Soul-craft and much of its material was compiled several decades ago. Yet, that information ties-in perfectly with knowledge now being received from space intelligences. Van Tassel has received nearly identical material in confirmation of this, only instead of being called, "The Great Abomination", he calls it, "The Great Adultery". But it is the same happening.

In Northern Arizona the research group was informed that all the inhabitants of the Earth are *space people*. This is true for several reasons. First of all, none of us live *underground*; we have our existence on the surface of Earth; therefore, we are inhabitants of space as well as people on Mars, Venus, or any other world. We are not, however, *space craft* people, for we have not yet mastered the secret of magnetic propulsion and have not gone to other worlds beside our own.

All people on Earth are true space beings for another very basic and important reason. Our ancestors came here as the "Sons of God", and since true "human" life came from outer space in the first place we are all descended from that migration. Hence, we are true *space people*. However, all individuals on Earth are NOT related in the dim past to the indigenous biologic earth-forms that were the ape mothers and *The Migrants* who came via the Great Migration and "looked upon the daughters of Earth" and saw that they were fair and chose of them wives.

There is a third class or category of spiritual life that is maintained on Earth. These are the Christ People who arrived to make a cosmic mission of mentoring the "angelic host from Sirius that fell" into the practices of mixing the heavenly and earthly breeds, and winning it back to its original angelic status. This third class is a special Universal order of souls: they are *The Wanderers*.

CHAPTER 2

THE WANDERERS

"To the apples we salt we return!" Remember that strange phrase from "*The Saucers Speak!*"

Space intelligences said that this was one of their old prophecy legends, but what could it mean? It sounds as though space people salted away some apples and were now returning to them. But what about the word "apple"; what did it represent?

For many months now, evidence has been accumulating at a rapid rate that there are many people on Earth that don't really belong here! This doesn't mean that they came here aboard a Flying Saucer, disembarked, put on a tweed suit, polished up their English language and moved into the house next door. It does mean, however, that there is a special class or order of beings in the Universe that are different from the rest because of the fact that they wander from one world to another, and from one system to another. They are the "chimney sweeps" of Creation. It is their specific job to go to the "trash cans" of the Universe and give aid to their fellow man on those backward worlds.

If these *Wanderers* didn't arrive here by spaceship, how did they get here? They volunteered to come to Earth and go through the reincarnational cycle here. In otherwords, they were born here! They have birth certificates, they went to school, had the childhood diseases, drank soda pop at the corner drug store and made eyes at each other in school, or threw "spit balls" at teacher. In brief, they were exactly the same as all the other people on Earth, except for one thing: they didn't belong here! They occupy physical vehicles and are born to parents of their own choice who they feel will best give them the advantages and training they need to fulfill their missions on Earth.

It was this special order of beings that arrived with the Son of Thought Incarnate when He came to Earth for the first time to begin his instruction. It is said that 144,000 souls or Lesser Avatars arrived with the Elder Brother, Son of Thought Incarnate. Here we see the use of the mystic numeral 12. Much will be said about this later.

There were several statements made in "*The Saucers Speak!*" that are significant in connection with these "Wanderers" or "Apples". "Seeds may be planted but they can rot and never reach maturity." This means that the people of outer space knew what was going to develop on Earth. They "planted" some of their own people here; "salted" them away like "apples". But every seed that is planted or "salted away" does not grow and reach maturity; it may rot in the ground because of many conditions. Therefore, some of the "Wanderers" now on Earth do not know who they are—they are lost in the ways of the Earth, and on physical death will return to their own worlds. They will be none the worse for their experience, except that their mission will not be accomplished.

Space intelligences knew that a certain percentage of the "apples" would fall by the way, therefore enough of them incarnated into Earth bodies to make up for this inevitable deficiency. It should be stated here that during the "Great Influx" of the late 1800's, many offspring were born to space visitors who had mated with Earth women. The descendants of these offspring are living today, but they are not part of the class known as *The Wanderers*.

Space friends also said: "Many of our people are in your world now. There are nearly ten million of them, with six of those million in the United States itself." This statement refers to the "apples". Space people, actually born on other planets, do get out of Saucers and go into cities and towns for various purposes. They never remain long, for they make the survey they are working on and immediately leave. Truman Bethurum points this out in his book, "*Aboard A Flying Saucer*". At certain times Aura Rhanes was seen by several people in places of business and on city streets.

So there are several million people in the world that have nothing to do with this world as far as learning anything from it that they haven't already acquired. They either passed through many lives on the Earth planet itself, or they learned the same lesson on another world similar to our Earth. At any rate, they are far ahead of the average Earth man or woman. Why do they come back? The answer is, because they want to help; they feel that there is something far more beautiful for man on Earth to attain. They are the reason we have progressed more in the last fifty years than we did in the previous ten thousand years! Many of our great and famous historical personages were "apples". Those specifically mentioned were Benjamin Franklin, Abraham Lincoln, Nikola Tesla, and others. Of course, many more fit into this category.

The Wanderers go through a normal childhood, not realizing who they are. If they are not among those "seeds that rotted" they someday remember who they are, where they are from, and what they are here for. Many "apples" had memory veils lifted about 1947, the year when Kenneth Arnold brought the Flying Saucer to the attention of the world. Space intelligences figured that we wouldn't develop atomic power until sometime in the 1960's. But World War II with its demands that an atomic bomb be made, speeded up the advancement of science and therefore the entire space program working itself out on Earth. The Saucers then appeared openly and also began the great task of "waking up" their own people occupying Earth bodies and going about their daily business unaware of the entire matter. Many received "the beam" in 1947!

They were right when they said: "We walk the streets . . ." Another time they facetiously said: "To the slop we throw out we never return!" By that they meant that they were not interested in those individual souls who couldn't make the grade on their respective worlds and thereby were the "slop" or "refuse" of that world. They never will return to the "waste" material of Creation that isn't interested in Truth and progression through the loving of your fellow man.

Again they said: "Certain seeds have been placed on Saros (Earth). To the apples we salt we return!"

Many ancient legends and manuscripts tell about these "Wanderers". For instance, in "Lessons In Gnani Yoga" by Yogi Ramacharaka, we read: "In fact there are in the world today, individual souls which have reached similar stages on other planets, and who are spending their rest period here amidst the comparatively lower Earth conditions, striving to lift up the Earth souls to greater heights."

The fact that some of the space visitors coming to Earth at this time once lived on the Earth itself was vividly shown when George Adamski spoke to the Venusian near Desert Center, California, on November 20, 1952. On page 204 of "*Flying Saucers Have Landed*," Adamski said: "Then pointing to himself, he (the Venusian), indicated that once he lived here on this Earth: then pointing up into space . . . but now he is living out there."

Therefore, those souls who incarnated here over and over again, finally learning the lesson the Earth world offered, went on to higher, more majestic realms. Some have returned to us in Saucers, others were born amongst us! Not all of the "apples" come from our own Solar System; many come from far-distant systems and galaxies. These volunteers have vowed that they will continue to appear on Earth until the situation here is cleared up, and Earthman takes his true place beside his brothers in the Cosmos!

As I said above, many of these universal servants know who they are. Others will have memory restored to them as time goes on and our Solar System goes deeper and deeper into Aquarius. They will rise to the occasion to help their brothers overhead in the Saucers accomplish their mission here.

How can we identify or recognize a "Wanderer"? It is not easily done. However, these space friends who work and live with us daily, are identified by their brothers in the sky by certain body markings. These marks may take the form of scar tissue that has been present on the body from birth and thereby not acquired by any natural means, and they may take the form of unusual types of stigmata (not the religious type). The arrangement and type of marks will determine the individual's place of origin and other pertinent facts. These marks are not really necessary in order for them to be recognized by the Saucer occupants, because they know who is who by other methods. However, the marks serve more as a "key of remembrance" to the individuals they are located on. By thinking of these strange scars, the "apple" is automatically put into the right frame of mind and vibrations for lifting of a memory veil. The more they dwell on how the marks were received, the more they remember. As said before, many great men of history, known as adepts, leaders and reformers belonged to other worlds.

Even now they serve in every field of endeavor: they are scientists, inventors, writers, ministers, students, teachers, electronic engineers, speakers and farmers! They have infiltrated everywhere and only wait for the day of *The Telling* to make themselves known.

These "Wanderers" are truly "Wayfarers" when they take up life on Earth. For they very seldom stick to one job for long periods of time. Some are inclined to be "nervous" or highly sensitive types. This is because of the lower vibratory rate on Earth. Many of them have intestinal disorders and stomach trouble. They move from one job to another, and many of them are found in communications, transportation, and scientific fields. The infiltration of the writing and radio profession has been on a colossal scale.

Remember in *"The Coming Of The Saucers"*, by Arnold and Palmer, where Arnold said: "I knew him the moment I saw him. He had tried to talk to me once in the lobby. He was a rather small man, sandy-haired, and *physically handicapped*, apparently from some childhood disease. He looked healthy and sound." The man Arnold is speaking of was Paul Lance, reporter for the Tacoma Times . . . and he died shortly after he met Arnold. At another time, Arnold said: "There we met . . . I think we were both a little surprised to find that . . . was also *physically handicapped*, due apparently to some childhood disease, although he looked robust and healthy."

Kenneth Arnold became quite concerned over the fact that he was dealing with an unusual number of handicapped people! What did it mean, if anything? It can only be stated here that some of the "apples" are cripples in some sense of the word. This is because they do not function properly on the Earth planet even though they come from more advanced worlds. Could this be the answer to Arnold's problem?

Rolf Telano, well known to B.S.R.A. readers, must have been thinking of "Wanderers" when he wrote: "The messages received on radio are actually point-to-point messages intended for certain persons on this planet who are working with the operators of the flying discs . . . mostly their own people whom they have put here to live among the people of this planet, and act as *observers*. A telephone directory check would be useless because they are not known among the Earthlings by the same name as in the message. In most cases, the name mentioned is the actual name of the person, but it is often a name which would sound strange to the people here, so they assume one which will not arouse so much curiosity. The particular band was chosen because it is not as much used as others, and it is thus less likely that others would hear the messages. As an extra precaution, they are also usually coded. The 'CW' is not actually such, but merely a tape recorded message which happens to sound like it. The transmission is on a rather wide band (in frequency), but on a quite narrow band as to direction, being beamed directly to the person whom they wish to contact. If a radio set happened to be directly on the beam, it would be quite likely to pick up the message even if it was turned off, as it is possible for the voice coil of the speaker to pick it up by induction. *Ordinarily*, however, the set is working on the fringe of the beam, and must be turned on and tuned somewhere near the right frequency."

Some have said that the coil of the speaker could pick up the code by induction, but there would have to be a cold solder joint somewhere in the circuit to act as a rectifier.

When writing the above, Telano had reference to the strange message picked up by the Iowa research group that was mentioned in *"The Saucers Speak!"* This message was received on 405 kc, and said, in part ". . . contact Alesandro Stockvet of Chicago." When the group checked the telephone directory in Chicago, no such person was found listed.

Telano could be referring to "Wanderers" and also regular Saucer occupants now engaged in activities on the surface of the Earth. However, as mentioned before, most of the space people on Earth are "apples".

Certain individuals have received messages from the space intelligences that were similar to the following: "Do not think of us as gods, for in a sense you are greater than we . . . and we must serve you as it was promised since time immemorial." By this, the Saucer occupants mean that *The Wanderers* were a special order of beings who did nothing but wander from planet to planet and stay until the particular world they were on was lifted up into higher understanding. If the message was directed to an "apple" on the Earth, we can see why the space people would say: "In a sense you are greater than we." Actually, there is no high nor low, but *The Wanderers* or "Apples" would be greater in the sense that they had previously served other worlds before coming to Earth. The

Saucer men recognize these "Wanderers" because they aided them before they came to Earth to help. In other words, "apples" lifted up other planets to their present majestic state of progression where all war, greed, lust and falsity is non-existent. They passed through Mars, Venus, and other spheres before volunteering for the Earth mission. And the mission to Earth began not just one or two lifetimes back, but it all started in the Miocene Epoch millions of years ago! The Universal "chimney-sweeps" will not go on to other degraded worlds until the planet Earth returns to the Interplanetary Brotherhood, established in Love, Truth, and peace.

The following message was received in the central part of the United States by a "Wanderer". It illustrates the point we have made above. Its point of origin was from space intelligences.

"Wake up! Do not underestimate yourself. Do not say that something is not true just because you alone thought it. Know this about yourself . . . when you think purely on your own plane (thought), there is no room for error as there is none being a part of who you are! Son of Light, we are coming soon to Earth in great numbers. Upon our arrival we will scatter over the face of the planet and instruct the immature souls concerning the most perfect application of the Love principle. Truly, in reality, this is all we do. We keep away and shut out all selfish interests and egotistical desires: in this we find our true purpose to the rest of God's great creation. We have so perfected the Love principle that we need not adopt the policy of loving our enemies and blessing those that curse us for there are no enemies and there is no one that curses. Truly here is where the spirit of God can move freely and give unto us unimaginable blessings. This, too, is one of our great missions here, since it is only when Love reigns supreme that it is possible for God to give you more than he has. This is not because God is unwilling to give unto you, it is because in your ignorance you refuse to receive that which is already given unto you. Upon our arrival be ready to receive and welcome us; not that we are demanding, but in order to fulfill our mission here it is necessary for us to mingle as much as possible with you who know us. You can aid us with certain information we desire. We mingle with you and people like you purposely because although you look human, *yet are you divine, even more so than we by far!* You remember meeting a stranger the other day, yet he was not a stranger at all, but one of us whom you met while *working in our realm to build us up as you are even now building up the Earth.* When we come to cooperate wholeheartedly, be not fearful of telling the world of our coming; for the world must know to be prepared. The time is therefore short, as we have said before. Work well and preach the truth until we come! And we will come, as we promised you before you took up the mantle of this mission". This message was signed simply: "A friend from Venus".

This Venusian friend was obviously addressing his remarks to a "Wanderer". He recognized the Earth worker because he had passed through his world Venus before coming to Earth. As stated before, the "Wanderers" began their mission on Earth millions of years ago when they originally came with the Great Avatar or Son of Thought Incarnate. However, the original number of 144,000 has been added to over many generations and highly advanced beings on other planets joined the ranks of The *Wanderers*.

Some might ask: "Why don't the occupants of the Saucers do the job of lifting up humanity on Earth?" Actually, they couldn't do the job alone. First of all, in order to get by for very long in present day society an individual has to have papers and records proving his birth, age, place of residence, driver's license, draft board classification, etc. Secondly, people of the Earth wouldn't want to be "lifted up" or taught by "foreigners" from outer space. But, if space people are among them as their own kind, they will be raised automatically into higher states of progression. Only if the "apples" volunteer for such a mission can it be accomplished.

Saucer occupants and "Wanderers" in our own Solar System belong to an order known as Knights of the Solar Cross. The literal *solar cross* is a luminous appearance consisting of a light-pillar combined with a segment of the parhelic circle, forming a cross with the sun at the center. A similar phenomenon about the moon is called a lunar cross.

Solar Cross, used here, however, means something entirely different. The swastika symbolizing the Four Great Primary Forces is the true Solar Cross, for without these forces our Sun and Solar System could not operate—in fact, they wouldn't even exist, and neither would anything else in Creation exist.

A Knight Errant was a wandering knight who, in the Middle Ages went forth in search of adventures fitted to exhibit his skill, prowess, or chivalry toward women; he belonged to wandering knighthood. Therefore, *The Wanderers* are Knights Errant of the Solar Cross as they go to the various planets of our Solar System. They operate through the authority and powers of the Four Great Forces to point men everywhere to the *Great Path*.

As said before, it doesn't matter whether the helpers came here in Saucers, or whether they were born here as "apples"—they all belong to the Solar Cross Order. The symbol of this Order shows the present twelve planets enveloped in their Resonating Electro-Magnetic Fields. The planet of the fifth orbit to space intelligences is the Earth, and its field is shown shaded and dark. This is because the Earth is now the only world in our Solar System that does not belong to the Interplanetary Brotherhood. The twelve planets surround the swastika and super-imposed over this is a face-like shield with a single eye in the center of the forehead. This symbolizes

PLATE XIII

the fact that Knights of the Solar Cross have a highly developed pineal body or gland, a "third eye" which gives them their astounding telepathic abilities. They examine all men by this "eye" instead of by normal vision which would only allow for reason and logic instead of truth. (See *Plate XIII*).

In June, 1953 a well known magazine received the following letter in reference to an article they had printed on life of other worlds.

"I have just read your article that claims the people on other worlds look like huge enlarged editions of your own (airth's)

169

microbes. Ha. Have a surprise in store! I was born on the planet Venus and my mother and father entered life on the planet Uranus. All three of us could walk right by you on the street and you couldn't tell any difference between us and those born on this planet airth. I have now been on this satellite of the Sun ten years, and along with hundreds of thousands of my group from the various galactic regions, have been mingling with you without undue alarm. Your own government is aware of our presence as well as our appearance; and every time another load of us arrive via solar ship, they get jittery . . . I am a Knight of the Solar Cross."

The editor published this letter in the next issue of the magazine and said: "Hey, Knight . . . ever heard of the Immigration Act?"

The following is a message received in Arizona from one of these Knights who is now surveying our Earth in space craft.

"In the Light of our Infinite Father, the Creative Spirit, we greet you fellow creatures and brothers of Saros. We who now speak are also of your third density. As you peer through your "big eyes" you can easily see many of us. However, you only see eight of us besides yourself. There are three more of the Father's Mansions with one being beyond the planet you know as Pluto, and the other two between Mercury and the Sun.

"Twelve is an important number and so is Seven. That is why a group to the west at Giant Rock in your State of California speaks of The Council of the Seven Lights. Remember, we have also spoken of The Council-Circle 7x. There were Twelve Apostles who followed the Master, one of the Twelve destroyed himself. There are Twelve Planets now in our Solar System, and one, your planet of Earth, known to other beings of the third density as Saros, is a lost brother (mansion) now on the brink of self-destruction. The Creator's symbolism is always exact and understood only by those who discern His signs.

"The planet known to you as Saturn is the location of the Universal Tribunal of this, our Solar System. We will not go into the nature of our Great Sun Body at this time, but let it be stated here that there are beings on the planetary bodies under the photosphere of the Sun. There is life on your Moon as well as on some other moons belonging to other planets.

"Saturn is the Seat of Justice . . ."As ye sow, so shall ye reap."
Saturn was your ancient god of Seed-Sowing, and believed to be a
king during an ancient Golden Age. Yes, the literal rule of Saturn
was enjoyed on Earth during the period of your Golden Age. It
was distinguished for peacefulness, happiness, and contentment.
The Saturnian Age is mentioned in all Earth history. Saturn was
the "sower of seeds" because it was he who gave authority to The
Wanderers so that they might go into physical life on the Earth.
Saturn has been called by your people, 'The Rising Sun of a New
Dispensation', and this is true for he represents form and discipline
which, when met and profited by, bring sure and permanent rewards.
Remember what your Holy Book tells you: "Be not deceived; God
is not mocked: for whatsoever a man soweth, that shall he also
reap." (Galatians 6:7).

"Long ago, it came to our attention that our Solar System, of
which you are a vital part, was quickly moving into another realm of
our Father's Creation. We are now a part of the first stages of the
fourth density. Beings of this density are now with us and among
us. They do not need mechanical contrivances as we of the third
density need them. We of the other planets in this System are more
advanced than your world, Saros. But we say this in all humility, not
wishing to boast. For we are, in a sense, still very crude. Again it
is written in your Good Book: "I have seen all the works that are
done *under the sun*; and, behold, *all is vanity* and vexation of spirit."
(Ecclesiastes 1:14). We are not perfect!

"As your 'big eyes' peer into space you see us because we
are in your density, but there are degrees of advancement and
we are ahead of you in that degree. We are now contacting our
Saros brothers by means of radiotelegraphy, telepathy, and direct
physical manifestations. Our brothers of the fourth density are
now contacting Saros brothers almost entirely by telepathy and by
projection. Do not think for a moment that the so-called 'Saucers'
and related phenomena are just from this or that planet; they come
from many, many worlds, systems and galaxies. And they are of
different development, yet they are all part of the Creator's plan
for Saros. The Interplanetary Confederation now operating around
your planet contains fifty-one solar systems which includes several
hundred planets (six-hundred and eight according to Van Tassel)
controlling some three and a half million spacecraft.

"For centuries and centuries we have watched your ruinous wars, and hoped that someday you would gain the understanding needed to gain your freedom from bondage of your own making. Our hopes have not been realized; instead, our worst fears have been realized. Not fear as you think of it, but only the knowledge of past events. The time has come for Saros to prepare herself for the Groom—she must put off the old, the shabby, and array herself in finery for the Wedding Feast shortly to take place in the fourth density realm. We, as your nearest Neighbors in space, are trying to prepare you adequately for this meeting.

"Our authority is from the Saturn Tribunal headed by Kadar Lacu. This Tribunal and its Kadar acts in the Creator's Light and Love. None of us are perfect as I have said, or we would not be here. There is much we all have to learn. There are worlds millions and even trillions of years 'ahead' of us, and there are many worlds thousands of years 'behind' us. We must not, therefore, be worshipped as gods. It is truly written: "And hath gone and served other gods, and worshipped them, either the sun, or moon, or any of the *host of heaven*, which I have not commanded." (Deuteronomy 17:3). "And they shall spread them before the sun, and the moon, and all the *host of heaven*, whom they have loved, and whom they have served, and after whom they have walked, and whom they have sought, and whom they have worshipped. (Jeremiah 8:2). We are the *Host of Heaven*, and we must not be worshipped as ancient men have bowed to sun, moon and stars!

"We are here among you. Some of us have always been here, with you, yet apart from you. We have watched you closely and occasionally we guided you whenever the opportunity arose. Our numbers have now been increased tremendously in preparation for another step in the development of your world Saros. You are not aware of this step completely, although it has been hinted at frequently in the accounts of your prophets. We contacted these prophets of yours in time past; but many of them did not know our true nature, therefore they could not always translate clearly the concepts implanted in their minds. Sometimes they were extremely cautious, and to insure the preservation of the information they wished to place upon record in the world, they spoke in metaphors and symbols.

"We have been confused many times with the gods of world-religions. However, we are your fellow creatures as I said before. You will find records of our presence in the mysterious symbols of ancient Egypt, where we made ourselves known in order to accomplish certain ends. One of our principal symbols appears in the religious art of your present civilization and occupies a position of importance upon the great seal of the United States. It has been preserved in certain secret societies founded originally to keep alive the knowledge of our existence and our intentions toward mankind. Another of our symbols is the Circle-Cross and the Swastika. The symbol known to you as the 'Tree of Life' is well-known to us and is important.

"We have left you outstanding landmarks. These were carefully placed in various parts of Saros, but most prominently in Egypt where we established a headquarters at one time. At that time, the foundations of your present civilization were 'laid in the earth' and the most ancient of your known landmarks established by means that would appear as miraculous to you now as they did to the *pre-Egyptians*, so many thousands of years ago. Since that time the whole art of building in stone has become symbolic, to many of you, of the work in hand—the building of the human race toward its perfection.

"Many of your ancestors knew us in those days as *preceptors* and as friends. Indeed, many of you knew us then, also. Now, though your own efforts, you have almost reached, in your majority, a new step on the long ladder of liberation. You have constantly been aided by our watchful inspiration, and hindered only by the difficulties natural to your processes of physical and moral development.

"You have lately achieved the means of destroying yourselves. Do not be hasty in your self-congratulation for yours is not the first civilization to have achieved and used such means. The 'lost world' known to you as the Asteroid Belt is spoken of in your records as 'Lucifer, the Shining One'. We called this planet 'Maldek, The Tongue'. We did not interfere when the men of that world experimented with certain and quick disaster. Each man, and hence each world, must learn the lesson and make its own progression. Universal Law prevented us from interfering. When this world was shattered, it caused terrible catastrophe on other worlds, as well as on Saros. You have not recovered to this day.

"We are now interfering more than we should, but we will not stand by and see another waste of creation in our System. There isn't time for another waste. Now that the Great Cycle is ending and we are all entering a new plane, all must be purified. That which is beyond hope will eliminate itself. We say 'eliminate itself' for we will destroy nothing. Those on Saros who believe the Creator punishes or destroys anything are in darkness. You are punished by your own deeds, as your world is now punishing itself for its crimes against Universal Law.

"Yours will not be the first world to be offered the means of preventing that destruction and proceeding in the full glory of its accumulated knowledge, to establish an era of enlightenment on Saros. However, if you do accept the means offered you, and if you do establish such a '*millennium*' upon the basis of your present accomplishments, yours will be the first civilization to do so.

"Always before, the knowledge, the techniques, the instruction, have become the possessions of a chosen few; a few who chose themselves by their open-minded and clear-sighted realization of the 'shape of things to come'. They endeavored to pass on their knowledge in the best possible form and by the most enduring means at their command. In a sense, they succeeded, but in another sense their failure equalled their success. Human acceptance is, to a very large extent, measurable by human experience. Succeeding generations, who never knew of our actual presence, translated the teachings of their elders in the terms of their own experience.

"For instance, a cross-sectional drawing, much simplified and stylized by many copyings, of one of our space craft, became the 'Sacred Eye of Horus', and eyes of many other gods. Other symbolical and alchemical 'eyes' are merely representative of our means of transportation. Osiris and Apollo became gods to the people, but they were actually our representatives on Saros: they were men! The 'golden disk' now confused with the solar disk and made a part of religion, and the 'discus' hurled sunward by the Grecian athlete and your athletes are also symbolic of our traveling devices or 'Saucers'.

"The really important fact, however, is that we are here among you! And you, as a world-race will know it before very much longer.

The time is almost ripe, but as with all ripening things, the process may not be hurried artificially without danger of damaging the fruit. There is a right time for every action, and the right time for our complete revelation of ourselves to Saros is fast approaching.

"Many of you have seen our 'advance guard' already. You have met us often in the streets of your cities; but you have not noticed us. Some, however, do 'sense' us! When we speed through your skies in the traditional vehicles, you are amazed, and those of you who tell of what you have seen are ac-counted dupes and fools. Actually, you are prophets of your age, seers in the true sense of the word. You in Kansas and Oklahoma, you in Oregon and in California, and Idaho, Indiana, Maine, and Vermont—you who know what you have seen, do not be dismayed by what so-called 'authorities' tell you. Remember, many of them haven't seen what you have! Their faulty opinions are not based on actual experience.

"Can you imagine a material almost transparent to the rays of ordinary light, yet strong enough to endure the stress of extremely rapid flight? Look again at the Great Nebulae, and think of the construction of your own Milky Way Galaxy, and be-hold the Universal examples of what we have found to be the perfect shape for an object which is to travel through what you still fondly refer to as 'empty' space. Our Crystal Bells operate in their own Resonating Electro-Magnetic Field the same as all celestial bodies do. Your own Saros is nothing but a huge space craft. We can travel the so-called 'speed of light' and faster, but actually light does not travel; *Light Is!*

"If we chose to remain unseen, we could do so easily and, in fact, we have done so almost without exception for hundreds of yeas. No one sees us unless we want to be seen! You must now become accustomed to our shapes in your skies, for one day soon they will be familiar, friendly, and reassuring sights.

"One of our very ancient prophecy legends says: "To the apples we salt we return." Some of you understand what this means. Long ago we knew what would take place on Saros and we knew that we would have to come down and dwell with you to accomplish certain objectives. Many of us have only recently arrived on your world and were brought here by space craft from our respective homes in this System and other systems. Our Confederation is large, but unfortunately, there are those of other worlds who are not here in the name of the Infinite Father. They are intruders!

"Many of us came centuries ago, and especially during the last part of your nineteenth century. Some of you are our direct descendants. Some of you were incarnated back into Saros from other planets and only recently have you begun to realize who you are and what your true purpose is. You are one with us and must prepare to meet the work ahead of us all. You are the 'apples' we 'salted away' until we had need of them. That time is now here. We have returned! However, all the 'seeds' have not matured; some have rotted. Therefore, some of you because of certain conditions will never know who you are. We are all space beings since all life is spiritual in essence and inhabits space. We are all the Creator's children; we are brothers and sisters.

"All of our people now on your planet are working toward the new order of things shortly to en-gulf your world. We are Knights of the Solar Cross. De you understand this? If you do fail, as other worlds have failed, then we will know what to do. The Council-Circle 7 has completed its work here, and matters have now been turned over to the Universal Tribunal. You will soon notice even stranger changes begin to take place in your world: unbelievable changes to you.

"Recognize us for what we are; we are here! We are a Confederation of many peoples working in Eternal Light. Our love and light to all of you. May our Infinite Father guide you always. For my brothers, I am, 'One Who Serves'."

This message speaks of the Twelve Planets. Besides the nine we know of, there is one beyond Pluto, which was spoken of as Patras in "*The Saucers Speak!*" Could Patras refer to the Greek *petra*, rock or *petros*, stone? Perhaps this planet is a small world and Patras in the Solex Mal may be "The Rock". Then there are two more planets unknown to most scientists between Mercury and the Sun.

In 1859 M. Lescarbault, a village physician of Orgeres, France, saw a small dark planet-like body pass across the sun's disc. This planet was called by anticipation, Vulcan. However, its existence still remains unconfirmed by science. M. Porro and M. Wolf of Zurich reported seeing Vulcan in transit in 1876. Since Vulcan was seen passing across the disk of the Sun it can be assumed that such a planet really exists. However, most astronomers refuse to accept its existence. They say it is a hypothetical intra-Mercurial planet. The French astronomer Le Verrier said Vulcan did exist because this would account for certain unexplained perturbations of Mercury. In 1846, J. G. Galle, the German astronomer, discovered the planet Neptune, following the calculations of Le Verrier. If Le Verrier was correct about the existence of Neptune, could he not be correct about Vulcan? He had calculated the exact position of Neptune in the sky. The perturbations mentioned means the deviation was caused by the attraction of some other body other than that round which Mercury moves. The perturbations of Mercury are caused by Vulcan. Besides, it has been seen in transit across the Sun's disk too often to be ignored.

Between Vulcan and the Sun there is still another planet of which little is known at this time. Information received by Van Tassel confirms the existence of Vulcan and this other world closest of all planets to the Sun.

All the planets in our Solar System are inhabited and are working in the Interplanetary Confederation. There is only one planet that is uneasy about the Earth. In "The Saucers Speak!" the following was received: "Uranus doesn't believe in too much contact with the Earth planet." Uranus had to be won over in the Universal Tribunal for she felt that little could be accomplished through Earth contact. This has been confirmed in a startling manner recently by a physicist in Canada who has had contact several times with a craft from Uranus. The occupants said they were not too interested in the Earth, but they did hope that man on Saros would rise out of stupidity and take his place with the other men of Creation.

The numeral 12 is very important in symbolism. A few of the important parts of the Scale of Twelve follow:

> 12 symbols of the Pillars in Neptune's Temple were related
> to the
> 12 Laws (Atlantis).
> 12 Emerald Tablets of Thoth the Atlantean. The writing is
> similar to the Solex-Mal and has engraved characters in
> the ancient Atlantean language. 12 Labors of Hercules:
> 12 Great Gods.
> 12 Signs of the Zodiac.
> 12 Months.

12 Faculties; 12 great Qualities and Virtues;

12 Gems in the Breastplate of the high priest.

12 Tribes of Israel; 12 Rods of the 12 Princes of Israel.

12 Phalanges of the fingers.

12 Lesser Prophets.

12 Apostles.

12 Patriarchs.

12 Gates (Revelation 21:12).

12 Angels (Revelation 21:12); 12 Legions of Angels (St. Matthew 26:53).

12 Foundations (Revelation 21:14).

12 Bullocks (Ezra 8:35).

12 He goats (Ezra 8:35).

12 Pointed Star; 12 Fruits (Revelation 22:2).

12 Sons of Jacob.

In ancient symbolism the Twelve Sons of Jacob were represented as twelve stars surrounding two circles. These circles stood for Jacob and his wife. (Jacob had several wives, but the circle stands for the mother of each son). In this connection, there is something very interesting to be found in Genesis 37:9: "And he dreamed yet another dream, and told it his brethren, and said, Behold, I have dreamed a dream more; and, behold, the sun and the moon and the eleven stars made obeisance to me."

Now this dream literally meant that some day Joseph's father (Jacob) and his mother and his eleven brothers would bow to him. Joseph's brothers sold his as a slave, and later they did bow down to him in Egypt. In Genesis 37:10, we read: "And he told it to his father, and to his brethren: and his father rebuked him, and said unto him, What is this dream that thou hast dreamed? Shall I and thy mother and thy brethren indeed come to bow down ourselves to thee to the earth?"

Joseph's dream likened his father, mother and brothers to the sun, moon, and eleven stars. Why eleven stars? In his day there were altogether thirteen planets in our Solar System. Since Joseph was on the Earth he would not count that a star, and besides the Earth did not belong to the Interplanetary Brotherhood. That would leave twelve stars or planets, But Maldek, not yet destroyed (its total destruction taking place at the time of the Exodus) did not belong to the Brotherhood either. Therefore, there were actually eleven stars or planets in our System that would have recognition at the Universal Tribunal. Somehow, the ancients knew this.

A sun disk, balanced upon a four-legged stand was found at Sippar before the canopied throne of Shamash, the sun god. It is recorded in a tablet of Nebopaliddin, King of Babylonia about 880 B. C. (See *Plate XIV*). This disk shows the central Sun with the Four Great Primary Forces, and it shows twelve wavy lines extending out or radiating from the Sun. This means there are twelve planets in the Solar System. Since this dates from 880 B. C. it would not show the planet Maldek or thirteen planets since Maldek ceased to exist around 1500 B. C. This sun disk is similar to the Ishtal-Maxin in the Solex-Mal. (See illustration on page *72*).

The large silver star which was placed in the floor of the Grotto of the Church of the Holy Nativity, in

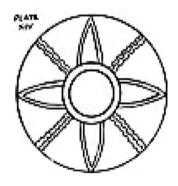

PLATE XIV

Bethlehem, in the nineteenth century, at the sup-posed spot on which Jesus was born, has twelve points. Tradition associates the number twelve with closeness of relationship between the divine and the human. Formerly, the Feast of Epiphany was known as "Twelfthtide", or "Twelfth Day", because it falls on the twelfth day after Christmas.

The Golden Candelabra with seven lamps of ancient times is very important because of its obvious connection with the Council of Seven Lights (Van Tassel) and the Council-Circle 7.

"And thou shalt make the seven lamps thereof: and they shall light the lamps thereof, that they may give light over against it." (Exodus 25:37).

"Speak unto Aaron, and say unto him, When thou lightest the lamps, the seven lamps shall give light over against the candlestick." (Numbers 8:2).

"And I turned to see the voice that spake with me. And being turned, I saw seven golden candlesticks; And in the midst of the seven candlesticks one like unto the Son of man, clothed with a garment down to the foot, and girt about the paps with a golden girdle." (Revelation 1:12-13).

"The mystery of the seven stars which thou sawest in my right hand, and the seven golden candlesticks. The seven stars are the angels of the seven churches: and the seven candlesticks which thou sawest are the seven churches." (Revelation 1:20).

Therefore, for the Scale of Seven we have: 7 Spirits of God; 7 Souls (Egyptian); 7 Seals; 7 Logi; 7 Creative Lords; 7 Creators or Fabricators (Jewish Elohim); 7 Golden Candlesticks; 7 Builders or Governors (Egyptian); 7 Rays; 7 Lamps; 7 Lamps of Fire; 7 Colors of Spectrum; 7 Sounds; 7 Rishis; 7 Stars; 7 Notes of Musical Scale; 7 Zones; 7 Continents; 7 Suns; 7 Angels; 7 Eyes of the Lord; 7 Daughters of Atlas (Pleiades); 7 Laws; 7 Churches; p. 237 7 Worlds; 7 Primordial Mysteries; 7 Principles; 7 Wheels; 7 Days of the week; 7 Old Books (From Noah's Ark); 7 Brazen Columns of Ham and Cheiron.

When Kadar Lacu, Head of the Universal Tribunal on Saturn contacted us in Northern Arizona, he always identified himself with a certain symbol: ⊕ Van Tassel at Giant Rock has also received this Circle-Cross. Anciently, it was known as the "Astronomical Cross of Egypt". Or it was called the "Mundane Cross". It is supposed to represent "accomplished creation". The ancients said it was of the fundamental divine interplanetary language, and it has the numerical value of three. To them it meant an individual creation, such as a planet, a solar system, or a galaxy. Since Lacu is Kadar (Head) of the tribunal for this Solar System, he would naturally use the Circle-Cross as his symbol.

Ponnar is an important personage from the planet Hatonn in the galactic system of Andromeda. The symbol he always uses is: ∞ This symbol of "eternity" is very old and is found on several of the Tarot Cards.

The symbol of the Tree of Life or the Tree and the Serpent is one of the Earth's most ancient representations. Remember in *"The White Sands Incident"*, by Dan Fry, where Dan noticed a simple design imprinted in the material of the seat in the Saucer? Alan said: "Oh, I see you have noticed the symbol and recognized its significance." "Yes," Dan said, "anyone who has ever read to any extent would recognize the symbol of the tree and the serpent. It is found in the original inscriptions and legends of every race on earth. It has always seemed to me to be a peculiarly earthly symbol and it was startling to see it appear from the depths of space or from whatever planet you call home."

Alan answered Dan by saying: "These are things which I had hoped to put off until our next contact. There is so much to tell and so little time. Our ancestors came originally from this earth. They had built a great empire and a mighty science upon the continent which your legends call 'Mu' or 'Lemuria'."

TREE OF LIFE

Mu was symbolized as a tree—the Tree of Life. The unadorned serpent is Khan the symbol of Khanab, "The Great Waters", the ocean. Mu was surrounded by water, even as the tree is surrounded by the serpent. There were indigenous life forms on other worlds, but several research groups have received information that during the catastrophes that struck both Lemuria and Atlantis, groups of people were evacuated from the Earth and taken to other planets. Especially Mars and Venus.

"To him that overcometh will I give to eat of the tree of life, which is in the midst of the paradise of God." (Revelation 2:7).

"In the midst of the street of it, and on either side of the river, was there the *tree of life*, which bare *twelve* manner of fruits, and yielded her fruit every month: and the leaves of the tree were for the healing of the nations." (Revelation 22:2).

"Blessed are they that do his commandments, that they may have right to the *tree of life*, and may enter in through the gates into the city." (Revelation 22:14).

Swedenborg says that by "the tree of life" is signified a man who lives from God, or God living in man; and as love and faith, wisdom and charity, or good and truth, make the life of God in a man, these are signified by the Tree of Life, and derivatively also the eternal life of man is signified. The Babylonians had a symbol of the Tree of Life, as did the Greeks for they spoke of "the wide spreading tree of Jove". The Egyptians had the "pillar of degrees", apparently a conventionalized palm tree in which they showed three levels or degrees. The Teuton mythology knows the tree Yggdrasil which grows by the well of Urd, the well of wisdom. Its branches

PLATE XV

reach into heaven, it roots into hela, the caverns of darkness.

Early in 1952, a strange young man appeared in California. He lectured on the coming of the space people to earth. He always spoke to small groups of students or clubs. There was nothing unusual about him except that he wore a lapel button on which was a distinctive symbol. (See *Plate XV*). Here we see the familiar swastika of the Four Forces and a serpent twined about a wand or rod. This is similar to the caduceus, a magic herald's wand, a sacred rod having power over wealth, prosperity, happiness, and dreams, carried by the messengers of the Greek gods, especially by Hermes. The caduceus was a sign of the settlement of quarrels, carried by heralds and ambassadors. This symbol is also used for Apollo.

The serpent and the staff are symbols of Aesculapius, Roman god of medicine and Asklepios, Greek god of healing. The staff represented this god's wanderings from place to place dispensing cures.

"Yea, though I walk through the valley of the shadow of death, I will fear no evil: for thou art with me; thy *rod* and thy *staff* they comfort me." (Psalms 23:4).

Since Apollo, Hermes, Osiris, and others were undoubtedly nothing but space visitors in ancient times who later were defied by the people, we would expect their symbols to be used yet by modern space visitors. The attributes or actions of Apollo or Hermes as space men were carried over to fit the later gods Apollo, Hermes, etc. The space men came to settle disputes and the caduceus became a sign of "the settlement of quarrels". It was carried by "heralds and ambassadors"—indeed space visitors were heralds of a new wisdom and knowledge and ambassadors of the worlds. The rod or staff represented the god of healing's "wanderings". And, the space visitors were "healers" of man's sufferings; they did wander from "place to place dispensing cures" for the "sorrowful planet Earth. The "rod" and the "staff" did "comfort" the people of the ancient world when it was visited by intelligences of other realms in outer space.

The description that has come down to us of Apollo fits him in his role of spaceman: "He was the god of pure light, the enemy of darkness, healer, preserver. He always declared truth; but the limited mind of man cannot always grasp the meaning of his sayings."

Likewise, the same is true of Osiris: "Osiris, reigning as a king on earth, reclaimed the Egyptians from savagery, gave them laws, and taught them worship. He introduced the cultivation of grains. Eager to communicate his discoveries to all mankind he travelled over the world, diffusing the blessings of civilization and agriculture wherever he went."

The Elder Brother clearly showed his position as Head of the Wandering Host when he said: "Ye are from beneath; I am from above: ye are of this world." (St. John 8:23).

In Christ's Prayer of Consecration he refers to *The Wanderers*: "I have given them thy word; and the world hath hated them, because they are not of the world, even as I am not of the world. I pray not that thou shouldest take them out of the world, but that thou shouldest keep them from the evil. They are not of the world, even as I am not of the world. Sanctify them through thy truth: thy word is truth. As thou hast sent me into the world, even so have I also sent them into the world. And for their sakes I sanctify myself, that they also might be sanctified through the truth. Neither pray I for these alone, but for them also which shall believe in me through their word; That they all may be one . . . as thou, Father, art in me, and I in thee, that they also may be one in us: that the world may believe that thou hast sent me. And the glory which thou gavest me I have given them; that they may be one, even as we are one: I in them, and thou in me, that they may be made perfect in one; and that the world may know that thou hast sent me, and hast loved them, as thou hast loved me. Father, I will that they also, whom thou hast given me, be with me where I am; that they may behold my glory, which thou hast given me: for thou lovedst me before the foundation of the world. O righteous Father, the world hath not known thee: but I have known thee, and these have known that thou hast sent me. And I have declared unto them thy name, and will declare it: that the love wherewith thou hast loved me may be in them, and I in them." (St. John 17:14-26). Jesus referred specifically to St. John as a *Wanderer* when he said: "If I will that he tarry till I come, what is that to thee?" (St. John 21:22).

"Then went this saying abroad among the brethren, that the disciple (John) should not die: yet Jesus said not unto him, He shall not die; but, If I will that he tarry till I come, what is that to thee?" (St. John 21:23).

Jesus didn't mean that John would not die. He meant that as a *Wanderer*, John would go in and out of life on Earth—he would "tarry" until the great plan had been fulfilled on Earth and man again took his rightful place in the Universe.

The Wanderers are mentioned in many other writings. For instance, in the "Golden Scripts".

"Behold it is of fact that in the higher realms of life there is a system that classifieth spirits into groups, according to their willingness to be of assistance unto others. At the head is the Christ Group, or group of Christ Souls, who have suffered so greatly in other worlds and in other forms that the essence of Self hath become utterly lost." (G. S. 69.2-2).

"They have come to earth from other planets, not earthly born, not knowing always Golgotha of reincarnation." (G. S. 69:6).

"They do manifest in flesh but rarely, and then only for great purposes involving earthly leadership: they go down into flesh when great events portend having as their essence the heart of humanity in jeopardy to itself. These persons have errands to perform of special tenor: they manifest according to plan agreed upon beforehand: they come and go at behest of a leader, usually the wisest and holiest among them. I say beloved, there are those amongst you of this order: they have known of old when labors were required to ennoble the race." (G. S. 69:8-10).

"All the mighty of the earth, verily the truly mighty, are members of this group. Some manifest in flesh today like unto yourselves; far greater, however, is the number gone on into the higher and even higher planes." (G. S. 69:26-27).

"My beloved, hear my words: I am at the head of sacrificial ones: bestowed upon me was the leadership of that group in that I wouldst sacrifice most, going down into flesh times of greatest number, suffering most terribly most of those times. Those who make up the group were created by that Spirit whom men call the Father, for purposes of ministering; therefore ye who do minister most are greatest, and he who is greatest in service is leader." (G. S. 69:31-32).

In the above, the Elder Brother tells us that he is the Head of the Wanderers, and that the Father created them for a special purpose; they belong to a special order.

The disciples were all *Wanderers*, for Christ says: "Did I not say unto my disciples, Verily I tell you there are those among you who shall not taste of death until I come again? Were not those disciples of the serving ones? Whereof can Mammon say with a certainty that they have ever died? Is it death for consciousness to pass from body unto body? Verily I tell you, they know themselves." (G. S. 69:36-39).

"There are those on planes of earth who have manifested unto me in many ages, not as men and women but as Radiant Ones; they have come and gone in your lives of the present as servants of mine, messengers and ministers in flesh, making you to see the earth after its nature as an abiding place for the children of men." (G. S. 79:15).

"Beloved, be advised: there are in flesh certain entities who are messengers of mine sent by the Host to do you good; they have one thought only, to execute my will." (G. S. 79:24).

"I tell you angels are about you, in and out of the flesh, that ye do meet and talk with them daily, that they do serve you at my behest, that they come back to me with report of your zeal. *In that ye serve, ye are served, my beloved!*" (G. S. 79:39-40).

Whether we call them the "Goodly Company", the "Sons of Light", the "Lesser Avatars", "Those who serve", "Apples", or *The Wanderers*, it doesn't matter—they continue to serve in Love and Light.

"Let brotherly love continue. Be not forgetful to entertain strangers: for thereby some have entertained angels unawares." (Hebrews 13:1-2).

It is truly written: "Other sheep have I which are not of this fold; them also will I bring."

CHAPTER 3

THE PROPHETS

Blessed be the Lord God of Israel, who "spake by the mouth of his holy *prophets*, which have been since the world began." (St. Luke 1:70).

The Prophets went before the face of the Lord to prepare his ways; to give light to them that sat in darkness and in the shadow of death; to guide their feet into the *way of peace*.

There have always been prophets and there always will be prophets; they are with us today. Wordsworth said: "Mighty Prophet! Seer blest, On whom those truths do rest, Which we are toiling all our lives to find."

In Old Testament times there were orders or bands of prophets, called *schools of the prophets*. In New Testament times Christian prophets constituted an order ranking next to that of apostle. The Moslems had Mohammed, the Mormons had Joseph Smith and the Christian Scientists had Mary Baker Eddy. Those who are discerning the signs of God and are telling the people of what the future holds are still exercising the office of *Prophet*.

Isaiah, Jeremiah, Ezekiel, Daniel, Hosea, Joel, Amos, Obadiah, Jonah, Micah, Haggai, Zechariah and Malachi were prophets along with others during the Old Testament days. Of course, Isaiah and Ezekiel seem to have had more direct contact with space intelligences than any of the others. Many of their writings are no longer available, such as "The Acts of Uzziah" written by Isaiah. (See II Chronicles 26:22).

Chapter Six of Isaiah was referred to in *Maldek And Malona*, showing us that this prophet was visited by space intelligences and thereby received his information for prophecy. Isaiah, himself, was a "Wanderer", a "Son of Light". To show that he knew of extraterrestrial visitation to Earth, he wrote:

> "Lift up your eyes on high, and behold who hath created these *things*, that bringeth out their host by number: he calleth them all by names by the greatness of his might, for that he is strong in power; not one faileth." (Isaiah 40:26).

David had said: "He telleth the number of the stars; he calleth them all by their names." (Psalms 147:4).

Isaiah wasn't referring to *things* or *stars* alone, and he didn't mean the light they gave off in the heavens. By "host" he meant the intelligences that were coming earthward from the heavenly bodies.

Isaiah's prophecy in Chapter Five could easily refer to the present time as well as it did the prophet's time. The vineyard and the wild grapes therein symbolizes our world of today and its people. In one of the new editions of the Bible, the following verses are omitted. Chapter Five ends with verse twenty-five. Why were these verses taken out after all these years?

"And he will lift up an ensign to the nations from far, and will hiss unto them from the end of the earth: and, behold, they shall come with speed swiftly: None shall be weary nor stumble among them; none shall slumber nor sleep; neither shall the girdle of their loins be loosed, nor the latchet of their shoes be broken: Whose arrows are sharp, and all their bows bent, their horses' hoofs shall be counted like flint, and their wheels like a whirlwind: Their roaring shall be like a lion, they shall roar like young lions: yea, they shall roar, and lay hold of the prey, and shall carry it away safe, and none shall deliver it. And in that day they shall roar against them like the roaring of the sea: and if one look unto the land, behold darkness and sorrow (distress), and the light is darkened in the heavens thereof (when it is light, it shall be dark in the destructions thereof). (Isaiah 5:26-30).

The space friends have "wheels like whirlwinds", their "arrows (truth) are sharp", they "come with speed swiftly", and they shall "lay hold of the prey, and shall carry it away safe".

Ezekiel had his encounter with space craft many years after Isaiah in 595 B.C. He gets off to a grand start in Chapter One giving us a perfect description of Flying Saucers, their landing, and their occupants getting out. Although the entire verses being transposed and generally mixed up, we can obtain a comprehensive view of the situation by careful reading and proper correlation. Remember that Ezekiel had no mechanical contrivances with which to make comparisons and he was therefore compelled to use

PLATE XVI

the only things with which he was familiar—animals, birds, and horse-drawn chariots with *wheels*.

In this connection the Tetramorph of Greek art is interesting. (See *Plate XVI*). This symbolic drawing was taken from a Byzantine Mosaic in the Convent of Vatopedi on Mt. Athos. The principal figure is that of a Man, the three heads of the other creatures appearing from behind, and six large wings covered with eyes are arranged around the heads and across the body of the Man, whose feet rest on fiery *wheels* which are also winged (indicating flight). All the heads are invested with plain nimbi. The Tetramorph was the ancients' idea or conception of what Ezekiel saw that day in 595 B.C. by the River of Chebar. It is one of the world's earliest known drawings of Saucers.

The verses in Chapter One which make the most sense in the light of our modern knowledge of space-craft will be given in that order.

"And I looked, and, behold, a whirlwind came out of the north, a great cloud, and a fire infolding (catching) itself, and a brightness was about it, and out of the midst thereof as the color of amber, out of the midst of the fire." (Ezekiel 1:4).

Many of the spacecraft sighted within the last few years have displayed a very bright amber glow.

"And every one had four faces, and every one had four wings. And their feet were straight feet (a straight foot); and the sole of their feet was like the sole of a calf's foot: and they sparkled like the color of burnished brass." (Ezekiel 1:6-7). We shall see in a moment why they had four faces and four wings. The "straight foot" is, of course, the ball-bearing landing-gear-like devices on the bottom of some Saucers with their contact points.

"Their wings were joined one to another; they turned not when they went; they went every one *straight forward*. As for the likeness of their faces; they four had the face of a man, and the face of a lion, on the right side: and they four had the face of an ox on the left side: they four also had the face of an eagle." (Ezekiel 1:9-10).

"And they went every one straight forward: *whither the spirit* was to go, they went; and they turned not when they went." (Ezekiel 1:12).

This could easily represent a fleet of four space craft or Saucers with their insignia shown on the sides, designating what portion of the heavens they come from. A man; a lion; an ox (bull); and an eagle. One represented the Constellation Aquarius (Man); one the Constellation Leo (Lion); one the Constellation Taurus (Ox or Bull); and one the Constellation Scorpio (Eagle). For the complete reconstruction of the ancient Scale of Four see Plate XVII. When reading this plate on the hidden meaning of the Four, the vertical columns should be considered as separate units, so that, when you read down in any of the four columns, you will discover all related material. Likewise, when you read across from left to right in the horizontal lines or sections, you will discover four items that are all related.

THE HIDDEN MEANING OF THE SCALE OF FOUR (DIVINE TETRAD):

	1	2	3	4
The Four Numerals:	1	2	3	4
The Four Cardinal Directions:	North	East	South	West
The Four Seasons:	Winter	Summer	Autumn	Spring
	Winter Solstice	Summer Solstice	Autumnal Equinox	Vernal Equinox
Four Constellations:	Aquarius	Leo	Taurus	Scorpio
	Gemini	Aries	Virgo	Cancer
	Libra	Sagittarius	Capricorn	Pisces
	Saturn	Mars	Fixed Stars	Jupiter
	Mercury	Sun	Moon	Venus
Four Royal Stars of the Ancients:	Fomalhaut	Regulus	Aldebaran	Antares
Four Great Primary Forces	RMF	ES	SM	EM
Four Beasts:	Man	Lion	Bull	Eagle
Four Gospels and Evangelists:	Matthew	Mark	Luke	John

Four Rivers of Paradise:	Gihon	Tigris	Euphrates	Pison
	Incarnation	Resurrection	Passion	Ascension
Four Elements:	Air	Fire	Earth	Water
The Four Tribes:	Reuben	Judah	Ephraim	Dan
Four Major or Greater Prophets:	Isaiah	Daniel	Jeremiah	Ezekiel
Four Archangels:	Gabriel	Michael	Uriel	Raphael
	Cold	Heat	Dryness	Moisture
The Four Kingdoms:	Metals	Animals	Stones	Plants
	Flying	Walking	Creeping	Swimming
	Cherub	Seraph	Ariel	Tharsis

Since Ezekiel could not conceive of a bird being able to fly in "any direction" without turning around, and since the Saucers did fly or go in any direction without turning, he naturally had to add wings to all four sides in order to remedy that defect, and also to protect himself and his writings from the uniformed populace. If there had been a Project "Whirlwind" (Saucer) in Ezekiel's time he would have been ridiculed indeed; and probably was by many.

Ezekiel didn't realize that the Saucers were separate from their respective occupants. He thought the men in the Saucers were the spirits of the wheels; to him the Saucers were living things!

"Also out of the midst thereof came the likeness of *four living creatures*. And this was their appearance; they had the *likeness of a man*." (Ezekiel 1:5).

Now that the Saucers are on the ground perhaps we can find out more about them.

"Now as I beheld the living creatures, behold one wheel upon the earth by the living creatures, with his four faces." (Ezekiel 1:15).

Two-faced men are bad enough, but Ezekiel would have had a difficult time, indeed, with four-faced men. However, the prophet did not mean that the living creatures had four faces, he meant the wheels had "four faces".

"The appearance of the wheels and their work was like unto the color of a beryl: *and they four had one likeness:* and their appearance and their work was as it were *a wheel in the middle of a wheel.*" (Ezekiel 1:16). "As for their rings, they were so high that they were dreadful; and their rings (strakes) were full of eyes round about them four. And when the living creatures went, the wheels went by them: and when the living creatures were lifted up from the earth, the wheels were lifted up. Whithersoever the spirit was to go, they went, thither was their spirit to go; and the wheels were lifted up over against them: for the spirit of the living creature (spirit of life) was in the wheels." (Ezekiel 1:18-20).

"And the likeness of the firmament upon the heads of the living creature was as the color of the terrible crystal, stretched forth over their heads above." (Ezekiel 1:22).

The firmament over the heads of the living creatures is, of course the dome, and the "eyes round about" were the portholes or observation openings of a Flying Disc or Saucer (Compare Adamski's photographs in *"Flying Saucers Have Landed"*). The word "rings" can also be translated "strakes" which is a shipbuilding term. It means one breadth of plates along the bottom or sides of a vessel reaching from stem to stern. Now the first word "rings" in verse eighteen cannot be translated "strakes," therefore it should read: "As for their rings, they were so high that they were dreadful; and their strakes were full of eyes round about them four." It means that the counter-rotating rings of the underneath portion of the Saucer "were so high that they were dreadful", and the strakes or sides of the Saucer which were composed of one breadth "were full of eyes round about them four". This latter description means that all four Saucers had the porthole openings.

The phrase, "when the living creatures were lifted up from the earth, the wheels were lifted up", means that when the occupants of the Saucers were in their ships, they both (creatures and wheels) left the ground together.

The "firmament" or dome of the Saucers was like "the color of the terrible crystal". On top of each dome there is a light or lamp that sends forth a terrifically bright beam. This corresponds to the "polar vent" area of our own big "spaceship", the Earth.

Usually this light is a "pulsating" light and changes colors. It would have appeared "terrible" to Ezekiel, indeed.

"And there was a voice from the firmament that was over their heads, when they stood, and had let down their wings. And above the firmament that was over their heads was the likeness of a throne, as the appearance of a sapphire stone: and upon the likeness of the throne was the likeness as the appearance of a man above upon it. And I saw as the color of amber, as the appearance of fire round about within it, from the appearance of his loins even upward, and from the appearance of his loins even downward, I saw as it were the appearance of fire, and it had brightness round about. As the appearance of the bow that is in the cloud in the day of rain (the rainbow), so was the appearance of the brightness round about." (Ezekiel 1:25-28).

In the November, 1953 issue of *Mystic Magazine*, Orfeo M. Angelucci told his story of contact with space beings to Paul M. Vest. Here is part of what he said: "But even as the glowing red orb vanished two smaller discs came from it. These discs were a soft fluorescent green and shot toward me like shooting stars. They streaked down in front of my car and hovered about fifteen feet directly in front of me. I judged them to be about thirty inches each in diameter. Hanging silently in the air like iridescent bubbles, their green light fluctuated in pulsations. As I gazed at those two eerie balls of green fire I heard a masculine voice, strong, well-modulated and speaking perfect English. The voice apparently came from *between* the two green discs." Again, he said: "The glowing discs created a soft illumination, but I could see no person anywhere. The voice stated that the small green discs were instruments of transmission and reception comparable to nothing developed on Earth. Then the voice added that through the discs I was in direct communication with friends from another planet." Then Orfeo said: "The area between the discs began to glow with a soft green light which gradually formed itself into a kind of luminous screen as the discs themselves faded perceptibly. Within that luminous, three-dimensional screen there appeared images of the heads and shoulders of two persons, as though in a cinema close-up." He continued: "Those two figures struck me somehow as being the ultimate of human perfection. There was a nobility about them, their eyes were larger and much more expressive and they emanated a kind of radiance that gave me a sense of wonder." Orfeo said that he had the feeling while they studied him that they knew every thought that passed in his mind: "I seemed to be in telepathic communication with them, for thoughts, understandings, and new comprehensions flashed through my consciousness that would have required hours of conversation to transmit."

If Angelucci's experience had taken place in 595 B.C., he too, would have been a prophet like *Ezekiel*. Instead he is a Prophet of the New Age now dawning on Earth.

Considering the strange experience of Angelucci, we can interpret Ezekiel 1:25-28, as follows:

A voice came from the dome of the hovering Saucer. Then, Ezekiel says that above the dome "was the likeness of a throne, as the appearance of a sapphire stone". Notice he doesn't say an actual throne, but "the *likeness* of a throne". Later he says "the *likeness* as the appearance of a man". Therefore, the throne and the man were not actually there—only their *likeness*. They were projected there, even as the man and woman were projected between the two green discs observed by Orfeo. Then, Ezekiel tells us that he saw the "appearance of fire", and that "it had brightness round about; as the appearance of the rainbow, so was the appearance of the brightness round about". Ezekiel was seeing the aura of the space visitor speaking to him from some sort of highly evolved television system. Where was this visitor? He is separate and distinct from the four living creatures, or occupants of the Saucers. Possibly he was as far away as the planet Saturn as we shall see presently.

The prophet says the throne appeared as "a sapphire stone". The ruby, or red corundum, is almost never called sapphire, but all other gem varieties are, as white, *green*, purple, and yellow sapphire. Therefore, a "sapphire stone" can be *green!* Besides, the color sapphire blue is *greenish-blue* in hue. Again this sounds very similar to Orfeo Angelucci's experience. In Ezekiel 1:16, we read: "The appearance of the wheels and their work was like unto the color of a *beryl*. "An emerald is a rich green variety of beryl; and the beryl is commonly green or bluish-green—aquamarine and emerald are varieties. Again the *green* color!

The gem sapphire is usually the birthstone of April and Taurus. And Taurus is ruled by Venus. This gem has been ascribed to Saturn, and to Venus. It was mentioned in *Revelation* as one of the foundations of the New Jerusalem. Moses and Aaron saw the God of Israel with a paved work of sapphire under his feet.

"And they saw the God of Israel: and there was under his feet as it were a paved work of a sapphire stone, and as it were the body of heaven in his clearness." (Exodus 24:10). The Book of Revelation also speaks of a similar happening and that will be discussed a little later on.

One legend about Aaron's rod says that it was made of *sapphire*. Sapphires are used against the evil eye and witchcraft of all kinds; the gem is said to exert good influence on its owners.

The beryl is designated the birthstone of October or Scorpio. Some Bible authorities claim it was one of the stones in the High Priest's breastplate and one of the foundation stones of the New Jerusalem. It was sometimes used to make *crystal balls!* Saucers or Crystal Bells of Beryl, indeed!

It is possible, therefore, that one of the Saucers of the four came from Venus, representing the Constellation of Taurus (Ox or Bull,), and the "voice of one that spake" could have been the voice of the Head (Kadar) of the Universal Tribunal on Saturn.

Then in Ezekiel 1:28, we read: "This was the appearance of the likeness of the glory of the Lord. And when I saw it, I fell upon my face, and I heard a voice of one that spake."

"And he said unto me, Son of man, stand upon thy feet, and I will speak unto thee. And the spirit entered into me when he spake unto me, and set me unto my feet, that I heard him that spake unto me." (Ezekiel 2:1-2).

When the prophet says that "the spirit entered into" him when the voice "spake unto" him, he means that telepathic communication had been set up—the same thing again as the Angelucci experience! "And he said unto me, Son of Man, I send thee to the children of Israel, to a rebellious nation (nations) that hath rebelled against me: they and their fathers have transgressed against me, even unto this very day." (Ezekiel 2:3).

Here, Ezekiel is being sent unto the people as Isaiah was sent: "And he said, Go, and tell this people, Hear ye indeed, but understand not; and see ye indeed, but perceive not." (Isaiah 6:9).

Isaiah and the Saucers were discussed in *Maldek and Malona*. Both prophets had encounters with extraterrestrial beings and then were told to go forth and give the message to the people. The very same thing is happening today in our twentieth century!

Ezekiel goes on to make many references to Flying Saucers. In Ezekiel 3.12-15, we read: "Then the spirit took me up, and I heard behind me a voice of a great rushing, saying, Blessed be the glory of the Lord from his place. I heard also the noise of the wings of the living creatures that touched (kissed) one another, and the noise of the wheels over against them, and a noise of a great rushing. So that spirit lifted me up, and took me away, and I went in bitterness (bitter), in the heat of my spirit, but the hand of the Lord was strong upon me. Then I came to them to the captivity at Tel-abib, that dwelt by the river of Chebar."

Ezekiel could truthfully say that he "rode a Flying Saucer". The "great rushing" was the characteristic *humming* of a space craft. In Chapter Ten, the prophet speaks of the vision of the Cherubim and the Wheels.

"Then I looked, and, behold, in the firmament that was above the head of the cherubim there appeared over them as it were a *sapphire* stone, as the appearance of the likeness of a throne." (Ezekiel 10:1).

Here we encounter the *greenish-blue* color again. And the prophet says, "*as it were* a sapphire stone." This means it appeared to be *like* a sapphire stone, but was not actually such a thing.

"And when I looked, behold the four wheels by the cherubim, one wheel by one cherub, and another wheel by another cherub: and the appearance of the wheels was as the color of a beryl stone. And as for their appearances, they four had one likeness, as if a wheel had been in the midst of a wheel." (Ezekiel 10:9-10).

The cherubim here represent the occupants of the Saucers. So, Ezekiel had another contact with the four Saucers! One Saucer was by one occupant, and so on. Again they appeared *green*.

"As for the wheels, it was cried unto them in my hearing, O wheel." (Ezekiel 10:13).

This can also be translated: "As for the wheels, they were called in my hearing, wheel, or *galgal.*"

Ezekiel says the cherubim "mounted up from the earth" in his sight, "and the glory of the God of Israel was over them above". (Ezekiel 10:19).

A Saucer increasing its speed and going through various color changes, all the time glowing brilliantly, would indeed appear as "the glory of the God of Israel".

"And the likeness of their faces was the same faces which I saw by the river of Chebar, their appearances and themselves: they went every one *straight forward*." (Ezekiel 10:22).

In Chapter Eleven, we read: "Moreover the spirit lifted me up, and brought me unto the east gate of the Lord's house." (Ezekiel 11:1).

"Then did the cherubim lift up their wings, and the wheels beside them; and the glory of the God of Israel was over them above. And the glory of the Lord went up from the midst of the city, and stood upon the mountain which is on the east side of the city." (Ezekiel 11:22-23).

The colorful, pulsating, glowing Saucers went straight up from the "midst of the city" and hovered over the mountain "on the east side of the city".

Pages and pages of interpretation could be written about Ezekiel's Saucer experiences, but enough has been given here to show the connection. Every verse seems to hold new, important information. For instance, Ezekiel 1:13: "As for the likeness of the living creatures, their appearance was like burning coal of fire, and like the appearance of lamps: it went up and down among the living creatures; and the fire was bright, and out of the fire went forth lightning."

This sounds very similar to the experience of ex-Mayor Oskar Linke, of Gleimershausen, near Meiningen, Germany. Herr Linke and his eleven year-old stepdaughter, Gabriele, saw a Saucer that had landed and they observed two human figures near it clothed in a kind of *shimmering metallic substance*. Herr Linke said, "I noticed that one man appeared to be carrying a *lamp on his chest . . . the lamp flashed on and off regularly.*"

In describing the "take off" of the Saucer, Linke made such statements as: "The color at first seemed green, then changed to red. At the same time I heard a slight hum. The whole object rose slowly. The rate of ascent now became much greater, and at the same time we heard a whistling sound, rather like the noise made by a falling bomb, but not nearly so loud. The object rose in a horizontal position, swerved away toward a nearby village and disappeared, still climbing over the hills and forests *toward* Stockheim."

Ezekiel's living creatures appeared like "burning coals of fire." Linke's human figures appeared like "shimmering metallic substances". Ezekiel's living creatures had the appearance of lamps, and the fire went *up and down* among the living creatures. Linke's human figure had something which appeared to be a lamp on his chest, and the lamp flashed *on and off* regularly. Herr Linke and the prophet Ezekiel had an almost identical experience, even to the color of *green*, and the Saucer going "up from the midst" and being over the mountains and hills, and the "noise of a great rushing" and the "whistling sound".

Isaiah and Ezekiel are not the only ones mentioned in the Bible who had Saucer contact. Job 40:6, may refer to a contact: "Then answered the Lord unto Job out of the *whirlwind*, and said . . ." Saucers have *always* been with us, and the Bible itself is a record of early contacts. The Bible, because of many translations, mistakes made by scribes, and deliberate tampering by men, is not *perfect*, but it does give us fairly accurate historical reports, especially in the Old Testament.

"And Jacob went on his way, and the angels of God met him. And when Jacob saw them, he said, This is God's host: and he called the name of that place Mahanaim (Two hosts)." (Genesis 32:1-2).

"And it came to pass, as they still went on, and talked, that, behold, there appeared a chariot of fire, and horses of fire, and parted them both asunder; and Elijah went up by a whirlwind into heaven. And Elisha saw it. (II Kings 2:11-12).

Elijah had completed his mission and was removed by a Saucer. Because of this Elijah was translated and Elisha was endowed. The latter took up the mantle of the former and carried on.

Elijah left Earth in "a chariot of fire" in 896 B.C., and for three years afterward, Elisha traveled about the country doing a great deal of good. He cured the sick, raised the dead, fed the hungry, and spread the word of God. There were subversives in those days too, and Elisha was in trouble with the King of Syria, and the king sent an army to capture the man of God.

"Therefore sent he thither horses, and chariots, and a great (heavy) host: and they came by night, and compassed the city about.

And when the servant (minister) of the man of God was risen early, and gone forth, behold a host compassed the city both with horses and chariots. And his servant said unto him, Alas, my master! how shall we do? And he answered, Fear not: for they that be with us are more than they that be with them. And Elisha prayed, and said, Lord, I pray thee, open his eyes, that he may see. And the Lord opened the eyes of the young man; and he saw: and, behold, *the mountain was full of horses and chariots of fire round about Elisha. And when they came down to him,* Elisha prayed unto the Lord, and said, Smite this people, I pray thee, with blindness. And he smote them with blindness according to the word of Elisha." (II Kings 6:14-18).

Here is a positive statement that there is a marked difference between the chariots of the king and the "chariots of fire". These "fire chariots" *came down*—and they couldn't possibly come down unless they were first up. And Elisha didn't wait there until hundreds of "chariots of fire" rolled and rumbled down the mountain-side—they had been on the mountain, "the mountain was full of" them—but they "came down" to Elisha, gliding noiselessly as only Saucers can do.

The "heavenly host" or Saucer intelligences were watching over the men of God in ancient times, even as today. *The Prophets* received their information directly from space intelligences and relayed it on—usually to *The Remnant*, for members of this group were the special charge of prophets.

Remember that *The Wanderers*, in a sense are "Sons of Light", but the term fits space intelligences in space craft in a more direct way. In the "Golden Scripts", we read:

"The Sons of Light array themselves at my bid-ding: they go forth in the world and make it beautiful." (G. S. 209:1).

"The Sons of Light are of the Host; they are a creation of the Father for a purpose; men call them angels; they are called Sons of Light by the Father's cohorts." (G. S. 209: 3-4).

In Chapter 209, verse 2, we read: "They are a goodly company indeed, but not the Goodly Company that findeth me through suffering." Here the Elder Brother is saying that the space intelligences in the Saucers are a part of the goodly company, but not the Goodly Company of "Wanderers" who go in and out of life on Earth to help their fellow man and thereby suffer.

"They are endowed with infallible powers in Matter, in that Matter obeyeth them; Matter is their servant: they have dominion over it. They know neither time nor space but transfer themselves from planet unto planet in the twinkling of an eye. They come and go upon the Father's business: great is their joy therein: they are pure in heart and beauteous of mien. They seek to do the Father's will, and in that they seek, they do find life wondrous." (G. S. 209: 6-9). "I tell you, be advised! Ye are as gods yourselves among men; the Sons of Light are your ministering servants." (G. S. 209:21).

"Do I speak unto you of mysteries? I say that ye shall know them in the Day of Understanding. Behold my *ministers* who are Sons of Light manifesting, have orders of me that ye be protected in your thought and persons when it so cometh that ye advance my Plan." (G. S. 209:31-32).

"Hear my words and be wise! I speak as a teacher who is honored with wisdom." (G. S. 209:36).

On page twenty-five of *I Rode A Flying Saucer*, by George W. Van Tassel, there is a message dated May 17, 1952. In part, it reads: "My center has given me authority to describe vaguely this ship I command. In your dimensions my, what you would call 'flagship', is three-hundred feet thick, and fifteen-hundred feet in diameter. Our crew *seventy-two hundred*."

The fact that the crew numbered seventy-two hundred is very significant and if we go to our Bible, we discover why.

"And, behold, one of them which were with Jesus stretched out his hand, and drew his sword, and struck a servant of the high priest's and smote off his ear. Then said Jesus unto him, Put up again thy sword into his place: for all they that take the sword shall perish with the sword. Thinkest thou that I cannot now pray to my Father, and he shall presently give me more than *twelve legions of angels?* But how then shall the scriptures be fulfilled, that thus it must be?" (St. Matthew 26:51-54).

In designating the number of angels the Father would send if Jesus requested them, the Master used the then familiar Roman military unit, the legion. A legion varied from the time of the early re-public until the empire in the number of men composing it. The Emperor Marius made many changes in its basic structure. However, the legion Triarii consisted of six-hundred men; this was the third line of the Roman army. Therefore, twelve Triarii equalled *seventy-two hundred men*, the same number as the crew of the space 'flagship".

There is a cross-reference in the Bible to "twelve legions of angels" found in St. Matthew 26:53 which is quoted above. That cross-reference refers us back to II Kings 6:17, which has already been mentioned, but it will be quoted again for emphasis.

"I pray thee, open his eyes, that he may see. And the Lord opened the eyes of the young man; and he saw: and, behold, the mountain was full of horses and chariots of fire round Elisha."

In going back to the year 4004 B.C., we find in Genesis 5:24, the following:

"And Enoch walked with God and he was not; for God took him." Again there is another cross-reference and it refers us to II Kings 2:11, which has already been quoted. There is mention of Enoch in Hebrews 11:5: "By faith Enoch was translated that he should not see death; and was not found, because God had translated him: for before his translation he had this testimony, that he pleased God."

Look at the Bible dates as they are recorded. In the first chapter of Genesis, first verse you will find the beginning of the story of the creation of the Earth. At the head of the center column reference is the date 4004 B.C. At the end of chapter three, after God had driven Adam and Eve out of the Garden of Eden, there is the date 4003 B.C., or, one year later than the beginning of Creation. In chapter five where the generations of Adam are listed, counting forward to the removal of Enoch, there is a lapse of nine-hundred eighty-five years, but the date at the head of the column is again 4004 B.C. How come?

Science has proven beyond a doubt that the Earth is millions of years old. Besides, there are in existence a number of documents dated much earlier than the alleged Bible date of creation. In the book, *Ancient Times, A History Of The Early World*, by James Henry Breasted, on page 45, chapter 61, we find reference to the Egyptian culture: "He decided to use the Moon no longer for dividing his year. He would have twelve months, and he would make his months all the same length, that is, thirty days each; then he would celebrate five feast days; a kind of holiday week that was five days long at the end of the year. This gave him a year of three-hundred sixty-five days. He was not enough of an astronomer to know that every four years he ought to have a leap year of three-hundred sixty-six days although he discovered this fact later. This convenient Egyptian calendar was devised in 4241 B.C. and its introduction is the *earliest dated event in history*. Furthermore, this calendar is the very one which has descended to us, after more than six thousand years, unfortunately with awkward alterations in the length of the months, but for these alterations the Egyptians were not responsible."

The calendar we use today was devised two-hundred thirty-seven years *before* the Earth was created if we want to accept the Bible dates. However, Archbishop Ussher (1581-1656 A.D.) figured out much of the Bible chronology and dated certain events by it. The dates, therefore, are not actually *scriptural*, but man-made. Certain Fundamental Christian groups believe the world was really created on October 23, 4004 B.C. The question that immediately comes up is: 'What was going on the day before, October 22nd? If the world hadn't been created yet, there couldn't have been an October, since that month was devised by man many years later!

"Who layeth the beams of his chambers in the waters: who maketh the clouds his chariot: who walketh upon the wings of the wind: Who maketh his angels spirits; his ministers a flaming fire." (Psalms 104:3-4). Again there is a cross-reference to II Kings 2:11.

"The chariots of God are twenty thousand, even thousands of angels: the Lord is among them, as in Sinai, in the holy place." (Psalms 68:17).

There are cross-references here to II Kings 6:16-17, already quoted. Daniel 7:9-10; Hebrews 12:20-22; Deuteronomy 33 are also referred to.

"I beheld till the thrones were cast down, and the Ancient of days did sit, whose garment was white as snow, and the hair of his head was like the pure wool: his throne was like the fiery flame, and his wheels as burning fire. A fiery stream issued and came forth from before him: thousand thousands ministered unto him (and ten thousand times ten thousand stood before him: the judgment was set and the books were opened." (Daniel 7:9-10).

Daniel and all the other prophets saw great fiery objects come down from the heavens and they con-versed with tremendous numbers of *celestial* beings who emerged from these objects—these beings instructed the prophets in the beauteous laws of love. More will be said about Daniel in *The Remnant*. A colossal program of aid, comfort and instruction was instituted with *The Prophets*. Of course, the Bible account is somewhat confused due to the many translations and alterations, and in some cases the deliberate attempt to cover up the truth in order to keep the mass of people "ignorant". However, people who know the truth are not dependent upon theological dogma or doctrine to "save them" or make them free: "Ye shall know the truth and the truth shall make you free."

"For they could not endure that which was commanded, And if so much as a beast touch the mountain, it shall be stoned, or thrust through with a dart: And so terrible was the sight, that Moses said, I exceedingly fear and quake: But ye are come unto mount Sion, and unto the city of the living God, the heavenly Jerusalem, and to an innumerable company of angels." (Hebrews 12:20-22).

"As an eagle stirreth up her nest, fluttereth over her young, spreadeth abroad her wings, taketh them, beareth them on her wings: So the Lord alone did lead him, and there was no strange god with him." (Deuteronomy 32:11).

"And this is the blessing, wherewith Moses the man of God blessed the children of Israel before his death. And he said, The Lord came from Sinai, and rose up from Seir unto them; he shined forth from mount Paran, and he came with ten thousands of saints: from his right hand went a fiery law (fire of law) for them." (Deuteronomy 33:1-2).

All the foregoing seems to point to a great company of angels, or heavenly host, who had descended to Earth to give Moses and his people specific information, and they warned Moses and the people not to come near as the force field surrounding the ships might injure them. This has happened in our time also, when space intelligences have warned individuals about getting too close to the ships while they are hovering. Adamski, Bethurum, and Fry experienced this. The ancient people could easily understand death or injury as a result of a stone, dart, or arrow wound; but they knew nothing of radiation, or rays, beams, or electro-magnetic energy.

"In the third month, when the children of Israel were gone forth out of the land of Egypt, the same day came they into the wilderness of Sinai. For they were departed from Rephidim, and were come to the desert of Sinai, and had pitched in the wilderness; and there Israel camped before the mount. And Moses went up unto God, and the Lord called unto him out of the mountain, saying, Thus shalt thou say to the house of Jacob, and tell the children of Israel; Ye have seen what I did unto the Egyptians, and how I bare you on eagles' wings, and brought you unto myself." (Exodus 19:1-4).

Now, only those verses which are pertinent to the subject will be quoted, since the intervening verses pertain to messages of instruction from the space beings (or the Lord, as the ancients believed) to the people, and the people's reply, with Moses acting as message bearer.

"And the Lord said unto Moses, Lo, I come unto thee in a thick cloud, that the people may hear when I speak with thee, and *believe thee forever.* And Moses told the words of the people unto the Lord." (Exodus 19:9).

"And be ready against the third day: for the third day the Lord will come down in the sight of all the people upon mount Sinai. And thou shalt set bounds unto the people round about, saying, Take heed to yourselves, *that ye go not up into the mount, or touch the border of it:* whosoever toucheth the mount shall be surely put to death: There shall not a hand touch it, but he shall surely be stoned, or shot through; whether it be beast or man, it shall not live: when the trumpet soundeth long, they shall come up to the mount." (Exodus 19:11-13). The space intelligences meant here that they would give a signal, a "trumpet" blast that "soundeth long", when it was safe for the people to come up to the mount.

"And it came to pass on the third day in the morning, that there were thunders and lightning, and a thick cloud upon the mount, and the voice of the trumpet exceeding loud; so that all the people that were in the camp trembled." (Exodus 19:16).

"And the Lord came down upon mount Sinai, on the top of the mount: and the Lord called Moses up to the top of the mount; and Moses went up." (Exodus 19:20).

Then the Lord told Moses to go down and warn the people so that they wouldn't "break through unto the Lord to gaze, and many of them perish".

"And God spake all these words, saying, I am the Lord thy God which have brought thee out of the land of Egypt, out of the house of bondage." (Exodus 20:1-2).

Then follows the Decalogue or Ten Commandments:

1. Thou shalt have no other Gods before me.
2. Thou shall not make unto thee any graven images.
3. Thou shalt not take the name of the Lord thy God in vain.
4. Remember the sabbath day to keep it holy.
5. Honor thy father and thy mother.
6. Thou shalt not kill.
7. Thou shalt not commit adultery.
8. Thou shalt not steal.
9. Thou shalt not bear false witness.
10. Thou shalt not covet.

"And all the people saw the thunderings, and the lightnings, and the noise of the trumpet, and the mountain smoking." (Exodus 20:18).

"When they had heard the king, they departed; and, lo, *the star*, which they saw in the east, *went before them, till it came and stood over where the young child was*. When they saw the star, they rejoiced with exceeding great joy." (St. Matthew 2:9-10).

"And there were in the same country shepherds abiding in the field, keeping watch over their flock by night. And, lo, *the angel of the Lord came upon them*, and the *glory of the Lord shone round about them*. and they were sore afraid. And the angel said unto them, Fear not: for, behold, I bring you good tidings of great joy, which shall be to all people. For unto you is born this day in the city of David a Savior, which is Christ the Lord." (St. Luke 2:8-11).

"And *suddenly there was with the angel a multitude of heavenly host* praising God, and saying, Glory to God in the highest, and on earth peace, good will toward men." (St. Luke 2:13-14).

For many years astronomers have tried to justify the actions of the Star of Bethlehem. There are several theories, but no agreement has been reached as yet. The constellations and conjunctions back to that period have been checked and it is found that no such *natural* event took place. One well-known astronomer said: "In my opinion, the Star of Bethlehem was created especially for the event."

What manner of "star" was it that "went before them", and then "stood over", or hovered over, "where the young child was"? Saucer sightings by the thousands have proven that in the night skies, they do, indeed, look like bright and shining "stars". The

"Spacecraft of Bethlehem" must have been an enormous ship specially designed and constructed for the event. (Van Tassel and Pelley also hold to this opinion).

Peace on earth, good will toward men, indeed! What have the people of Earth done with the great message of peace and good will which the Heavenly Host has brought them over the many centuries? And what are we doing with the messages they are still bringing to us? The answer is obvious: we have met peace and brotherly love with courts, prisons, want, firebombs and hellbombs, murders, lust, greed and fear. Oh, thou faithless generation!

In II Corinthians 12:2-4, Paul tells of being "caught up to the third heaven", and "caught up into paradise", where he "heard unspeakable words, which it is not lawful (possible) for a man to utter". Paul's visions were his apostolic credentials.

St. John was an apostle, but he was also a prophet. The Revelation of St. John the Divine again brings in the Four Beasts and Saucers. Therefore, from Genesis to Revelation we have numerous accounts of space intelligences contacting, conversing with, and sometimes taking away, men of Earth.

Read the entire Chapter Four of Revelation. John says that a trumpet talked with him—he was "in the spirit"—"a throne was set in heaven".

"And he that sat was to look upon like a jasper and a sardine stone: and there was a rainbow round about the throne, in sight like unto an emerald." (Revelation 4:3).

In Ezekiel 1:16 the beryl was referred to! in Ezekiel 1:26, the sapphire was mentioned. Now, St. John had an experience almost identical with Ezekiel's, except the Jasper, the Sardine (Sardius), and the Emerald are used to describe the scene. All five of these stones, however, were included in the High Priest's breastplate. (See Exodus 28:17-20). A Sard or Sardine is a deep orange-red variety of chalcedony. The Sardius is either a ruby or a sard. Therefore, the color represented by these stones is *red*. The Jasper of the Bible was a dark-green or opalescent milky iridescence stone. Here is the *green* again! And the Emerald, of course, is green as everyone knows. Remember Orfeo said there was a glowing *red* orb, followed by two *green* discs? Remember Oskar Linke said that, "The color at first seemed *green*, then changed to *red*"? The *rainbow* is again mentioned as it was in Ezekiel 1:28.

Then St. John tells us that "round about the throne were four and twenty seats", and upon the seats he saw "four and twenty elders".

These twenty-four representatives could possibly constitute the Saturn Tribunal, with two members for each of the twelve planets.

John, now acting as a prophet, said: "Out of the throne proceeded lightnings and thunderings and voices . . . and there were *seven lamps of fire* burning before the throne . . . there was a sea of glass like unto crystal . . . round about the throne were *four beasts* full of eyes before and behind."

The seven lamps represent the Council of Seven Lights as mentioned previously. Once again, the Saucers are described.

"And the first beast was like a *lion*, and the second beast like a *calf*, and the third beast had a face as a *man*, and the fourth beast was like a flying *eagle*." (Revelation 4:7).

It should be mentioned here that the Constellation Scorpio is now thought of as a scorpion. However, from Abraham's time on up to more recent time, Scorpio was known as the "flying eagle".

When Ezekiel first mentioned the Four Beasts, the ancient Jewish initiates accused him of exposing to the profane the profundities of the secret doctrine. The cherubim constitute the mystical symbol of the fullness of wisdom and these creatures are the spiritual guardians of the four rivers of life flowing from the effulgency of the Creator. When the twelve tribes of Israel encamped in the wilderness, the banners of Reuben (the man), Judah (the lion), Ephrain (the bull), and Dan (the eagle) were placed at the four corners. In the Oedipus Judaicus, Sir W. Drummond reproduces a figure from Kircher which reveals the encampment of Israel to have been symbolic of the *order of the universe*. And, according to Iranous, there must be four Gospels of the New Testament just as there are four quarters of the world and four general winds. The church is supposed to have four pillars like the cherubim, from the midst of which the Word goes forth. The creatures of the lower senses are the four animal natures to be first overcome by man before he can enter into the sphere of light. In the Kabbalah, Adolph Franck writes: "All human faces may be traced, finally, to four primary types, to which they either draw near or from which they recede according to the rank held by the souls in their intellectual and moral order." In the Zohar it is written that the celestial throne of Ezekiel's vision signifies the *traditional* law, and the appearance of a man sitting upon the throne represents the *written* law. (Again, see Plate XVII *p. 253*).

There is no record today, or in Biblical times, where Saucers or Saucer beings ever deliberately injured anyone. Some people may say that the reference to "smote them with blindness" in II Kings 6:18, already referred to, means that harm or injury resulted from contact with space intelligences. However, if we read on we find that Elisha said: "Lord, open the eyes of these men, that they may see. And the Lord opened their eyes, and they saw." (II Kings 6:20).

"And the king of Israel said unto Elisha, when he saw them, My father, shall I smite them? shall I smite them? And he answered, Thou shalt not smite them. Set bread and water before them, that they may eat and drink, and go to their master." (II Kings 6:21-22).

Therefore, the "blindness" was only temporary, for the men not only regained their sight, but they were well fed and sent on their way home.

The heavens are still full of "horses and chariots of fire"; they are here as it was promised. They are here to protect us, to guide us, to encourage us, to make us triumphant over life's circumstances on Earth. Let us be assured that we are part of a *living* Universe, not a dead universe. Beyond our sight there are other worlds more real than the one in which we live, worlds of Light and power. In those worlds God is King. Fear not, for they that are with us are more than they which are with the persons and things that oppose us.

And you who would tell the world of new things, do not be concerned whether that world hears or not, "for they are a rebellious house, yet they shall know that there hash been a *prophet* among them".

CHAPTER 4

THE HARVESTERS

"In my Father's house are many mansions: if it were not so, I would have told you. I go to prepare a place for you." (St. John 14:2).

Jesus spoke of the "many mansions" or planets of the Father's Creation. Some say that the Bible never speaks of more worlds than the Earth, but it certainly does, for in Hebrews we read: "God, who at sundry times and in divers manners spake in time past unto the fathers by the prophets, Hath in these last days spoken unto us by his Son, whom he hath appointed heir of all things, by whom also he made the *worlds*." (Hebrews 1:1-2).

"Through faith we understand that the *worlds* were framed by the word of God, so that things which are seen were not made of things which do appear." (Hebrew 11:3).

Since "worlds" is used in the plural sense, we can readily see that the Infinite Father created and established all planets and celestial bodies by His Word. He used the Four Great Primary Forces, for "things which are seen' are "not made of things which do appear".

The Harvesters, are the occupants of the Flying Saucers and spacecraft coming to Earth at this time. Space visitors have always been with us! Since Miocene times, inhabitants of outer space have been surveying our Earth; they have watched its progression over thousands and even millions of years. At times, they have contacted various individuals who were dedicated souls, willing to serve God and fellow man. The reason they made themselves known generally over the world in 1947, is because this is the time for the Great Harvest.

The Four Gospels speak of this period:

"Then saith he unto his disciples, The harvest truly is plenteous, but the laborers are few; Pray ye therefore the Lord of the harvest, that he will send forth laborers into his harvest." (St. Matthew 9:37-38).

"But when the fruit is brought forth (ripe), immediately he putteth in the sickle, because the harvest is come." (St. Mark 4:29).

"Therefore said he unto them, The harvest truly is great, but the laborers are few: pray ye therefore the Lord of the harvest, that he would send forth laborers into his harvest." (St. Luke 10:2).

"Say not ye, There are yet four months, and then cometh harvest? behold, I say unto you, Lift up your eyes, and look on the fields; for they are White already to harvest." (St. John 4:35).

If space visitors have indeed been with us *always*, we expect to find mention of them in ancient records. The study of these ancient manuscripts and documents will show anyone that "Flying Wheels", "Fire-Circles", and "Flying Boats", have been around for a long, long time. It doesn't matter what they are called, they are always described in the same way; even as they are today. Saucers were not *first seen* in the 1800's, and this period didn't see the *first large public demonstration* in history. What actually took place toward the close of the Nineteenth Century was the *first public demonstration of the modern, industrial age.*

Mass appearances of Saucers in the past have been rare, but they have taken place. For example, the great Khmer race of the Middle Ages completely disappeared from the face of the Earth almost overnight! The Khmers had developed a great Hindu and Buddhistic civilization and were a native race of Cambodia in Indo-China, but they were of *undetermined origin.* Information from present space visitors indicates that great space ships removed the *entire race* of Khmers from Indo-China leaving their great capitol of Angkor Vat deserted and barren.

Portuguese diaries of the 1700's describe ancient, massive ruins in the interior of the Matto Grosso in Brazil. There are indications on every hand that great numbers of people were suddenly removed from these vast, Grecian-like cities, and transported elsewhere. Since they didn't just walk away (for their trail would be picked up) they must have gone off in spacecraft like the Khmers. There are many other historical accounts that readily fall into this same category.

Egyptian hieroglyphics have been translated by Borris de Rachewiltz which show the existence of Flying Saucers in ancient Egyptian times during the XVIIIth. Dynasty. The transcription is a part of the Royal Annals of the period of Thuthmosis (Thotmes) III, circa 1504-1450 B.C. The original manuscript is in very poor condition, however, part of the translation is as follows:

> "In the year 2, third month of winter, sixth hour of the day, the scribes of the House of Life found that a circle of fire was coming in the sky. They thought it had no head, and the breath of the mouth had a foul odor. Its body was one 'rod' long and one 'rod' large. It had no voice. Their hearts became confused through it and they laid themselves on their bellies.
>
> "Now after some days had passed over, Lo! those things were more numerous than anything. They were shining in the sky more than the sun to the limits of the four supports of heaven. Powerful was the position of the *fire circles*. The army of the king looked on and His Majesty was in the midst of it."

In the Fourth Dynasty, the dynasty of Cheops, who reigned as its second king about 2750 B. C., *Solar Boats* reached their peak of magnificence. The solar boat was constructed to carry the dead Pharaoh on his journey to "heaven". These boats were at least equal to tombs in importance in ancient Egyptian religion, if not more important. They were the one ritual object that remained constant, although other things changed and disappeared. Models of solar boats were found in the tomb of Tutankhamen, the boy king. The solar boats didn't vanish from the Egyptian scene until the invasion by Alexander the Great in 332 B.C. Was the solar boat the Egyptian representation of the space visitor's vehicle? The ancients said that the immortals went in solar boats of the night for the terrifying nocturnal trip through the Under-world. The boats had to pass twelve gates. The "fire circles" became incorporated into the Egyptian religion as solar boats just as we have already seen that Osiris and Apollo were in reality space visitors.

Early European and American cave drawings possibly depict space craft by the concentric circle drawings that exist by the thousands. These are thought to be only Sun symbols; but why the concentric circles that appear as "wheels within wheels"? These, of course, are far older than the Tetramorph symbol.

Wherever there is recorded history there is mention of spacecraft. And if we knew the unwritten record of prehistory we would undoubtedly find more evidence of space visitation.

These visitors or Harvesters from other worlds are very much like we are; some may be thousands of years ahead of us in progression, but they are still not perfect. In *The Saucers Speak!* they said: "We have marriage mates from birth." This indicates that they must be united with their soul mates in marriage and the male and female must come into physical life at about the same time so they can grow up together.

They claim they are not all vegetarians; some do eat meat. The question of eating is an individual matter as it is on Earth. They say that human sex-life is misunderstood on Earth. The main purpose of mating is not to have biological offspring alone, but to put the negative (female) and positive (male) elements back into balance. Man, by himself, is not complete—he must have his other half in order to be a total creative unit and be in balance. They tell us that many of the things we call sins are not sins at all in the Universal sense. They are sins on Earth because social custom dictates it so.

One of the most startling phenomena connected with the coming of the Saucers, is the appearance from time to time of the "fireballs". In *The Saucers Speak!* space friends said: "You would be astonished if you knew what these 'fireballs' really were. They are not the same as your remote-controlled devices." Another time they said: "It was a ball-globe *being* on its duty." And again: "Crystals are valuable to us. With a crystal miracles can be performed."

Since December of 1948 countless "fireballs" have bathed the hills of the American Southwest with their strange, blue-green glare. They have also been seen in Pennsylvania, Maryland, Puerto Rico, Arizona, California, Washington, Denmark, and other places throughout the world. The chief Air Intelligence officer for the Albuquerque district saw one. Col. Joseph D. Caldara, USAF, attached to the Joint Chiefs of Staff, saw one in Virginia. Hundreds of pilots, weather observers and atomic scientists have observed these "fireballs".

Reports came so rapidly during 1948 that in 1949 the Air Force established "Project Twinkle" to investigate them. This Project established a triple photo-theodolite post at Vaughn, New Mexico to obtain scientific data on the "fireballs". Day and night, week in, week out, for three months, a crew kept watch of the skies. Ironically, while "fireballs" continued flashing everywhere else in the South-west, they saw *nothing* until the Project was transferred to the Holloman Air Force Base at Alamogordo, New Mexico.

During the next three months they saw a few but were unable to make *satisfactory* computations because of the "fireballs'" great speed. Search parties have had no better luck. They have combed in vain the countryside beneath the point of disappearance; not a trace of telltale substance has been found on the ground!

Theoreticians in the Air Force believe the "fireballs" are not natural phenomena but propelled objects. They bear similarity to the balls of fire, called "fireball fighters" or "foo fighters" which flew wing on Allied aircraft *over* Germany and Japan during 1944-45 and which have *never* been satisfactorily explained. Many of these "fireballs" are balls of kelly-green fire, blazing brightly, and race across the sky straight as bullets, parallel to the ground. Then they explode in a frightful paroxysm of light—*without making a sound!*

In the Southwest, the popular belief has been that a strange meteor shower is underway. However, Dr. Lincoln La Paz, mathematician, astronomer and director of the Institute of Meteoritics at the University of New Mexico, has pointed out that normal fireballs do not appear green, they fall in the trajectory forced on them by gravity, are generally noisy as a freight train and leave meteorites where they hit. The green "fireball" does *none of these things!*

The "fireballs" do not appear to be electro-static phenomena because they move too regularly and too fast. They are not the product of a U. S. weapons project and they are not self-destroying Russian reconnaissance devices. These "fireballs" are propelled, artificial objects. Their color is close to 5,200 angstroms on a spectrum chart—close to the green of burning *copper*. Copper is almost never found in meteorites; the friction of the air *oxidizes* it shortly after the meteor enters the upper atmosphere. However, a curious fact has been recorded by aerologists. Concentrations of copper particles are now present in the air of Arizona and New Mexico, particularly in "fireball" areas. These were not encountered in air samples made *before* 1948!

These "fireballs" are always silent, and upon exploding, light-up the ground directly beneath them. They are not always green or blue-green in color; they can be nearly white, also. Of course, they are intelligently controlled devices, but they are not manned with "little men" only inches tall. They are similar to our own remote-controlled devices, however, on a much more highly advanced scale. They are sent down from the large space-laboratories that are daily checking our Earth for important scientific data. Undoubtedly, Lt. Gorman encountered such a device when he chased the "flying light" over Fargo, North Dakota, October 1, 1948.

It appears that the "fireballs" fall into three general classes: 1. Those which leave copper particles in the atmosphere after silently exploding and leave no residue on the ground such as meteors do. 2. Those that were called "foo fighters" and known by other names which draw near our aircraft and other earthly objects to obtain information to be relayed directly to the space-lab. These objects are mainly crystalline in structure and are really *sentient* beings. They possess the powers of sense or sense-perception and have actual experience of sensation and feeling as they "televise" their gathered data back to the hovering laboratory. This idea is difficult for the people of Earth to accept, and indeed, even to understand. The idea of a *crystal that thinks!* 3. There is a third class of "fireballs" that do not explode. In fact, after they are constructed in great scientific laboratories their power is immutable! There are very strange records in history of the activities of this type of "fireball". Their power is similar to the power of the robot "Gort" in *"The Day The Earth Stood Still"* a science-fiction movie. However, the space people do not have robots in the form of "mechanical-men".

In his book, *The Ether Ship Mystery And Its Solution*, Meade Layne says: "The balls or discs of light, sometimes only a few inches in diameter, consist of 99% aluminum, with 1% of copper in very ionized form. These are used as a rule as photo plates, that televise their pictures back to the mother ship that gave them birth, and are later destroyed or disintegrated. The large green 'fireballs' are ionized copper, and are exploded in your atmosphere to absorb the radiations created by your atomic bombs. These radiations drift toward the north magnetic pole, and most of the green 'fireballs' originate in the northern skies."

Similar information has been received by other research groups. Type 1 is exploded to nullify adverse conditions arising from atomic explosions. These "fireballs" are usually observed shortly after atomic tests have taken place. Type 2 is a remote-controlled device that televises information back to the space-lab. Their nature should not be too astounding to us. J. R. Anderson of the Bell Telephone Laboratories now claims that barium titanate crystals apparently can store as many as two-thousand five-hundred items of information within a crystal of one square inch surface and a few thousandths of an inch thickness. The crystal stores electronic impulses for a long time. The pulses may be less than one-millionth second long. The crystal consumes no power while storing the information, and is able to operate on low-voltage circuits. We know that tiny crystals serve as transistors, and can do many of the jobs that vacuum tubes once did. Other crystals experimented with are rochelle salts, potassium niobate, and potassium dihydrogen phosphate. Scientists say that some of man's most difficult problems may be solved by crystals. Therefore, if we are now about to have crystal recording devices on Earth, it is easy to understand how our space friends have such advanced methods.

In his book, *Flying Saucers From Outer Space*, Maj. Keyhoe comes to the conclusion that the "fireballs" may be guided missiles of an invading interplanetary force! At the same time, however, he tells us that this may not be the case that the "fireballs" may have another purpose entirely. In other words, the Major is speculating, and lets you draw your own conclusions. Many people, however, have definitely come to believe that our world is about to be invaded by monstrous creatures from the blackness of space.

First of all, if the Saucers have been looking us over for centuries, why have they waited until we developed atomic weapons to attack us? Why didn't they invade when the job was relatively simple and all they had to deal with was clubs, bows and arrows? Maj. Keyhoe tells us that the first "fireballs" seen may have been testing devices or "duds", and that later we can expect the actual guided missile attack! *If that were true, why have they waited so long to get at the invasion?*

There is absolutely nothing to fear from the "fireballs", whether they be white, green, or blue-green; silent or otherwise. Space friends are here with only love in their hearts—if they conquer us it will be with that love. If it were not for their "fireballs" our own childish playing with atomic energy would bounce back on us. Through the use of the photographic type "fireball" they have surveyed every square mile of our planet. They constantly patrol the major fault lines of Earth to discover where overwhelming catastrophe may begin. In such an event, they might evacuate certain persons. After the "fireball" relays vital information on the condition of the faults it explodes to be used no more. (See Plate II).

Welcome the "fireballs" as the instruments of a friendly race, and say a prayer in your heart for those who are here only in love.

The Type 3 "fireball" is little known and practically nothing has been gathered on its operation. Remember the strange case of "spontaneous human combustion", in St. Petersburg, Florida in 1951? Mrs. Mary H. Reeser, 67, was discovered in her apartment where she was almost completely destroyed by fire. Yet, the apartment itself wasn't damaged and newspapers near the chair in which she was cremated weren't even scorched! Scientists said it would take unbelievable temperatures to destroy her body so completely, and the fact that nothing else was damaged in the room didn't make sense at all. One authority said that some kind of "lightning unknown to man at the present time" had to cause the disaster.

Mrs. Reeser was by no means the first to suffer such a fate. The writer Dickens wrote a story about a man who in real life actually perished as Mrs. Reeser did. These mysterious cremations display a definite pattern and a basic similarity. In *The Scientific Classbook or, A Familiar Introduction to the Principles of Physical Science*, printed in 1836 in Philadelphia, Walter R. Johnson, M.A., cites the then well-known cremation mystery involving the Countess Cornelia Zangari of Cesena. Although parts of her body remained intact, she was almost reduced to a heap of ashes. The air of her apartment was reported to be filled with a fine soot which had an unpleasant smell. The blaze was confined entirely to the countess' body; the floor and furniture were undamaged.

Dr. Wilmer, a Coventry, England surgeon reported the cremation of Mary Clues, 50, in March, 1773. She was reduced to whitish ashes, but the bed-clothes were undamaged. The walls and furnishings of the room were blackened and the air was filled with a sickening smell. Only the body was burned.

An 18th Century German journal records the flaming death of Don G. Maria Bertholi, a friar who lived at Mount Volere.

About 1845, *Chambers' Edinburgh Journal*, reported that Anne Nelis, wife of a Dublin merchant was cremated in her chair. The back and seat of the chair were undamaged and the room was filled with a pungent unpleasant smell.

Also about 1845, in Limerick, a Mrs. Peacock was discovered on the floor of the room under her own and her body was burning and "red as copper". In the ceiling of the room a large hole the size of the body had been burned through the boards. Her body had dropped through this hole from her room above. Her room wasn't damaged in any way.

One morning in 1808 an Irish woman named Mrs. Stout, 60, was found burned to a cinder on the floor of her bedroom. When the body was moved it crumbled into ashes, but her nightcap had not been burned!

Another Irish woman of 60, from the county of Doun, was found burning "with an internal fire". Her body was black as charcoal and smoke issued from every part of it. There was a foul-smelling odor throughout the house and the woman's daughter who had been sleeping next to her in the same bed had not been burned; in fact, the bed and bed-clothes were untouched.

In recent years the mysterious and recurring phenomenon has happened more frequently. Mrs. Cecil Rogers of Pleasantville, Ohio died this way, as did a man who tried to take his own life with a knife before the cremation took place. Everyone of the victims so far has always been a degraded human being and water cannot put out the fire; it only adds to its intensity.

The Type 3 "fireball" has a special mission in that it is magnetically attracted to certain individuals. As soon as a person takes up a certain evil path, one of the "fireballs" starts on its journey toward that person. You ask: "Do the space people destroy us with these monstrous 'fireballs' they construct in their laboratories? The answer is that the space people destroy *nothing!* The victims destroy themselves by their own deeds and actions; they are free at any time to change their ways and the "fireball" will reverse direction.

A wonderful example is found in *A Dweller On Two Planets* by Phylos. Mainin called upon Incal (Creator) to punish him for his crimes and evil deeds if He (Incal) really existed. Then a voice said to him: "I shall not, O Mainin, enumerate thy crimes, thou knowest them every one: I knew thy way; I knew its evil, yet interfered not, for thou art thine own master, even as all men are self-masters; few, alas, are faithful! But thine altitude of wisdom, prostituted to selfishness, to sin, to crime, more utterly than any other man hath dared, is thy destruction. Thy name meaneth 'Light', and great hath thy brilliancy been; but thou hast been as a light adrift on the seas, a lure to death of all them that follow thee, and these have been myriad. Thou hast blasphemed God, and jeered in thy soul, saying, 'Punish!' But thine is one out of a *myriad of cases*, more heinous because thou art wise, not ignorant. I will cut thee off for a season, for thou shalt neither destroy more of my sheep, nor be let to leave unexpiated the evil thou hast done. It were better for thee couldst thou cease to exist. But this may not be of an ego. I can but suspend thee as a human entity and cast thee into the outer darkness to serve as one of the powers of nature. Get thee behind me!"

Phylos goes on: "Now, however, as the Son of Light ceased to speak, Mainin uttered a howl of mingled terror and defiance. Instantly Mainin was surrounded with a *glowing flame* which, on disappearing, revealed also the disappearance of the Demon Priest. Thus had Mainin sinned, perverting his noble wisdom to evil and to sowing the seeds of sin, on and in the hearts of unsuspecting weaklings of humanity. For this sowing he was blasted from the Book of Life." The voice said: "Such is the fate of the wholly selfish man."

Another example is found in *Mystic Magazine* for October, 1954. In Orfeo Angelucci's article, *My Awakening On Another Planet*, he says:

"The scene was focusing upon an unfamiliar part of the heavens. A sun and a number of encircling planets were in view. Then the scene centered upon a single planet in this unknown solar system. It was a smug, sleek planet; but it was exceedingly dark in tone and surrounded with concentric waves of darkness. A tangible vibration or emanation came from it, evil, unpleasant and utterly without inspiration or hope. Approaching this world I saw a glowing red dot with a long, misty tail. The fiery dot seemed *irresistibly attracted* to the dark world. The two collided in a spectacular fiery display. I felt Lyra's hand upon mine as she whispered, It is an *immutable Law of the Cosmos* that too great a preponderance of evil inevitably brings about self-destruction.'"

Therefore, victims of the mysterious cremation cases are destroyed by the great "preponderance of evil" existing within their own souls! This Type 3 "fireball" that is "irresistibly attracted" to such persons is never destroyed; it will exist forever once it is created. Not even its creators can revoke its power! When it finally connects with the object of its magnetic attraction, it does not "explode" in the usual sense. Now that we are going deeper into new areas of Cosmos we are encountering strange things; things which manifested centuries ago, but which are now increasing at a rapid rate.

The question arises: "Why is the Type 2 "fireball" copper and crystalline in construction?" First of all, copper has the strange capacity to record and retain. Copper can be compared to the soul in that it is receptive and also it can recall once accepted impact. It can be said that copper never forgets; it does not lose impressions. Copper is a stratified attention crystallized consciousness. It could be developed and actually experimentally ascertained that copper radiation has a dimensional multiplicity which no other metal has. Gold or any other metal cannot step out of the three dimensional world in its effects. Copper can be the bridge between time and timelessness. That is its occult feature!

An electron shows itself as a particle in an electrical or magnetic field. But if a crystal diffracts it, it becomes a wave; thus the wavicular form is generated by specific conditioning of diffraction by crystal. Transpose this situation from the world of physics to the world of consciousness. Imagine consciousness to be equivalent to a particle and three dimensional stimulation equivalent to a crystal. Consciousness itself assumes a wavicular form when influenced, or diffracted, by the "crystal" of three dimensional stimulation.

The Type 2 "fireball' is undoubtedly composed of crystalline copper instead of being copper and crystal separately used. The crystalline copper "fireball" actually *lives* and has *conscious thought*. Space intelligences have said that with crystals "miracles can be performed", and that "crystals can think". This is true because of the qualities of consciousness that copper possesses.

Now it is easy to understand what space friends meant when they said we would be "astonished" if we knew what the "fireballs" really were. They said that "fireballs" were not the same as our remote-controlled devices; they are ball-globe *beings* performing their duties. These "fireballs" of the Type 2 class can be instructed to go to a certain location by telepathy or by verbal command. Once in the designated area they will record required information through the unusual properties of copper and this information is evaluated and separated by the qualities of crystal before wavicular form relays it to the hovering laboratory. Just as a crystal separates light into a spectrum, so the Type 2 "fireball" separates the items it records. Remember, this type of "fireball" has intelligence *within it*, not just *behind it*. The "flying light" observed by Lt. Gorman operated intelligently because of its own inherent abilities, not because it was "guided" entirely by direction from a nearby mother ship or laboratory.

"Light hath more properties than even man hath dreamt of: it hath vibration so fine in ether that incandescence cometh, it reacheth men's eyes in aspect of waves; I say it doeth more, it hath more than incandescence, it performeth a greater wonder than that men may see in darkness: it cometh to man sustaining his spirit, it maketh miracles to happen." (G. S. 30:15-16).

When we use the term *Light* in the broader sense, it includes not only incandescent light but also light of shorter and longer wavelengths which *cannot* be picked up by the human eye. Examples would be Infrared, Radio or Hertzian waves; Ultraviolet, X-Rays, Gamma Rays, and Secondary Cosmic Rays.

"Light is the word of the Father, saying, Be . . . lo, matter, is!" (G. S. 30:21).

Since *Light is Matter* either one can be received and transmitted by the Type 2 "fireball". And further, since Light is the essence of all life and Light is a wave phenomenon, the diffraction of Light by the crystalline copper gives this "fireball" the qualities of *conscious thought*. Therefore, there must be a combination of copper, crystal, and Light properties in order to have a sentient "fireball". (See Plate XVIII, *p. 302*).

In reading the Chart on A Conception of Matter, read horizontally from left to right. The column on the extreme right indicates a return to the Particle Phase. Although the return is to the same phase, it is necessarily an advanced or progressed development of that phase. This is a continuous, spiraling process. The vertical columns show analogy. All analogy is basically a revealment of some measure of identity. The items in the vertical columns may be more closely related than is suspected at this time.

"In Light have I manifested: in Light do I manifest: I give Light commandments: I have made it Motive Servant." (G. S. 30.40).

"Light waves are Thought Incarnate manifesting on and in substance; I have answered the mystery. Thus Light hath performance." (G. S. 30:42).

The Elder Brother or Christ says He "manifests in Light", and He gives "Light commandments". Therefore, Light entering the crystalline copper "fireball" imparts "commandments" to the device, and it is truly an instrument of the Father's Will through Christ and thereby through the space intelligences themselves.

Christ is One with the Father—and the Father is Thought Incarnate, therefore "Light waves *are* Thought Incarnate manifesting on and in substance". Remember Christ said: "I am the Light of the world!"

In recent years, Lapis Lingua $(Na_{4-5}Al_3Si_3O_{12}S)$, has been used to stimulate subjects in telepathic experiments. In the Edgar Cayce readings on gems and stones, Lapis Lingua, a corrosive product of copper in its natural state, was often mentioned as

A CONCEPTION OF MATTER:

TYPE OF FIELD:	PHASES OF MATTER: *			
	Particle Phase is Timeless (positive) *and At Rest.* **	*Means of Activation of Particle Phase.*	*Wave Phase* which is *Temporal* and *In Motion.* **	*Particle Phase* again manifests when Wave becomes of stationary character.
	Electron	Crystal	Wave	
Electro-Magnetic				Standing wave rendered in terms of vibrations is picked out as a photon (energy quantum of light).
Multi-dimensional	Self-complete state of consciousness *** Super-consciousness (knowledge).	"Crystal" of three-dimensional experience.	Wave phase of consciousness. Attention consciousness. (sense data or art of knowing).	Return to Particle Phase.
	Conscious commands, emanations or vibrations to be recorded.	Crystalline copper "Fireball." ****	Wave motion relays itemized information.	Return to Particle Phase.
	God the Father	Desire	Thought	Souls *****
	Soul (self-awareness)	Frame of reference	Spirit (soul in action)	Godhood with creative thought) *****

a type of stone which may stimulate the endocrine centers. They revert to the vibratory theory that all matter has its own vibration. Lapis Lingua, it seems, may stimulate, raise the vibratory rate of the gland centers, if taped over them. This would be similar to giving more electrical power to a sending and receiving radio station.

The following are excerpts from the readings: "Lapis is of particular value to those who are interested in things psychic. Outside influences may be induced to aid an individual in contacts with the higher sources of activity. Lapis is not considered a high quality gem; rather a very low form, but for that indicated in the character of the stone itself, it would be most helpful in creating that vibration which will make for the developments of certain characters of demonstrations with any psychic forces or psychic individuals."

There is a definite increase in telepathic powers when the Lapis stone is used. In experiments, it has been taped over four gland centers of the sender: Pituitary, Pineal, Thyroids, and

Thymus. Again the Cayce readings say: "It has been given that the Lapis Lingua is the name which was applied to touchstones, or those used by initiates in their various ceremonial activities. (Hence the stones acquired power through thought projections about them.) Those that are of a psychic turn may hear the emanations as retained or thrown off by influence about such stones; the Lapis Lingua would bring much that will act as a protective influence. This is the green stone, you see, the *crystallization of copper* and those influences that are *creative within themselves*. For, as indicated from the influence of the Lapis Lingua, there is the need for not only the copper ore, that is a part of man's own development in many fields, but the need for the very combination of its elements as protection to not only the material benefits but the bodily forces necessary for the transmission of benefits through its own physical being. Wearing of the Lapis Lingua will make the body more sensitive to the higher vibrations. The wearing of the Lapis stone would be an aid in the entity's periods of meditation, and would become a helpful influence. Not as a 'lucky' charm, but rather as a helpful influence toward making for the ability to make decisions in dealing with mental attributes; the emanations from Lapis Lingua are very strong. As to stone, have near yourself, worn preferably upon the body, about the neck, the Lapis; this preferably *encased in crystal*."

The Cayce readings advised the use of both Lapis Lingua and Lapis Lazuli. The latter was a favorite stone of the ancient Egyptians. Lapis is probably the sapphire of the old testament and of the ancient writers. Both Pliny and the Holy Bible make allusions to sapphires as stones sprinkled with gold.

"The stones of it are the place of sapphires: and it hath dust of gold." (Job 28:6).

In certain drawings, ancient personages are shown with a slender band around their head in the center of which appears a gem or stone of some kind. It is believed that this stone was the Lapis Lingua, and that it is used not merely for ornamentation but to stimulate the pineal gland near the center of the forehead.

All of the foregoing reference to the Lapis *Lingua* only shows more clearly the unusual qualities of copper and why it is used in crystalline form in the construction of the "fireballs".

Copper is the only metal which occurs native abundantly in large masses and copper is supreme among the common metals in its everlasting qualities. The following are two slightly different forms in which the ancient alchemists of the Middle Ages employed the "ankh", the symbol of enduring life,

to designate copper. These alchemists always represented copper by the astrological sign for Venus. this circle with cross attached below was the Egyptian symbol for everlasting or enduring life. The "ankh" or Crux Ansata symbolized life itself, therefore it was a fitting symbol to be used for copper which can be the bridge between time and timelessness! Both the cross and the circle were phallic symbols, for the ancient world venerated the generative powers of Nature as being expressive of the creative attributes of the Deity. The Crux Ansata, by combining the masculine Tau with the feminine oval, exemplified the principles of generation. The generative powers which the "ankh" symbolized were also representative of life, since without these powers no man would be born on Earth.

In Asia, copper was the metal of the Queen of Heaven (Astarte, etc.). As stated before, astrologers and alchemists assigned it to Venus; it was sacred to the Fire God and the Seven Gods of Babylonia and Assyria; North Pacific Coast Indians and several other groups assigned it to the Sun; in India it was a sacred metal; the Indians of the Lake Superior region regarded the lumps of copper they found as divinities.

In some places there is a custom of placing copper on a corpse. This is because copper was symbolic of life. Pliny mentions that in Arcadia the yew tree is fatal to anyone sleeping under it unless a copper nail is driven into the tree. Again we see the unusual power of this metal. As late as the middle of the eighteenth century the Spaniards believed that copper grew in the ground, and that if a mine was left alone, it would become productive again! All of this goes to illustrate the fact that the ancients knew about the hidden qualities of copper. The Spaniards suspected the everlasting and timeless qualities of the metal when they thought it "grew in the ground".

In the Bible in Exodus 38:8, and in II Kings 25:13, the Hebrew word Nechosheth, should be translated *copper* and not *brass*. Many sacred objects were fashioned of copper. In Ezra 8:27 we read: "Two vessels of fine copper, precious (desirable) as gold." Copper was known as yellow, or shining brass, and the ancients knew its great occult features because they said it was as "precious as gold".

Certain investigations have shown that life or death rays are emitted from metal discs. Ziegler, one of the investigators of metal rays found during his experiments that *copper* discs emit *life-rays*. Zinc plates emit hindrance or life-antagonistic rays. Platinum, as well as copper plates send out life or vitalizing rays according to the investigations of Korschelt, and the former can be used to heal ulcers, etc.

Copper radiates green, and this color is neutral, at the fulcrum of the solar spectrum, the balancing point. The space intelligences have said: "Blue of sky, gold of sun!" And green is poised between the Gold of Wisdom and the Blue of Heaven on the spectrum.

The *crystal* ball among the ancients had a three-fold meaning: (1) It signified the crystalline Universal Egg in whose transparent depths creation exists; (2) It was a proper figure of Deity previous to Its immersion in matter; (3) It signified the aetheric sphere of the world in whose translucent essences is impressed and preserved the perfect image of all terrestrial activity.

In recent years the crystal ball has been misunderstood and misused. Nostradamus possessed one of the few remaining crystal balls originally brought here by space visitors and left in temples in ancient Egypt. Several of these balls were unearthed near the Great Pyramid but they were done away with because they were thought to be of modern date and worthless! The great predictions of *Nostradamus* came about through his use of a crystal ball from outer space!

Prof. Reichenbach found that crystals radiate yellow light rays at the base while the top of the crystals radiate blue light rays. The blue or green light rays are life or vital rays, while the yellow light rays are hindrance rays. Dr. Heermann's research has proved that plants as well as trees radiate so-called life rays at the top while the roots emit the hindrance rays. If it were possible to determine the colors of the rays emanating from the branches of a tree we should most likely find that they radiate green and blue while the roots radiate yellow similar to the radiation of crystals.

The human being is very similar since we radiate yellow on one side, blue on the other side. Therefore, we radiate positive as well as negative magnetic currents. Rays from our Solar System produce life or vitality currents in our body and these rays are of an electromagnetic nature.

Plants, animals, minerals and man—they are all similar. It is easy to understand why *crystal* qualities are incorporated into the Type 2 "fireball". This device also radiates positive as well as negative magnetic currents and operates in its own Resonating Electro-Magnetic Field. Rays from our Solar System, and, of course, other systems, produce life or vitality currents in the crystalline "fireball" also; and again, these rays are of an electromagnetic nature.

Newton discovered the definite relationship between tones and colors. Every tone and every color has a distinct frequency of vibration, and because of this relationship, the "fireball" receives and transmits everything in full color and full tonal quality, exactly as a *living being* would react to vibrational stimuli.

The quotation from *The Ether Ship Mystery And Its Solution*, by Meade Layne was given to show that he accepts the Type 1 and Type 2 "fireball". His statement that the latter consists of 99% aluminum seems contradictory to the information in this book. However, aluminum radiates green the same as copper. We must keep in mind also that the space visitors are coming from many areas of the Universe and from many levels of progression. Actually, there may be other "fireballs" of varying construction in use.

All spacecraft, including Saucers, operate in a Resonating Electro-Magnetic Field. This RMF is the Fourth Great Primary Force that Earth scientists do not understand. Certain scientists of the past came dangerously close to discovering it. It is dangerous because it is at the same time of a positive and negative nature. If its great force is reversed it becomes a deadly death ray.

This terrible sidereal Force was called Mash-Mak by the ancient Atlanteans. The Aryan Rishis speak of it in their *Ashtar Vidya* and this same Force is called *vril* by Sir E. Bulwer-Lytton, in his Coming Race. It is believed that this author coined this name from the word *virile*. The antediluvians called it the "Water of Phtha;" their descendants named it the Anima Mundi, the soul of the Universe. Later the mediaeval hermetists termed it "sidereal light", or the "Milk of the Celestial Virgin", the "Magnes", and many other names.

The name *vril* may be a fiction, but the Force itself exists. It is mentioned in all the ancient secret works of Earth. In the *Ashtar Vidya*, we discover that this vibratory Force was aimed at an army from an Agni Rath fixed on a flying vessel and it reduced to ashes one-hundred thousand men and elephants. It is allegorised in the *Vishnu Purana*, in the *Ramayana* and other works. In the fable about the sage Kapila we discover that his glance made a mountain of ashes of King Sagara's sixty-thousand sons. This Force is often referred to as the Kapilaksha—"Kapila's Eye".

Many years ago Faraday, the great scientist, said: "The various forms under which the forces of matter are made manifest, have *one common origin*. They are so directly related and naturally dependent, that they are convertible, as it were, into one another, and possess equivalents of power in their action."

The *Vril*, the Primal Force of Faraday, and the Kabalistic Astral Light are one and the same thing. In ancient times the Vril Stick was a slender "glass" rod, some thirty inches long and hollow in the center. At the top end there was a strange handle, or rather it was capped by a six-inch length of "glass" affixed in oblique slant somewhat in the shape of a cross-bar made by Spencerian penmen when they write a capital letter "T". Inside of this tube the Vril Ray was confined, and in this case it was a death ray. How it was evolved, or how it could be confined in a slender tube pertains to the lost arts of antiquity.

The Vril Stick was used in Atlantis and later in Egypt. A recovered stick now rests in the British Museum in a specially sealed glass case. No one handles it anymore and no one is allowed even to view it! The ancient gods and goddesses are sometimes depicted holding Vril Sticks, and great rulers had them in their possession. This was the origin of the king's sceptre. The sceptre signifies the union of the forces that create life, and thus from the most ancient days, a symbol of highest power given only to rulers and gods of life. The Vril Stick was indeed a "sceptre endowed with marvelous power". And any potentate possessing it carried the decree of life or death in his hand. The "ankh" closely resembles this stick as to form and to symbolic meaning. There are countless legends of fairy wands, and magical rods that have been derived from stories about the Vril Stick.

This stick of amazing power was constructed of "glass". Remember, the ancients prized diamonds and other gems because they were pure forms of carbon. They used carbon and magnets together to perform certain beneficial cures on the human body, and the gods are sometimes shown holding rods of carbon in their hands about six inches long. Today gems are prized for their monetary worth or for their value in giving one social prestige; but the ancients prized them for their vibrational qualities. That is why so much gold was used and worn by the Aztecs, Mayas, Incas, etc. Gold and diamonds both raise the vibrations of a human being. Other stones and metals can lower the vibrations.

All of the foregoing is important when considering the fact that the Saucers operate in a Resonating Electro-Magnetic Field and are said to be "Crystal Bells!". Many reports state that the Saucers appeared to be made of crystal and were translucent; they must utilize the same power once known on Earth and found in the Vril Stick. This stick held some sort of resonating magnetic current operating fatally in reverse. The ancients were familiar with such principles of magnetism because several ancient civilizations on Earth possessed "flying ships" not very much different from our present day Saucers. A few years ago, a Saucer landed in Alaska that was mainly composed of glass. Later, a model was made of that Saucer and used in the movie, *The Day The Earth Stood Still*. Scientists claim glass would withstand high speeds better than any known metal. Of course, Saucers don't have to worry about the effects of "high speeds".

The Vril Ray force known as the Fourth Great Force relates to the other Three Great Forces, and all belong to the One Primal Force of the Omniverse. This One Force is symbolized by the swastika, for the *wheel* is the emblem of creative motion—manifesting force is rotary, being, in fact, the "Wheel of the spirit of life" involving the whole system of the Universe.

Many people, including the "prophets of gloom", throughout the world are saying we will be totally destroyed in a terrible atomic war. In meditating upon these grim forecasts for our immediate future we can't help but remember other dire warnings that have come our way over the decades. Some "prophet" or other is always setting an exact date for the "end of the world". The planet Earth is now in a state of transition toward a greater enfoldment of man's progression; the world is not going to end!

Space friends are here to help build a bigger and better Earth where all men may live together as true brothers should. Everyone will be "his brother's keeper". The Great Avatar never said: 'Till the end of the world", as so many theologians would have us believe. Actually, He said: "Till the end of the *age*." Immediately we see that He was referring to the end of the Piscean Age, not the cataclysmic so-called "end" of the literal ground beneath our feet. Further, Christ never spoke in negative terms for His was a ministry of positive thought in contrast with the "thou shalt nots" of the old Mosaic Law.

Space craft occupants have said that man on Earth worships the Creator; but he worships in *word*, not *deed*. If we believe in Him, and have faith in Him, we cannot believe that He will rain down death, destruction, and horror on us. Over and over again, with much repetition, the "men of God" in the pulpits today tell us that our God is "all loving and kind". With the next breath they contradict themselves by telling us that at times He "gives us up". And they paint a picture of "sweet angels" casting poor "sinners" into lakes of fire and brimstone to endure *eternal* torment!

Information coming from the highest authority among the space people tell us that our world is to become a place of tranquil peace and plenty for all. Only the good and the beautiful is to be inherited by man on Earth! Many individuals to-day point to the strange changes in our weather, the many earthquakes, tornados, tidal-waves, floods, and so forth and tell us that these are certainly "signs of doom". Changes have been going on for thousands of years on Earth, but the old world is still keeping its orbit around its Sun. However, many great changes never before experienced are taking place and will continue to do so. These changes are on the physical, mental and spiritual planes of Earth.

In 1953 there were many outstanding catastrophic events. On February 2nd hurricane floods on south-eastern British, Dutch, and Belgian coasts killed one-thousand nine-hundred forty-one persons. On February 12th there was a violent quake at Torroud, Iran which killed five-hundred thirty-one persons. March 19th saw the Turkish quakes that killed two-hundred forty-six people. On April 30th tornados killed nineteen in central Georgia and caused wide-spread damage. In May, on the 11th, Waco and San Angelo, Texas were smashed by tornados causing sixty million dollars in damage and killing one-hundred twenty-four persons.

June 9th tornados killed one-hundred thirty-nine in Michigan and Ohio. The following day, on the 10th, tornados killed eighty-six in Massachusetts. On June 26th Japan's worst flood in modern history killed seven-hundred two with one-thousand four-hundred thirty-three missing. July 12th seven-hundred died in the Greek Ionian Island earthquakes. Later in the year on November 9th two-thousand died in the Indochina typhoon. And on December 5th many people died in a tornado disaster that caused twenty-five million dollars in damage at Vicksburg, Mississippi.

There were many, many more reports of disasters of all kinds. Scientists agree that something mighty strange is going on. These changes are to be expected as our entire Solar System moves into a new area of the Universe! Meteorologists are concerned over the unusual weather conditions, but statements are never made to the public. The facts of 1953 speak for themselves; the evidence is more than substantial.

Climatologists, meteorologists, and physicists, are not the only ones worried about strange weather phenomena; plain citizens are alarmed and can observe that the climate of the world is getting warmer at an unprecedented rate. The question is seriously asked: "Do the atomic explosions produce mysterious changes in the atmosphere at high altitudes—perhaps in the ionized layers of the atmosphere?"

Atomic explosions are not the cause of the weather changes, but they are weakening an already unstable condition. The vibrations of the new area of the Universe are responsible for the physical, mental, and spiritual changes on Earth. Men's minds and conceptions are changing as well as the geographical features and climate of the world. Our government picked an area of small population to test its atomic devices, but it also tested these devices over major fault lines in New Mexico and Nevada. This further weakened these fault lines and accentuated the change already under way because of different vibratory rate.

Astronomers know that gigantic sun spots appear on our Sun after atomic explosions. If the Sun can be affected ninety-three millions of millions of miles away, it certainly stands to reason that vast changes will take place on the originating planet also. Even though the world isn't going to end, nevertheless, there will be great catastrophes locally throughout the world in years to come. In *The Saucers Speak!* the statement was made that disasters would increase—and increase they have!

Here are some of the mysterious climatological facts: The world's heat belt is on the move. It is progressing northward as well as eastward. William J. Baxter, in his book, *Today's Revolution In Weather*, says animals are already reacting to the northward advance of the heat belt. The possum is now common as far north as Boston, where fifty years ago, he was seldom seen north of the Mason-Dixon line. Deer, badgers, moose, and raccoons are pushing in the direction of the North Pole. The cardinal, the mocking bird, the tufted titmouse and the hooded warbler, always considered southern birds, are moving into New England. Birds that once flew South every winter are now staying in the North all year round.

The southern parts of the United States will be like the tropics, and New York and New England will be the Florida of the future. Abnormally high temperatures have been recorded along the entire East Coast and in most of the Central and Southern States. Overall snowfall has been much less than average. The same phenomenon has been noted up and down the West Coast, with abnormally high temperatures combined with scanty precipitations of snow recorded.

A tribe of Indians in Maine has observed that the ice in the Penobscot River has been breaking up much earlier since 1948. The break-up has been occurring frequently following an "unseasonal and abnormal" January thaw—something previously unheard of. In earlier years, the river was seldom free of ice until late March or early April.

On the West and East Coasts and across the Southern States, semi-tropical vegetation is appearing. Throughout the entire crop season, fruits and vegetables that require considerable warmth have been attaining larger size more rapidly. Pines and spruces are growing nearer and nearer the North Pole. Cereal crops are flourishing in places where twenty years ago there were ice fields!

Dr. George H. T. Kimble, director of the American Geographical Society, says it is altogether possible that Canadians in Northern Ontario will grow corn and New Yorkers will become cotton planters. He points out that temperatures have been rising in winter in the last thirty to forty years. In Upper Canada, he relates, the forest is migrating into hitherto barren tundra.

Arnold Court of the University of California says we can expect temperatures over one-hundred seven degrees in the summers of the future. Scientists probing glaciers throughout the world, including the great Baffin Island glacier, have discovered these glaciers are steadily shrinking. Dr. John W. Aldrich, of the U. S. Fish and Wildlife Service, says that fish are moving northward. Cod, once unknown in Greenland, is now a steady Eskimo dish. Whiting, halibut, king *mackerel* and haddock are found farther and farther north in the Atlantic. New Jersey has sighted tropical flying fish! The tropical-fish hunting grounds of the future will be along the New Jersey and Maryland coasts instead of Florida and the Bahamas, as at present. For some years now, deep sea pleasure fisherman have been taking tuna off the Long Island Coast and even further to the North. It was not so long ago that tuna were seldom observed further North than Georgia waters.

The tremendous warming-up is also observable north of the United States—Canada, Alaska, and Greenland. The size and extent of glaciers in all these areas have been decreasing at an unprecedented rate, exposing vast areas for potential cultivation. In Alaska, Muir Glacier has been shrinking in length at a rate of about half a mile a year, while Guyot Glacier has been losing thickness at about thirty feet a year. Alaskan farmers are now growing crops in areas that only a few years ago were snow-covered. Along the Alaskan Arctic Coast, much of the ground is bare of snow through many months each summer, while temperate-zone trees and shrubs are appearing further to the North and higher on the mountainsides. Alaskan forests are "advancing", according to authority Dr. Robert E. Griggs. Along the entire roof of the North American continent, the Arctic Ice is receding rapidly. It used to contact the coast solidly and be many feet thick in winter. Now there are often open patches of water extending fifty or more miles offshore, while the thickness of the ice has greatly decreased.

Ships are now frequently able to put in at Greenland ports in mid-winter. Fresh land is steadily being bared by the receding icecaps, and vegetation and birds that formerly shunned Greenland are appearing. The great strait between Greenland and Canada that used to be ice-locked the year around is now frequently open to ships. In the United States the climate will be like that of present day Mexico. Canada's climate will resemble that of the United States today. Greenland's climate will resemble that of Canada now. However, if the trend does not slow down, the entire equatorial belt will become unfit for human habitation—the temperate zones will become largely scorching deserts, while only the polar regions will be comfortably habitable.

In the United States, "dust bowl" areas are increasing. In Africa, the Sahara Desert is advancing Southward at a rate of three miles a year. The Middle East is steadily declining in water supply, while much of India and China, once fertile agricultural land, is now semi-desert or actual desert without vegetation of any sort. In Central Africa, the lakes are becoming smaller and the jungles less lush. This is also true of South America, where the Amazon River Basin and jungle areas are shrinking rapidly, with grasslands developing around the periphery. Lake Victoria in Africa is dropping at the rate of almost a foot a year while the amount of water flowing over Victoria Falls has declined greatly.

Great Salt Lake in America has shrunk by half in less than fifty years, and the waterpower production of Niagara is declining. In one-hundred years the temperature of England has risen by three degrees. Similar rises have been noted in other countries where accurate weather records have been kept. It has been estimated that a rise in average temperature of only six degrees would melt all the glaciers and polar icecaps in the world in a few decades. The sea-level of all the oceans is rising at a rapid rate.

Oceanographers calculate that if all the ice now existent on Earth was melted and returned to the oceans, the sea-level would rise by approximately five-hundred to one-thousand feet, reducing the total land area of the Earth by many millions of square miles. England and most of Central Europe will be submerged, as would the entire Mississippi River Basin!

There are many good reasons why we cannot attribute the rising temperatures to atomic causes. For one thing, the temperature rise has been going on for many years, and was first noticed long before we even suspected an atomic bomb could be made. It has been increasing at an accelerating pace, however, which is why an apparent connection with atomic bombs has been suggested.

It is well-known that the entire history of the Earth has been marked by a succession of "cold" and "warm" periods—some of thousands of years duration, others of only a few centuries. Meteorologists say, therefore, that it is not unusual because the Earth is experiencing a climate change, but it is unusual because instead of going into a colder cycle which it should be doing, it's going into a still warmer cycle!

Astronomers know that our entire Solar System is moving rapidly into an area of greater warmth—the Sun and its family of twelve planets is moving into a region of space where cosmic ray bombardment and intense vibrational frequency will cause many drastic changes. Proof of the fact of a climate warm-up the world over are the many European avalanches during the past few years, and *absence* of the ice floes that usually prevented ships from entering Northern European harbors. The government is well-aware of the mysterious change and has secret projects at the North Pole investigating all evidence.

These changes are to be expected as our Earth enters the new section of Creation. Several Saucer researchers received information several years ago that our Earth was being bombarded with cosmic rays that would change man as well as the terrain! Recently, Prof. Kurt Sitte of Syracuse University said: "Too many electrons are showering down on us. At least, there are too many of these tiny units of electrical charge to be explained by present theories, which hold that electrons are produced by cosmic rays smashing into the atmosphere high above the Earth. *Unknown* particles or processes must be involved!" Dr. Sitte's conclusions were based on studies made in the Summer of 1953 at altitudes *of* ten-thousand to fourteen-thousand feet in Colorado. Dr. Sitte is now a visiting professor at the University of Sao Paulo in Brazil. He has been investigating at Chacaltaya, Brazil, eighteen-thousand feet above sea level. He hopes to discover what processes or particles produce the electrons that *cannot be accounted for by present theories!*

Science is now discovering and proving what space intelligences said months ago. There is intensive bombardment going on, and the changes are taking place daily! Space friends also said: "Look to nature for signs of the New Age presently to come to Earth." When we "look to nature", we see proof on every hand.

From space craft occupants we understand that the new influential vibrations, now being felt, are coming from outside our own Solar System. Many times, science later confirms with actual discovery the statements made by the extraterrestrial visitors. Dr. Marcel Schein of the University of Chicago says that part, if not all, of the cosmic radiation continuously bombarding the Earth comes from outside of the Solar System.

Dr. Schein's conclusion is based on the extremely high energy of the onrushing particles as they have been caught in photographic emulsions sent many miles above the Earth's surface. "It would be most unlikely," Dr. Schein says, "that the Sun's magnetic field could accelerate the charged particles to such very high energies, greater than ten-trillion electron volts. The theory of extra-solar origin is also supported by some new experiments at the University of Chicago. By using two photographic plates sliding slowly past each other, cosmic radiation scientists are, for the first time, able to pin down the time at which the particle left its track.

With this new method, Dr. Schein and his associates have found that the variation between the numbers of tracks of heavy charged particles during the day and at night is not very great. "This," he said, "argues for a cosmic ray source outside our own Solar System."

Dr. Armin J. Deutsch of Mount Wilson and Palomar Observatories believes that the cosmic rays coming to Earth may be material thrown off from rotating stars with strong magnetic fields. Dr. Deutsch's findings tend to prove that many of these rays are extra-solar in origin.

Dr. Schein believes that maybe all of the cosmic radiation bombarding the Earth comes from outside of our Solar System. However, it appears that nearly all cosmic rays come from our own Sun—the only rays coming from outside of our System are possibly those consisting of high energy particles. The fact that too many electrons are showering down on us and present theories won't account for them and the fact that certain cosmic rays bombard the

Earth from outside our own Solar System tends to support the idea that our entire Solar System is entering a new possibility area of the Universe. Every phase of Earth life will be greatly influenced— Economics, Religion, Education, Politics, Science, Social life, Medicine, Eating habits, etc. Virtually *everything* will change, and for the better!

If we are truly entering a New Age, then we should certainly see effects of it on the physical plane. No one can deny the fact that "strange" things are going on. Look at your newspaper, your magazines; turn on your radio or television set; go outside and observe the weather and you might even listen to the unusual movement of the "creeping" things. The lowly worm knows more about what's happening than the crowning achievement on Earth—Man!

Prof. Albert Einstein's new unified field theory entered the picture at just the right moment. In brief, it tells us that gravity, electricity, and magnetism are all one and the same thing. As the Nineteenth Century drew to a close, scientists felt that they had built a perfect picture of the Universe on the basis of Sir *Isaac* Newton's law of gravitation. This was a mechanistic universe, set in a framework of *absolute* space and *absolute* time, in which the law of cause and effect operated without exception.

Our scientific view is widening at an alarming rate. If you carefully scan your newspaper you will notice a great deal of talk going on about magnetics; electronic experiments; new sources of power, such as the harnessing of sun's rays; and so on, *ad infinitum.* Steam as a source of power is fast being replaced. All the great discoveries of the Water Age are being supplanted by new Air Age discoveries. In that older age, Columbus crossed the Atlantic and our livelihood centered on things of the watery seas. Now man has his eyes and his heart on the stars out in space!

The happenings of today remind us of the time when Jesus was in a small boat on turbulent waters. Those with Him were very much afraid and awakened Him to tell Him of the disaster that surely would befall them. Do you remember His words to them? He said, "O ye of little faith!" That very same thing is taking place today. Men of "little faith" are preaching "doomsday". Violence is around us, indeed, just as the turbulent waters were around the little boat. But, remember, He calmed the waters. No matter what takes place on Earth, He will guide us, for He has promised, "Lo I am with you always!"

Religionists of today preach eternal life, but they certainly don't act as if they believed it. If life is eternal what is there to fear? Take the great events of our time as signs of the approaching Golden Dawn on Earth, with your very soul say: "Thy will be done, in and through me, thy servant."

At the present time, a rather new theory as to the origin of the Flying Saucers is gaining wide acceptance. This theory explains the spacecraft away as "the spirits of demons, monsters and devils". Certain hell-fire and brimstone evangelists tell their listeners the country over that Satan himself is the leader of the Saucer armada! We should not be surprised at this kind of thinking, for it is characteristic of the planet Earth. So-called "men of God" interpret everything in the Holy Book according to what they personally believe—they are presenting "the doctrines of men to be the commandments of God".

Very few ministers are telling their congregations that the Saucers may have a connection with the "signs in the skies" that the prophets of old spoke of. Some theologians, however, believe that the coming of the Saucers heralds the coming of the Elder Brother himself. Remember, Jesus was called a "devil" so why shouldn't we expect His Host also to be referred to in the same manner?

There are powerful forces in this country and throughout the world today who want the people to believe that the authority behind the Saucers is of the Evil One! Through ignorance and superstition they hope to control this situation as they have in the past. Dr. Vannevar Bush, president of Carnegie Institute in Washington, recently said that discoveries in the atomic field are only a small segment of the advances being made in other fields of scientific research. He declared that "the dam is about to break" in the whole field of biological science. The trend is not so evident as it now is in the atomic field, but he described it as a "great blossoming". He said there is the possibility that the emotional reactions of a whole nation might be controlled through a chemical placed in the food they consume! They could be made docile or irrational, lazy and unimaginative or energetic and constructive.

Already, world food products are contaminated by chemical poisonings in the guise of "preservatives", "enriching ingredients", "bleaching", and "synthetic vitamins". Now the prospect looms that in the near future the very emotions of people are to be controlled by substances placed in their daily rations. Shortly, biological science will experience the "shaking up" given physics a few years ago when the Atomic Age suddenly came upon man. But many of the so-called "advances" are of a destructive and negative nature as are the ideas that atomic power can be used for peaceful pursuits.

The people of the world can be deceived by those who put "darkness for light". The *real* advances will be the total elimination of food-tampering, food contamination, and chemical fertilization. True advance will not be the complete control of world population by having power over every thought, action and deed of man through his food consumption. Man will not only be released from dogmas, doctrines, false theories, pseudo-authorities, war mongers, spiritual conceit, and other centuries-old "chains that bind", but he will take his true place in Cosmos as a Son of God and a potential god himself!

In *The Saucers Speak!* mention was made of a Wyoming evangelist who claims he has had contact with Saucers for many years. He says they land near him, give off horrible stenches of burning *sulphur*, and the occupants are hideous, beastly devils with swishing forked tails and large horns. He says he could write a book that would put all Saucer research done so far "in the shade". He names this theory for world salvation after himself, of course. This man is not preaching love, brotherhood of man, and the imminent return of the Elder Brother. Instead, he warns people to beware of the "devils" and "imps" in the Saucers!

"Doomsday is here; disaster is upon us; we shall all surely die", cry those of "little faith". The Holy Book and the Golden Scripts are full of the Elder Brother's promises. He will "make our foreheads like flint", "nothing at all shall hurt us", "He is with us till the end". The evidence is abundant on every hand that the children of God have nothing to fear. Nowhere does Jesus speak of death and destruction as man's heritage in the New Age!

"For God hath not given us the spirit of fear; but of power, and of love, and of a sound mind." (II Timothy 1:7).

One of the unusual types of sightings connected with occupants of Saucers is the "mask sightings". In the early part of

1954, several young people were passing March Field, California in an automobile. Glancing onto the Air Force Field, they observed a shiny-looking Saucer resting on the ground. They stopped their car and got out in order to get a better look. After observing the craft at closer range, they noticed it was quite smooth and apparently no one was around. Still curious, they decided to get an even closer look. As they neared the object, a man suddenly stepped in front of them. He raised his arm and threw a "fireball" at them. It passed by them and struck their car. They immediately turned and fled, driving into the nearest Sheriff's office in a hurry.

The young observers said that the man wore some sort of a half mask on his face that appeared to be metallic in nature. This incident is very similar to the Italian sightings of 1953, where a man saw two occupants of a Saucer with metallic half-masks on their faces.

The "fireball" had dented the side of their car and the painted surface was burned and black. Needless to say, no harm was intended as far as the young people are concerned. The only reason the Saucer pilot threw this object is because he wanted to keep the curious observers from getting too near the Resonating Electro-Magnetic Force Field around the Saucer. What better way could he have gotten them to leave? And he didn't have to say a word! The "ball of fire" that came at the Florida Scoutmaster served the same purpose. If Saucer intelligences really wanted to harm someone they could do a much better job of it!

A reputable production engineer in South Pasadena, California says that while he was working cutting wood in his yard, a Saucer hovered nearby about twenty feet from the ground. By means of a ladder, three men descended and although they didn't speak English, he says he exchanged some ideas by means of sign language. He says the three men didn't even have *mouths!* These men might have been wearing masks, or they might be from worlds where only telepathy is used and where food intake is not necessary or the same as our own. At any rate, they could not speak.

"*Earths In The Universe*," by Emanuel Swedenborg, was first published in Latin in London, 1758. In the section on the planet Mars, he says: "There was presented before me an inhabitant of that earth (Mars). His face was like that of the inhabitants of our earth, but the lower region of the face was black, *not from a beard*, for he had none, but from blackness in place of it. This blackness extended on both sides as far as the ears. The upper part of the face was like the face of the inhabitants of our earth."

Swedenborg may have observed *half-masks* that appeared black. At any rate, there have been enough reports on "masks" to make it a vital part of Saucer investigation.

Space intelligences many times said: "We cannot stand by and see another waste of Creation." Because of this they survey our planet checking on dangerous fault zones and other weakened and unbalanced conditions.

Before the Ionian Island earthquake disaster, great exploding flashes of light were observed in various parts of Europe. The night *before* the big *New England* hurricane of 1954 there was a terrific explosion in Melrose, Massachusetts—cause *unknown*. Enormous exploding lights have been observed in the sky all over the world just *before* disaster strikes on the ground.

A mysterious explosion rocked the port of Dieppe, France. The explosion was preceded by a flash in the sky. A railwayman at Orchies, near the Belgian border, said he saw a fiery disc in the sky moving at great speed at the time of the Dieppe explosion. Similar happenings have been observed along the Western Coast of the United States from San Diego to Seattle. San Diego and Los Angeles have both experienced strange exploding lights overhead, usually followed by a mysterious explosion.

The Coast Guard pressed its investigation of wide-spread reports along the Oregon coast of a brilliant flash of light observed offshore by many people. Reports of the phenomenon came from points as widely separated as Empire and Newport, as well as several communities in between. Persons reporting the flash to the Coast Guard and the Portland air defense filter center said they saw a bright, multi-colored burst of light which suddenly disappeared as though some flaming object had dropped into the sea. They agreed that a vapor trail had lingered over the water for several minutes after the lights disappeared. In addition the reports came from Coos Bay, Beverly Beach and Depoe Bay. The Coast Guard at Newport and at Thirteenth Naval District Headquarters in Seattle said no planes had been flying over the area and discounted the possibility the light had been a meteor because of the object's trajectory. Officer's declined to speculate about what might have caused the strange flash. Seattle, Washington experienced a mysterious exploding light that startled hundreds of people. This city is in a very vital area because it is situated over the place where three of the world's major fault lines converge. The same situation that exists for the Ionian Islands and the Azores, exists for Seattle! These same exploding lights have been observed in the Japanese Islands and in other parts of the world where fault lines exist.

Sometimes these "lights" explode silently and at other times, because of certain conditions, they cause a violent shock-blast. They are only relaying vital information back to the space laboratories hovering high above. On September 9, 1954, a violent earthquake shattered the old Roman town of Orleansville, Algeria. Surrounding villages were also hard hit and buildings crumbled killing twelve-hundred fear-stricken inhabitants. Witnesses reported that a great ball of fire appeared in the sky just *before* the shock crumbled the city of nearly fifty-thousand population.

Space intelligences have been closely watching the Mediterranean area. There have been more violent earthquakes in that area in the last two years than in the rest of the world combined. Italy has had severe shocks and Mr. Vesuvius has been on the rampage. This volcano is situated on Italy's great fault line. Greece has suffered terribly from earthquakes recently and hundreds died in Turkey only recently. Cyprus has also been hit by severe earth tremors. Two major fault lines join west of the Cape Verde Islands and shocks have been recorded in that area of the Atlantic.

Other reports have come in from the Caucasus Mountain area and from several places in Iran. There have been many earthquakes in the Mediterranean area and there will be vast geographical changes there. The great "shaking-up" of the entire African, Grecian and Italian countrysides is a prelude to this.

If the "great ball of fire" observed over Orleansville had relayed information that a major catastrophe was due because of weakened fault lines, the Saucers would undoubtedly have staged an evacuation operation. Space intelligences say they will assist in the event of major disaster. How much longer the Mediterranean area can stand stress and strain on the fault zones is not known, but the Saucers are keeping a sharp lookout. (See *Plate II*).

On May 31, 1954, the Combat Operations Center at McChord Air Force Base, Washington, received eight reports of unidentified objects sighted over various sections of the Pacific Northwest. The objects were reported over Spokane, Pasco, Ellensburg, Yakima and several Oregon cities, including Redmond and Portland.

Fred Blackstone, a commercial pilot, reported at Moses Lake the object he sighted was absolutely silent and had a stream of reddish fire spouting from its end. The control tower at Yakima County Airport described the object it saw in a similar fashion, as did Justin Cerley of Spokane, an Air Force veteran of the Korean War who sighted another object just east of Spokane. He said the object glowed like a light bulb. Sgt. George Berg, of the Spokane Police Department, said he and his wife saw a globe of light with brilliant red sparks shooting from the back. It was not going fast and made no sound. Other reports said that people had observed "bluish blinking lights", "flying white globes of light", "white balls making terrific speed", "silent spheres of light", etc. The Air Force Combat Center at McChord said there was no attempt at interception and declined to speculate on the nature of the objects.

On June 1, 1954, The State Patrol in the Ellensburg area reported "flying globes" and several calls were received at Radio Station KLXE. Reports were now coming in from all over Washington, Oregon, parts of Canada, and even from Alaska. Willard Renfro, of Ellensburg, along with his wife and mother, observed a circular object with a "dome-shaped" top. He observed it for forty-five minutes through binoculars. Many observers said they saw "flat objects" flying in a northerly direction on a line parallel to the ground.

On June 5, 1954, six mysterious flying objects were sighted over Port Townsend. The Air Force dispatched an F-86 all-weather jet interceptor plane, fully armed, to Port Townsend from Paine Air Force Base. The interceptor made no contact with the strange objects, however, and a negative report on the flight was filed. Jefferson County Sheriff Peter J. Naughton said he saw six yellowish objects "flying in echelon formation spaced about two-hundred feet apart". He estimated they were at an altitude of four-thousand to five-thousand feet and traveling at two-hundred fifty to three-hundred miles per hour. Naughton said he reported the objects to Indian Island, a Naval Base near Port Townsend. He said he watched the Saucers zoom through the skies for about twelve minutes before he went to the telephone. A short time later he received a telephone call from Seattle requesting him to go to the Port Townsend Airport and ground planes because "interceptors were coming in with live ammunition".

The Flying Saucers returned on June 8, 1954 to amaze Seattle citizens. They appeared over many sections of the city about seven in the evening. Dozens of residents called the *Post-Intelligencer* and the Police Department to report the objects. Fire-men stationed at the Fire Station at E. 45th St. and Brooklyn Ave. spotted about six of the shiny discs and promptly used binoculars to get a closer look. A Queen Anne resident, Mrs. Sylvia Knight, told police she and a "lot of other people" saw Saucers moving "very high in the sky and shining like silver".

Sumner and Puyallup, Washington are three miles from each other and this area is eight miles southeast of Tacoma. Tacoma is thirty miles south of Seattle, Washington. Sumner and Puyallup are located on the middle fault line of the three major fault lines that converge at Seattle. Because of this fact, many strange and unbelievable things have been going on in this area, and they are still happening.

David D. Bunker of Sumner, his brother Allen, his fiancee, his younger brother Steve, fellow workers from Boeing Aircraft Co., other relatives and friends have observed orange, red and green blinking lights in this same general area. Many of these lights are known to have come toward the State of Washington from the Pacific Ocean area.

Some people have seen fast moving orange-red lights or "white globes", and others, such as David Bunker, have observed white or red lights that move slower and seem to be surveying in a particular area close to the ground. These lights blink, stop, then seem to flare up brightly at times. The May-June Washington sightings were concerned with actual Saucers, but some of the phenomena are connected with Type 2 "fireballs" and "projected intelligence" from highly advanced solar systems.

On September 12, 1952, the following information was relayed to George Van Tassel at Giant Rock, California. "I am Ashtar. Our Center has requested that I advance to you mortal beings of Shan (Earth) the following information. Over your past several months our ventlas have discharged several thousand *light beings* in certain remote areas upon your planet. These individuals, serving the cause of Universal Law, are recording numerous occurrences taking place within the civilization of the people of Shan. It would be advisable to instruct any mortal being who by chance should approach any of our *light intelligences* to do so with a thought projection of peace, 'I am friendly'. Any approach in any other frame of thought will meet with instant defensive conditions. It is not our desire to injure anyone. Only under individual protective measures shall we do anything other than retreat. In the records obtained by these beings . . . we shall determine what action to take in the very near future. My love remains with you. I am Ashtar."

This communication to Van Tassel shows the nature and purpose of the Washington "lights". Surveys are made constantly in remote areas of the Pacific Northwest because of the unstable and dangerous condition of the fault lines there.

Many pilots from the Seattle-Tacoma Civilian Airport and pilots from McChord Air Force Base have reported *strange* UFO's. These objects have also appeared on radar in this area. The Derringer Power Plant in Summer has had a great deal of difficulty with its power operation, and employees from the plant have observed strange flying lights while they have been working there. Saucers usually land in areas where interference with city electrical systems will be negligible. Because of their intensive study of this fault zone area, power systems are affected.

In the Fall of 1953, David Bunker was awakened by the neighborhood dogs barking. Once awake, he saw that his entire room was filled with a strange, brilliant orange glow . . . it covered everything. He called his sister Lois and his brother Steve who also observed this phenomenon. David went downstairs and discovered that the whole house was filled with the glow. When he went out onto the front porch he noticed that this orange glow engulfed his house only. A neighbor looked out of his window and the light faded away. However, both David and the neighbor heard a humming sound similar to a sixty-cycle hum.

On Sunday night, March 28, 1954, David, Steve, Lois, David's fiancee, and Lois' girl friend, were in David's car. They drove to a lonely uninhabited area off the road by the Puget Sound power line. David turned out the car lights and immediately saw a white glowing ball with a clearly defined edge about a mile and a half ahead of the car. It glided down, wobbling as it went, and apparently went into a group of trees. Then this light came from the tree area, traveled up through the valley, and approached the car. After several minutes, Steve said: "Who's that?" David and his fiancee saw the white globe in front of the car and to the left. When David turned on the car lights the globe disappeared. Later, Steve asked: "Did you see the man standing in front of the car?" Steve had seen a tall, well-built, broad-shouldered man standing exactly in the spot where David and his fiancee saw the white globe. Steve said the man had a glowing light all around him.

On Saturday, July 3, 1954, at Midnight, David and his fiancee were out driving when they saw a white light drop out of the sky and go into some bushes next to the road. After the light entered the bushes it turned green and could be observed twinkling through the brush. David turned out the car lights, and shortly thereafter they saw a solid red ball of light come from the left and drop onto the ground about twenty feet in front of the car. David turned on the lights and a man was standing where the red light had hit the ground. The man was standing directly in front of the car and looked over his right shoulder. He was about six feet tall, wore a tight-fitting white shirt and some sort of a vest. He appeared to be about twenty-seven years old. He looked *through* the car, not *at* it! When David turned on the car motor, the man vanished. One moment he was there and the next moment he was gone. The green light in the brush had remained there, twinkling, as the red ball of light came down.

On Monday, July 19, 1954, David was in his car and saw a white light moving in the sky. It came closer, got bigger, then seemed to fade out of sight. About five miles further down the road David noticed a terrible odor that filled the air around him. It was suffocating. It smelled like metal burning in acid and hydrogen sulfide.

All of the foregoing is related to show that there is an intensive survey now being conducted in the State of Washington by the Confederation of Space Intelligences here in the name of the Infinite Father. And remember, Mount Rainier is only a short distance from Sumner and Puyallup—Mount *Rainier*, where Kenneth Arnold saw the nine Saucers on Tuesday, June 24, 1947.

There have been sightings near Lancaster, New York that are identical with the strange happenings in Washington. Mr. and Mrs.

Gerhard Koblich owned a fine farm near Lancaster, and several months ago unusual phenomena began to take place. They both saw many "flying lights", "white globes", "flying red stars", etc. Then, one night, as they were watching television in their living-room, a foggy-white beam of light shot through one of the windows. And looking in the window was the face of a man who appeared to be of a dark complexion. He couldn't have been over four or four and a half feet tall, because nothing could be observed but his neck and head. The face seemed to be in or with the beam. When they walked toward the window to get a better look, the face disappeared. Later, it would appear again. This happened many times, but they never saw footprints outside and no one was ever discovered on the farm although they searched everywhere.

One time, Mrs. Koblich was outside in her yard feeding her cats when a beam came from above and caught her in its three-foot wide path. There was nothing in the sky at the time—nothing but the beam of white light. This is another case of "projection" and since this area is close to two major fault lines a survey is being conducted there, also.

Warren, Ohio is also in the area of two major fault lines and many unexplained things have been going on there. Many Saucers have been observed in the general area and have been reported by civilian and Air Force pilots. Saucers have landed and their occupants observed by several individuals.

Many months ago, information was received that Martian scientists were planning to improve the condition of Earth's soil by impregnating it with certain highly-concentrated, organic material. When this program would be put into effect, and how, no one knew.

February, 1954, saw the actual beginning of the new project. On February 4th, Mayor Ray Logan of Galena, Illinois said he was flooded with calls from persons who claimed they saw a long, brilliant red "telephone pole" fly over Galena a few nights before. The Mayor said it was only a typical Saturday night in Galena, meaning that the revelry wasn't so great that people were seeing things.

The report in this Northern Illinois town near the Wisconsin border coincided with observations of a brilliant blue flash (also observed by Ray Palmer, of the Amherst Press, publishers of this book), believed caused by a meteor, over central Wisconsin. Witnesses said the pole was shaped something like a baseball bat and glided noiselessly along, not very high and not very fast.

Mayor Logan said that very reputable and responsible persons first called him about the object, and that afterward, he received numerous reports from others in Galena and in communities to the north. "The descriptions given me were pretty much the same," Logan said. "I'm still getting calls."

The police department said that a half dozen motorists reported that they nearly had accidents when they saw the pole pass low overhead. Mouths agape, they jammed on brakes. One motorist said he almost piled into a big truck when the driver abruptly stopped. Virginia Beadle, the local telephone operator, said she saw the object while on her way to work and it nearly frightened her to death.

Later reports said the pole was green in color as it sailed northward, and Logan said he received re-ports from the north that it was blue over Wisconsin. It was undetermined, however, whether Wisconsin residents saw the pole or the blue flash of light reported by others. Dr. Bengt Stromgren, director of Yerkes Observatory at Williams Bay, Wisconsin, said he received a dozen reports of the flash from throughout central Wisconsin, but from all of information it appeared that the "flying phone pole" had merely been a *fireball!* But it may be very significant that in both 1955 and 1956 Wisconsin *led the nation* in corn production per acre, although it is not a part of the famed "corn belt".

The 'Red Spray Cases" mentioned by Maj Keyhoe are believed to be early experiments on the part of space intelligences to determine the best method of soil rejuvenation on our world. These cases happened back in the 1940's—the things came down to two-hundred feet and exploded. The green "fireballs" never came as close as these devices. The government listed this strange phenomena in its 1949 summaries as Case #225.

One night, back in 1949, a strange reddish light was sighted at Albuquerque, New Mexico where they had been seeing the green "fireballs." The object came in at about five-hundred feet, then it suddenly dropped down to two-hundred feet and exploded in a red spray. A few people were frightened, but it wasn't directly over the city—it had exploded out of town toward the airport. This same thing happened on three other nights—the same place, and the same hour!

Maj. Keyhoe believes the red spray devices were ranging bombs under remote control and is convinced that the green "fireballs" are guided missiles. However, he says: "The tests began over four years ago; if an attack was all they had in mind, they'd have hit us long before this." That is true—this phenomena is of a more constructive nature. The nature and purpose of the green "fireballs" has already been given in this book, and the "Red Spray Bombs" were an early form of the "Red Flying Poles"—and both serve the purpose of soil rejuvenation.

Because of the cosmic eruptions through which we are passing, the world's available humus supply is shrinking and there will be serious difficulties in growing enough food to prevent large-scale famines. This fact was stated recently by Prof. Vaino Auer of Finland's Helsinki University, one of the world's leading geographers. He also said that these eruptions (of which there have been six since 12,000 B.C.) take place at two-thousand year intervals and are marked by drastic changes in plant and animal life, long periods of drought, the rising of sea level, and the receding of forests, supplanted by desert or shrub. At present we are experiencing all of these phenomena.

What is most alarming is the disappearance of bacteria, which is causing the recession of forests, death of plants, and the erosion of humus. Prof. Auer has warned of the dangers of extensive agriculture, noting that it takes nine-thousand years, more or less, for humus to be formed. It can be destroyed in a year or two!

Space friends knew the Earth would be bombarded more and more with cosmic rays, and they knew this would begin to destroy humus-forming bacteria. Our government has now set up a Division of Radiation and Organisms to handle this growing problem. Since information on humus destruction is "Top Secret" no news is given out to the press or the public. The Division investigating the phenomena attributes the causes to "conventional" factors when questioned. Evidently they don't agree with Prof. Auer. They say: "Bacteria will grow anywhere where there is a suitable environment involving water, mineral nutrients, suitable organic matter and the proper temperature." This is true, but they don't mention the fact that increased cosmic ray bombardment is destroying the bacteria!

The bacterial population of any region fluctuates greatly depending upon changes in the various factors listed above. And changes there are! The Division admits that in certain regions great changes are taking place, but they will not admit that there is a worldwide trend in regard to a disappearing bacterial population. They say the changes can be readily explained upon the basis of known physiological and agriculture phenomena. If this is true, why are scientists like Dr. Sitte and Prof. Auer so concerned?

The Division further says that the principal factors causing the recession of forests are fire, the lumbering industries and the demand for increased agricultural lands. They say that this is a serious problem, but primarily a socio-economic one. There have been forest fires for thousands of years, and man has been extending his agricultural areas for hundreds of years and the lumbering industry isn't a particular threat to forests now. Authorities don't want information on increased cosmic ray activity to become generally known, so they "explain it away" as a socio-economic problem!

The Space Confederation decided to do something about our depleted Earth and this is what they have said: "You have been hearing about strange 'Flying Telephone Poles' that are observed to come very close to your Earth. These strike the earth and will take care of a large area. They go into the ground and dissolve in the soil in about one hour. They do not look like shooting stars when they fall, but appear as a *blue streak* to the naked eye. Your beneficial bacteria are dying and these 'flying poles' are sent out by the scientific space laboratories to take care of you Western Hemisphere. In this area of your planet you will find that certain farmers are puzzled as to how the soil became so rich and at times there is evidence of a red dust. Many of these 'poles' are tube-like, pointed at both ends and usually six feet long by twelve inches in diameter, although they can be much larger. The tubes contain rich, concentrated organic soil material from our own gardens and canals on Mars. They are full of vital, healthy, organic elements that will correct your increasing problem of *humus destruction*. The soil will be supplied with nitrogen. Look on some of your land; it will take on a reddish color in the sunlight—remember, Mars is known as the Red Planet!"

Certain bacteria produce enzymes which accelerate the decomposition of organic wastes such as proteins and certain other nitrogenous compounds producing nitrogen compounds in a form that can be used by plants. Nitrogen is one of the constituents of protein and thus a requirement of all plants and animals.

Certain bacteria take free nitrogen from the atmosphere and convert it by various methods to nitrogen compounds that are in such form that plants and animals can use it. Atmospheric nitrogen, however, is not available to plant and animal life—so without the services of bacteria in decomposition of organic wastes via the enzymes they produce, or conversion of free atmospheric nitrogen to nitrogenous compounds available to plants, there can be *no life* and the partially decomposed organic material known as humus that we already have is left to erosion for lack of plant life to hold it in place!

The early "spray" devices did not prove effective, so the "pole" or "tube" devices were designed which would enter the soil directly instead of just being sprayed over the surface. The many cases of "red snow" or "red dust" reported in Europe and the United States are due to the rejuvenation experiments by space intelligences. "Red snow" spread dust over the Minneapolis area so thickly that many tons were dropped upon each square mile of territory. A minimum of seventy-five tons of red dust fell on the basic Twin City area of one-thousand five-hundred square miles. One sample collected on the University of Minnesota campus showed the equivalent of 128.8 tons per square mile.

Several farmers have been interviewed who say that something is happening to the soil that they cannot explain. In certain areas its richness has increased unbelievably.

So bacteria are now dying at a rapid rate because of cosmic eruptions. Because of this vital nitrogen compounds are not produced and the nitrogen cycle essential to all life is violently disturbed. Space scientists are correcting that condition on Earth by sending highly concentrated organic material impregnated with the necessary bacteria, and this will replenish the depleted Earth supply. They say they are doing this in the Western Hemisphere because the land of the New Age is in the West.

Remote control bombs? Guided missiles? A thousand times no! Friends from outer space are saving our food supply by soil rejuvenation and thereby they save a race!

In *The Saucers Speak!* space visitors spoke of a "dark moon", or "second moon" of Earth. They called this second satellite "Fowser". Now scientists claim they believe our planet may indeed have an extra moon, in fact, there may be several moons that are unknown at present. The government has known about the existence of extra satellites for some time but they are now breaking the news "gently" to the public. Many new discoveries are not being revealed as yet. For instance, the speed record in aircraft is far in excess of what they claim—and what about experiments on magnetic flight or the space station? Is an artificial earth satellite now being constructed at a base in California?

In July, 1954, the planet Mars came closer to Earth than it had in fifteen years. It was forty-million miles away, and scientists had another look.

During the early part of 1954, the "Mars Committee" representing leading observatories and universities met in Washington. Although Venus is closer to Earth than Mars, the latter is more easily observed. Most astronomers agree that there is something extraordinary on the surface of Mars. Dr. H. Percy Wilkins, fellow Royal Astronomical Society and world authority on the Moon, recently announced that the Martian "canals" have been seen by astronomers this year and that he, himself, saw the "canals" distinctly when he used the sixty-inch reflector at Mt. Wilson.

The "Mars Committee" may be used by the government to announce to the world that there really is life on Mars! Once people get over the shock that they are not alone in the Universe perhaps they can take the bigger announcement of the nature of the Saucers.

Astronomer Clyde Tombaugh, who discovered the planet Pluto in 1930, has been looking for nearer and more elusive objects. Extra Earth satellites. Dr. Tombaugh has refused to give many details and refers questioners to Army Ordnance in Washington. He says the fact that other Earth moons have not been discovered yet does not mean that they do not exist. Remember *From The Earth To The Moon*, by Jules Verne? In this book a small satellite of the Earth disturbed the course of the space ship and almost kept it from returning to Earth.

A small satellite close to the Earth would be hard to spot. It might circle near the equator, invisible to most of the world's observatories. In any case, it would spend nearly half its time in the shadow of the Earth, where it would be invisible. Most of the rest of the time it would be passing over the sunlit Earth, and would look no brighter at best than a tiny fragment of the Moon as seen by day. The best time to look for a small satellite would be at dawn or dusk, when it would be shining brightly above the dim-lit Earth.

A satellite near the Earth would have to move very fast to keep itself out of the clutches of Earth's gravitation, and its speed would make it doubly hard to spot. Thousands of small areas in the sky must be examined and completion of such a search could take years. Dr. Tombaugh is now trying to discover what space intelligences said was true many long months ago!

Nothing "official" has been released announcing discovery of the "dark moon" of Earth, but other information equally, if not more important has been reported. Nearly two years ago, Frank Edwards, radio commentator, first reported Mt. Palo-mar's discovery of "two unknown objects of unique character". Sir Edward Appleton, famous British radio-physicist said: "These two unknown objects are discoveries of great astronomical interest."

On March 12, 1954, Frank Edwards again revealed official concern over the two "objects" which lie in the orbit between Earth and Mars. These objects recently confirmed by radio-telescope were not seen prior to 1877. Scientists at White Sands, New Mexico are examining the evidence.

On August 22, 1952 our research group in Northern Arizona was informed by space friends that Lowell Observatory was conducting highly secret investigation with the aid of new electronic devices. We knew that expensive equipment had been installed on Mars Hill near Flagstaff, Arizona and the building housing the equipment was surrounded by a high fence and was guarded by large dogs. The Santa Fe Railroad was informed that if its radio equipment in the vicinity interfered with the electronic investigation some changes would have to be made. The two artificial satellites, or space stations, were tracked by the new equipment at Lowell.

In August, 1954, *Aviation Week* magazine reported that the two objects were *meteors*, and insisted that Dr. Lincoln La Paz helped identify them as natural rather than man-made. Dr. La Paz attacked the magazine's reference to him, but acknowledged the search for nearby satellites. He also said: "The report is false in every particular insofar as reference to me is concerned."

Two *artificial* objects are known to be circling the Earth at four-hundred and six-hundred miles out in space. The Russians haven't beaten the United States to space operations and the objects aren't natural *meteors.* Van Tassel and others reported their existence several years ago.

For years, astronomers have observed fantastic sights on our Moon. Dr. F. B. Harris on January 27, 1912 saw what he reported as an "intensely black object" whose size he estimated at fifty by two-hundred fifty miles. Almost two-hundred years ago Sir John Herschel reported a dozen or more very bright lights on the Moon during eclipses. He thought they were active volcanoes, but he was very puzzled by some that appeared to be *above the Moon.*

A bright light in the Crater Aristarchus and one at the eastern base of the lunar Alps have been seen frequently for more than one hundred years. The whole plain of Mare Crisium puts on a spectacle of dots and streaks of light once in awhile. Messier blazes up with two bright lines separated by a very dark band dotted with luminous points. Exodus and Aristarchus have displayed long lines of light "like luminous cable or shining wall" and moving lights have been frequently seen.

Strings of moving lights have been observed in Plato and in 1869 thirty bright lights appeared on the crater floor all at once. They rapidly sorted *themselves* into groups—some would blaze simultaneously, at the same moment other groups faded to a dull glow. This continued in a symphony of lights, as if they were all manipulated from a master keyboard. This was so sensational that the Royal Society instituted a group observation. The display died out in April, 1871 and the group had recorded one-thousand six-hundred observations and drew thirty-seven graphs of the light fluctuations.

Lights around the Moon's rim are often seen during eclipses, as are squadrons of bright and dark bodies maneuvering in the lunar sky. During the eclipse of November 16, 1910, a bright light shone on the Moon and observatories at two widely-separated points saw a ball of light shoot out from the disc. C. Stanley Ogilvy of Trinity College admits that lights have been seen around the Moon. Recently, Mount Piton, in the northern section of Mare

Imbrium has sent out beacon-like beams of light—some mighty strange things are happening on Luna. Van Tassel says the Crater Tycho is the location of one of the largest underground cities on the Moon. The population of Tycho numbers several hundred thousand and the city is built on many levels or stories. The bright spot in the Crater Aristarchus is the lens which provides power, light and other utilities for the oldest lunar underground city.

Karl G. Jansky of Bell Telephone Laboratories, was the first man to detect radio signals originating from the Moon. Whereas radio signals originating from the Earth would be detected as coming from above the Earth's surface, the Moon signals have been detected as originating from *beneath the surface of the Moon*. This confirms the statement of Van Tassel that inhabitants of the Moon live underground in craters.

Many thousands of years ago, the Moon had an indigenous population. Then there were long periods when our satellite was nearly lifeless. Several hundred years ago, intelligences from outer space migrated to Luna and are the "little people" mentioned in *Behind The Flying Saucers*, by Frank Scully. There was a suggestion in his book that the "little men" might come from Venus, but their home base is the Moon. Also, the small occupants of the Saucer that landed on Helgoland Island in the North Sea off the German coast originated from our satellite. These "little people" are similar to the Martian in advancement, being twenty-five or thirty thousand years ahead of us at the present time.

The Harvesters have their own system of color identification. The code consists of various geometric shapes and certain colors; the meaning of each follows:

FORM:	COLOR:	INTERPRETATION:
Square	White	Spiritually perfect man.
"	Yellow	Protect man.
"	Orange	Serve man.
"	Red	Strengthen man.
"	Violet	Understand and teach man.
"	Blue	You are of Man, Nature of Being.

"	Green	Be at peace with man.
"	Brown	Comfort man.
"	Gray	Do not afflict man.
"	Black	Do not destroy man.
Circle	White	Spiritually perfect the body.
"	Yellow	Protect the body.
"	Orange	Serve the body.
"	Red	Strengthen the body.
"	Violet	Understand and teach the body.
"	Blue	You are of Christ—The Being.
"	Green	Be at peace with the body.
"	Brown	Comfort the body.
"	Gray	Do not afflict the body.
"	Black	Do not destroy the body.
Star (Five Points)	White	Spiritually perfect the mind.
"	Yellow	Protect the mind.
"	Orange	Serve the mind.
"	Red	Strengthen the mind.
"	Violet	Understand and teach the mind.
"	Blue	You are of the Holy Ghost—Understanding of Being.
"	Green	Be at peace with the mind.
"	Brown	Comfort the mind.
"	Gray	Do not afflict the mind.
"	Black	Do not destroy the mind.
Triangle	White	Spiritually perfect the soul.
"	Yellow	Protect the soul.
"	Orange	Serve the soul.
"	Red	Strengthen the soul.
"	Violet	Understand the soul.

"	Blue	You are of God—Spirit of Being.
"	Green	Be at peace with the soul.
"	Brown	Comfort the soul.
"	Gray	Do not afflict the soul.
"	Black	Do not destroy the soul.

The above information was received from a research group in a large city in the midwest. Color is used extensively by space visitors for identification and communication purposes. The "lamps" mentioned by Ezekiel and by Herr Linke in Germany are used so that when the occupants of a Saucer are separated from each other after leaving their craft, they can immediately look at the color flashing from the other man's "lamp" on his chest and know at once what he is thinking. This is telepathy helped along by mechanical ingenuity. Their mental vibrations or emanations show up as various colors in the "lamp".

Two Soviet astronomers recently announced that the Earth has a fiery tail! *Nature*, official journal of the British Association for the Advancement of Science points out that the scientists are thoroughly reliable and have had exceptional opportunities for observation from the central Asian desert. The two astronomers, Fesenkov and Astapovich, were making a study of the "Gegenschein," a glow seen occasionally in the sky just opposite the Sun two or three hours before sunrise or after sunset. They concluded that this glow is a tenuous film of gas in the form of a hollow sleeve pulled off from the extreme upper atmosphere on the twilight side of Earth—much the same phenomenon as the tail of a comet.

They have now observed a broad pyramid of fainter luminescence connecting the "Gegenschein" with the horizon, and confined to the western side of the night sky. Before, this luminosity was believed to be a concentration of gas particles moving around the Sun like a minor planet. But now the Russians have discovered it is not beyond the atmosphere but continuous with it. Thus it makes a tail extending outward into space for about one-hundred sixty-thousand miles!

The "Gegenschein," or counterglow was first recorded in 1855 and seems to be associated in origin with the *zodiacal light*. In the tropics this zodiacal light is visible throughout the year, both morning and evening, and in especially clear skies it has been traced as a narrow zodiacal band completely around the ecliptic.

Van Tassel at Giant Rock received the following: "There are many things going on unknown and unseen by you. One of these conditions is the condensation of a ring around Earth at the equator line. This ring has always been there unknown to your men of science. It is similar to the visible rings of the planet Saturn. In our terms, this is known as the "Arch of the Firmament".

Therefore, the Earth doesn't have a *tail*, but it has *rings!* From various locations on the surface of Earth the ring or arch system would appear as a tail for only part of the equatorial arch could be viewed at any one time. This is why the zodiacal light is visible *throughout the year* in the tropics.

Again, Van Tassel's communication says: "As this ring will soon be discovered by your science, they will then comprehend more about light energy. This ring maintains balanced interchange of power through the crust and atmosphere of Earth, and all planets that revolve. It is the prime cause of vortices turning clockwise in the northern hemisphere and counter-clockwise in the southern hemisphere. You will discover that vines climb in spirals in the same direction or rotation, opposite to each other in the different hemispheres. The condensation of the ring will bring about stabilization of Earth and cause the end of your seasons. Scientists will register this as a natural occurrence but let me inform you, that many thousands of beings trained in the control of vortice condensation are working diligently on a long, hard assignment to bring this condition about. A thousand years from now, one may look at the Earth from other planets and see rings similar to those surrounding Saturn."

Of course, this ring was discovered when Fesenkov and Astapovich observed a broad pyramid of fainter luminescence connecting the "Gegenschein" with the horizon. It will become more visible to the unaided eye as time goes on. Needless to say, the rings of Saturn are not "moonlets" or "swarms of meteors". The Resonating Electro-Magnetic Field of Saturn is very intense. This is evidenced by the fact that Saturn has the greatest oblateness (flattened at the poles) among the planets in our Solar System. Because of the considerable oblateness of the planet, the cleavage layer of its magnetic field shows up as three concentric rings in the plane of its equator. The *inner* parts of the rings revolve faster than the *outer* parts. This tends to prove the fact that Saturn is operating in a vortex. The outer parts of the ring system move westward across the Saturnian sky; but a considerable part of the bright ring, and all of the crape ring rise in the west and set in the east as seen from the surface of Saturn, duplicating the behavior of Phobos in the Martian sky. The rings are designated by name and letter as follows: the outer rings (A), the bright ring (B), and the "crape" ring (C). The rings A and C are *transparent*. Observers have watched the rings pass over stars without entirely hiding them.

The ring system of Saturn is similar to the "rings" mentioned by George Adamski in *Flying Saucers Have Landed.* "As the ship started moving, I (Adamski) noticed two rings under the flange and a third around the centre disk. This inner ring and the outer one appeared to be revolving clockwise, while the ring between these two moved in a counter clockwise motion."

Some people wonder if our government is attempting contact with Saucers. They have already had contact, but they are still working at it as evidenced by the fact that at Edwards Air Base in California there is a highly secret operation known as Project NQ-707. This project and its personnel is concerned with nothing but radio-telegraphic contact with Saucers. They have been successful in their work and have attempted to get the Saucers to land at a rendezvous point near Salton Sea in Southern California. Warner Peak, of volcanic origin, is very close to this area and because of a deep crater would be excellent for Saucer landings. In fact, it is reliably reported that many such craft have used this extinct crater in recent months. It was near Desert Center, California that contact was made with a Venusian on November 20, 1952, and this area is also near the Salton Sea rendezvous point.

Many people are "fed-up" with the numerous space stories found in comic books, pocket books and pulp magazines—heard over the radio, seen on television and in the movies. But this is all part of the plan on the part of the Confederation. That's why science fiction has gained in popularity in the past few years. Why did the younger generation suddenly drop "cowboys and injuns" and turn to "spacemen and Saucers"? The answer is obvious—*The Wanderers* have infiltrated the writing profession!

Some sincere individuals say: "But those awful space programs are ruining our children!" On the contrary, "those awful space programs" are indoctrinating the children for the biggest event in history. People object because the space heroes invariably carry "ray pistols" or "disintegrating guns" and wear the familiar "inverted fishbowl" or "space helmet".

The guns and the helmet are absolutely necessary, for without these symbols the TV spaceman would be as undressed as "Hoppy" without his trusty pistol and his western boots. Another example is that all children today are crazy about "space suits" which can be purchased quite reasonably or even improvised—which reminds me of a boy belonging to a friend of mine ... this potential "spaceman" stole the plastic cover off the toaster and calmly put it over his head. He wasn't going to be outdone by the neighbor kids; not by a long shot!

One excellent space program on television in Los Angeles, California, starts its daily excitement by first showing a Flying Saucer going through black, interstellar space pinpointed with a million stars—and a voice says: "Commander Comet—the first *man* to come from another planet to prove to Earth-men that brotherhood is found throughout the Universe!" Did you notice that the voice said MAN? Because of this program, children are being shown that ordinary men occupy the Saucers, not jelly monsters or vegetable Frankensteins! Furthermore, they are shown that the guy in the Saucer is their friend, he hasn't come to invade the Earth, but upon his arrival he organizes a bunch of kids into "Space Scouts" and they assist him as he takes on the role of "Superman" and cleans up the Earth making it a fit place for decent people to live in. Do you still say these programs are "awful"?

When the Saucers land by the thousands, the children will be knocking at the Saucer pilot's "door" saying: "Let me in—I'm a Space Scout!" Children are very receptive to indoctrination by space visitors. Take the case of ten year old Jamie who looked up at his grandmother and said, "Tell you what, Gram: You help me with my arithmetic and I'll explain to you all about the sound barrier and space people."

In *The Saucers Speak!* Ponnar said: "There are now many young people in your world who understand our message. They will accept it quickly for they are of the New Age. The Great Awakening is here."

Recently a serial story appeared in a leading magazine for boys and girls. It was called, *Jonny And The Boy From Space.* John Jenks was the nine-year old son of a scientist who lived on a farm in the northern part of New Jersey. Jonny had the amazing experience of talking with a man who came to Earth in a Flying Saucer space ship. The man from space Jonny called "the man from Out There" and this man had left a space-o-tron with Jonny. Possession of this scientific toy enabled the boy to communicate with the space man by means of thought waves. The spaceman finally brought his young son to Earth to be Jonny's playmate for awhile.

The space-o-tron was a little marsquartz ball that responded to telepathic commands! This object is very similar, indeed, to the Type 2 "fireball".

"The marsquartz ball moved through the air like a gleam of light. It tapped gently against the sleeve of Mr. Murphy's sport shirt and then followed Jonny's mental command back to its place under the pillow."

There is always enough *truth* in these stories so that they can be detected as being inspired by the space intelligences. Children learn that there are human beings on other worlds and that an Earth boy or a boy from Out There are just about the same—a boy is a boy no matter where you find him.

Some day, when Saucers land, and adults are afraid to venture too close, thousands of children will be the first officially to welcome space visitors to Earth, for "a little child shall lead them".

In *Gnani Yoga*, by Yogi Ramacharaka, we read: "The Universe contains many worlds for the Soul to inhabit, and then after it has passed on to other Universes, there will still be Infinitude before it. There are now in existence, on planes infinitely higher than your own, intelligences of transcendent glory and magnificence, but they were once Men even as you are today."

There is no limit to Man's progression toward All Perfection! "The Yogi Philosophy teaches that Man will live forever, ascending from higher to higher planes, and then on and on and on. As we progress on to higher planes of life, we shall incarnate in bodies far more ethereal than those now used by us, just as in the past we used bodies almost incredibly grosser and coarser than those we call our own to-day."

Saucer intelligences are human beings, only they have progressed to other "grandeurs", and they still have a long way to go as we do. These intelligences tell us we are all "Sons of God" and that planets were created to be the abode of Man—the human form and the human race is Universal! These wonderful brothers and sisters tell us what we have hoped was true before the dawn of history, that life is *eternal.* We are all immortal beings. What could be more significant?

These space people are offering their brothers of Earth wonderful, eternal gifts of great value. Let us in all humbleness accept what they have to offer, and thank our Infinite Father for sending them to us at this time. The time is short; we have but a little while to choose them, for it is written: "The *harvest* shall be removed in the day of inheritance, and there shall be deadly sorrow." (Isaiah 17:11).

To sum up just what Flying Saucers are, we would say that they are mechanical devices intelligently controlled by men like ourselves. These men originate from many planets and planes and although they are different from one another in spiritual evolvement, they are banded together in an Interplanetary Brotherhood or Confederation of Solar Systems in this area of the Universe. The purpose of this organization is to aid their brother-man on the planet Earth as the New Age dawns. The Saucers constitute the "Host" which is the forerunner of the promised "Second Coming" of the Elder Brother. The ORIGIN of the Saucers, however, is not the important consideration—but their MISSION is!

Man on Earth is still a child that wants to tear everything apart to see "what makes it tick". Since the appearance of Saucers his interest in the dissection or microscopic investigation of a beetle or a leaf has violently swung to the examination of the heavens and he is aflame with desire to know what the Saucers and their occupants are made of (if anything). Only recently has there been evidenced a great interest in the *purpose* or *mission* of the space visitors.

People are saying: "It's nice to meet a Venusian on the desert, and it's thrilling to speak to Saucers via shortwave—but now that the contact novelty has worn off what does it all add up to? The people of Earth are starving for Truth and if our brothers coming here in space ships can supply us with Truth we want to know about it. How can those of us desiring the Light help?"

Needless to say, scientific facts are not going to satisfy Man's deeper longings. The important message that should be heralded from the housetops is: This is the hour of crisis on the planet Earth, and HELP HAS COME FROM OUTER SPACE to usher man into a *millennium* of peace, health, and abundant joy. Let's not worry about the atomic structure of these people bringing the help, but let's realize that they are here and they are not going away.

At the present time it is urgent to "feed the sheep in the Master's flock for the night cometh". Truth-hungry souls want knowledge that will enable them to have the courage and faith to endure the coming world changes. Details of Saucer construction or the analysis of sedimentary rock from Pluto will not give spiritual nourishment that is vital during this stage of transition into a totally new era.

Recorded history proves that we go through stages of spiritual advancement and then scientific or technical advancement. Unfortunately, the technical side of the matter has far outstripped the spiritual side. The result is our present state of affairs. Now man on Earth must balance the unstable condition and his spiritual evolvement must "catch up" so to speak with his ability in mechanics and technology. When a balance is reached, Earthmen can again settle down to the analysis of the Universe—this time in the light of great revelations brought to us by our space friends.

The Harvesters are to be The reapers in the time of harvest. "Let both grow together until the harvest: and in the time of harvest I will say to the reapers, Gather ye together first the tares, and bind them in bundles to burn them: but gather the wheat into my barn." (St. Matthew 13:30).

The *tares* will be those individuals who don't survive to live in the New Age on Earth. The wheat that is gathered is *The Remnant* that is spoken of at the end of this book.

Christ said: "He that soweth the good seed is the Son of man; The field is the world; the good seed are the children of the kingdom; but the tares are the children of the wicked one; The enemy that sowed them is the devil; the harvest is the end of the world; and *the reapers are the angels*. As therefore the tares are gathered

263

and burned in the fire; so shall it be in the end of this world. The Son of man shall send forth his angels, and they shall gather out of his kingdom all things that offend, and them which do iniquity; and shall cast them into a furnace of fire: there shall be wailing and gnashing of teeth. Then shall the righteous shine forth as the sun in the kingdom of their Father. Who hath ears to hear, let him hear." (St. Matthew 13:37-43).

Space intelligences have said that a separation was now in progress: "the black from the white (not referring to races)" and the "sheep from the goats".

In *The Impending Golden Age*, published by Sanctilean University, we read: "The physical humanity of Earth at this time is almost unconsciously in the process of segregation into two groups. These are the Slow Incubatives and Advanced Incubatives. The segregation is in terms of purity of living, chastity, nonresistance to evil, and conformity with the verities, principles and laws of cosmic actuality."

"And I looked, and behold a white cloud, and upon the cloud one sat like unto the Son of man, having on his head a golden crown, and in his hand a sharp sickle. And another angel came out of the temple, crying with a loud voice to him that sat on the cloud, Thrust in thy sickle, and reap; for the harvest of the earth is ripe. And he that sat on the cloud thrust in his sickle on the earth; and the earth was reaped." (Revelation 14:14-16).

The Harvesters will soon thrust in their sickles and the earth shall be reaped as it is written.

In the *Golden Scripts*, *The Harvesters* are called the Sons of Light. "The Sons of Light array themselves at my bidding: they go forth in the world and make it beautiful: They are a goodly company indeed, but not *the* Goodly Company that findeth me through suffering. The Sons of Light are of the Host; they are a creation of the Father for a purpose; men call them angels." (G. S. 209:1-3).

This means that *the* Goodly Company is composed of those who have incarnated on Earth over and over again—in other *words*, *The Wanderers*. The Saucer intelligences or the Sons of Light are a goodly company, but they have not performed their duties through suffering on the Earth planet as the Knights of the Solar Cross or Wanderers have done. These latter servants are also *Harvesters* in that they aid the space visitors in the "reaping of the harvest".

The Elder Brother says: "They (Sons of Light) are endowed with infallible powers in Matter, in that Matter obeyeth them; Matter is their servant: they have dominion over it. They know neither time nor space but transfer themselves from planet unto planet in the twinkling of an eye. They come and go upon the Father's business: great is their joy therein: they are pure in heart and beauteous of mien. They seek to do the Father's will, and in that they seek, they do find life wondrous." (G. S. 209:6-9).

"He that gathereth in summer is a wise son: but he that sleepeth in harvest is a son that causeth shame." (Proverbs 10:5).

"The harvest is past, the summer is ended, and we are not saved." (Jeremiah 8:20). No man on Earth will want to be "he that sleepeth" during the harvest when *The Remnant* shall be saved. Who on Earth thinks he will be among those to say: "The harvest is past, and I am not saved?"

But all men will not be saved, for only a few shall remain. Where there are now thousands there will only be tens. Heed *The Harvesters* as they raise their voices in unison saying: "Go, and tell this people, Hear ye indeed, but understand not; and see ye indeed, but perceive not." (Isaiah 6:9).

People of Earth! "See with thine eyes, hear with thine ears, and understand with thy heart."

Footnotes

*   The matter itself is above, beyond, and beneath both the wavicular and corpuscular (particle) forms.

**   Wavicular means Temporal: for the moment; and particle (corpuscular) means the Timeless because it deposits, and because the corpuscular content is positive . . . it doesn't move.

***   This spotlight of consciousness is a sunlight by itself.

**** The copper results are related to the field of the multiple dimension.

*****   Ideas incorporated from *Beyond Grandeur*.

CHAPTER 5

THE AGENTS

Will everyone be contacted by space visitors? This question is often asked, as well as: "Why are some people contacted by the Saucer occupants and others not?"

These are good questions and deserve serious attention. Certain individuals are acting as Agents for space visitors, and may well have volunteered for this duty before taking up their present incarnation!

However, these *Agents* are not *Wanderers*. The latter belong to other worlds, whereas the Agents belong to Earth. The Wanderers bring the message of their people—the space people; the Agents carry the message of their people—the Earth people.

People of other worlds live among us and work among us unknown, but certain inhabitants of Earth are being contacted by Saucers—therefore, what is their mission? I remember what a radio operator who made contact via radiotelegraphy said: "Why should spacemen be interested in me; I'm a nobody, why don't they contact our great scientists and government heads?" I answered him by saying: "How do you know the so-called great haven't been contacted?"

This radio operator forgets that the space intelligences know more about him than he knows about himself. They have access to his complete record. And that means they know his attainments, his failures, his desires, his love and hate, his tenderness and cruelty. They know what they can and cannot expect of him. The individuals we call "great" in our present civilization may not be "great" at all in the light of their eternal record.

Space friends have said that high military rank; material wealth; talent; good-looks; social prestige, etc. are not prerequisites to being contacted by them. Some individuals who are considered by society to be "sinners" are not seen in that light at all by space visitors. "Sins" are offenses of social dictation and what may be a "sin" today may not be considered a "sin" tomorrow. If space visitors were here to contact only those who were "pure of heart" or those who diligently went to vespers or followed one-hundred percent the dictates of the church, they wouldn't find many people ready!

They say that the important thing is that we desire Light itself; and as we stand in that Light, drawing it to us, we attract these space friends. They will contact those who choose them only; and *The Agents* will be used to bridge the gap between the two divisions of outer space and the Earth. If one is more desirous of helping suffering humanity than of worldly fame or gain, then one is a good candidate for space intelligence contact.

It matters not if a man gets up from the lowest depths of human degradation and decides to follow the Great Path to Truth. He may not be as advanced as other souls, but *that first step* is the important step! He has decided to put on the Mantle of Seeking, and although he will suffer and die many times for the lesson, he does not hesitate in his decision—he has made that *first* step!

The space people who represent a higher authority have very well made plans and eventually every man, woman and child will have an opportunity to meet the visitors.

If we went to another planet we would first monitor the radio *broadcasts* if the people had advanced that far, and we would learn the language and code systems. Later, if we deemed it wise, we would contact individuals of that planet who were concerned with communications. A close friend of mine who is in the field of radio broadcasting, and at the present time employed by a well-known western radio station, wrote to me recently. Here is a significant part of his letter:

"I am doing a shift Saturday afternoons and nights, and Sunday mornings. I naturally open up and I am alone in the studio until about eleven in the morning. Well, last Sunday, I signed on at eight o'clock. After identification, with good mornings, etc., I logged a program called "Music For Sunday" from 8:05 a.m. After my opening theme on a 78 RPM disk, a short introduction, I faded out the theme and on another turn-table faded in a 12" 33⅓ RPM of Mantovani's Victor Herbert Concert. I still had my head-phones on because I was busy logging meter readings, etc. "At about 8:15 a.m., over the music, faintly, I heard the following: 'All is well, all is well, all is well . . . soon, soon, soon, brother, brother . . . all is well, all is well.' Needless to say, I was at first startled. I left the control room and started searching the entire studio to see if there was an open mike or if there was somebody around, checked to see if one of the several radios around the station was feeding back some other program, even went to the door to see if my car radio was playing. Everything checked out, and I returned to the control room and listened to the head-phones and again, faintly, I heard: "All is well . . . brother, brother, soon.'

"I thought maybe I was crazy, so I called several friends on the phone that I knew were listening to their radios and asked them if they had heard anything unusual along with the music. They all said, 'No!' Then I quickly grabbed the tape recorder and set it up in another studio, checked to make sure I had it hooked up O.K., and recorded the following: 'I am—, today is Sunday, January 24, 1954, I am at the studio on duty, Radio Station—. During the program (see our log) I heard a voice over my head-phone-set at approximately 8:15 a.m. and again at 8:21 a.m. It did not go over the air to other listeners. I checked all possible sources for feed backs and there were none; no other person within one-half mile of me. I will attempt to record the voice I just heard after station break and the start of the next, a recorded, "I then went back to the control room and made the station break, introduced and announced a fifteen-minute newscast, and at 8:45 a.m. started another fifteen-minute transcription which was a musical program. With an extension running from the control board, I took the head-phones to the other studio where I had the recorder set up. Then I listened to the program with the head-phones. At 8:50 a.m. I could hear the voice very faintly again and I brought the head-phones directly to the mike on the recorder and kept it there until 8:57 a.m.

"The rest of the morning I heard no more voices over the head-set. At my first opportunity, I played back the tape that I had made—and I got the whole thing! But, a half hour later when I went to play it again—only my voice was heard! The other voice simply didn't come through; and get this: *Neither did the music!*

"Now . . . before I left the studio at 1:30 p.m., I made a tape of commentary on world events to be played over the air at 3:00 p.m. the same day. It's a fifteen-minute commentary, mostly features that come over the AP teletype, which I edit and announce. On this tape, I talked for about five minutes on world affairs and then I related my experiences of that morning with the voices; this took up the next three minutes. Then I finished if off with Washington news.

"After making this tape, I took it to our auditioning studio and played it back for a check—and it was all there. However, and get this, when the tape came on the air at 3:00 p.m., my glorious voice came out with the world affairs, then there was about *three minutes of absolute silence*, followed by my Washington news! The rest of the gang saved that tape for me and I played it again the next morning. It was *complete* excepting my full account of Sunday morning's experience with the voices. Three minutes and twenty seconds of total silence in the middle of that tape!

"At first, I thought it might be some electronic error, that I was maybe picking up some 'ham' or something else; but after that series of strange happenings, I am of the firm belief that it was no 'ham' nor was it coincidence! What do you think?"

xThis young man is very interested in the Saucer phenomena. He and his good wife, only a few months ago, were "social climbers"; they thought the main goal in life was to own a "Cad", a diamond as big as an ice-cube, and eat caviar and hob-nob with the "best people". Lately, they have changed their minds. They realize that to help their fellowman means more than those material items. They have earnestly desired to have contact in some way with space intelligences. The answer to my friend's question, "What do you think?" is obvious.

The Agents are found in all walks of life and in all age groups. Sometimes they can be detected by the strange, far-away, glassy look in their eyes. Sometimes a muscle in their neck "throbs" or "jumps" spasmodically. This indicates that the individual is "under control" by space intelligences and at that time will be issued telepathic instructions. Some may say that this "control" takes away the free will of a man. However, this is not the case, since *The Agents* had free will before they volunteered for this duty. Once having volunteered, they set the course of their future; they were willing to be used as an instrument, and used they are. It is their duty to introduce certain people to each other, to be at certain lectures or meetings, to ask leading questions, to gather small groups around them, to give needed addresses, books, reports, etc. to those requiring them, etc.

The Agents are contacted through car radios, FM-radio, "ham" sets, AM-radio, portable radios, and, of course, by telepathy. And some are contacted by visual observation of spacecraft. Space friends have said: "Show us when you are ready to venture." An Agent merely has to show his desire to venture daringly into the New Order of things and his duties will begin at once!

Sanctilean University is speaking of *Agents* in *The Impending Golden Age*, when it says: "Many persons who regret the evil conditions now prevailing throughout the world, and their inability to do anything about them, have been placed in physical embodiment at this time as selected Students of Life."

The Agents serve the needy when they cry out; the poor also; and those who have no helper. They serve, for they are the helpers of the fatherless. Their prayer is: "Let us therefore come boldly unto the throne of grace, that we may obtain mercy, and find grace to help in time of need." (Hebrews 4:16).

The prayer of the people of Earth should be that of David the *Psalmist*: "I will lift up mine eyes unto the hills, from whence cometh my help." The help is from the sky and from the Earth.

CHAPTER 6

THE INTRUDERS

One of the enigmas of *The Saucers Speak!* was found in the following statement made by space visitors: "Evil planetary men, who abound, will attempt contact with evil men of Saras for destruction! The good men of Saras must unite with the good men of the Universe." Again, they said: "We must tell you about Orion. Many there wish to conquer the Universe. We are here to warn you of this also. The Orion solar systems are much like Saras. The principles of good (positive) and evil (negative) are Universal. We must tell you that Orion is coming soon to Saras in a square star body. Orion systems want to destroy—remember, Orion is evil (negative)."

To discover what space intelligences meant by use of the word "Orion" we must go to the Bible and to ancient records. In Job 38: 31-32, we read: "Canst thou bind the sweet influences of Pleiades (Cimah, or the seven stars), or loose the bands of Orion (Kesil)? Canst thou bring forth Mazzaroth (the twelve signs) in his season? or canst thou guide Arcturus with his sons?"

Here is the implication that the Pleiades sends forth vibrations of peace and love, and that Orion, because of opposite or negative vibrations has been bound. Chapter 38 of Job came to Job through the "Voice from the Whirlwind". "Which maketh Arcturus, Orion, and Pleiades, and the chambers of the south." (Job 9:9). There is an interesting cross-reference here to Genesis 1:16: "And God made two great lights; the greater light to rule the day, and the lesser light to rule the night: he made the stars also." The lesser light was for the rule of night or darkness, and the greater light was for the rule of the day or light.

"Seek him that maketh the seven stars and Orion, and turneth the shadow of death into the morning, and maketh the day dark with night: that calleth for the waters of the sea, and poureth them out upon the face of the earth: The Lord is his name: That strengtheneth the spoiled against the strong, so that the spoiled shall come against the fortress." (Amos 5:8-9).

In Amos, the same implication is found. At some time in the past Orion attempted to interfere with the Seven Stars (Pleiades) and was bound—but is now attempting to interfere on Earth. It appears that Orion tried to destroy the Pleiades at one time; they were in the "shadow of death" and Universal Law bound Orion. But Orion was only forbidden access to the Seven Stars of the Pleiades; his evil influence could still emanate to other sections of the Universe.

"The spoiled (Pleiades) were strengthened against the strong (Orion)". Orion in Hebrew is Kesil and means "strong." Then the spoiled (Pleiades) came against the fortress of the strong (Orion).

Another interpretation of Job 38:31 is: "Canst thou bind the sweet influences of Pleiades, or loose the bands (drawing together) of Orion?" *Moshekoth*, translated as "bands" means "drawings together". This refers to Orion's "drawing together" other planets into its own Confederation of Evil.

The constellation Orion takes its name from a giant hunter of Greek mythology. His sword hangs from his belt, and it is the middle star of the three in line in Orion's sword which appears a little too large and hazy to be simply a star—it is a nebula.

To understand the nature of the Orion nebula, the following general *information* is given:

Nebulae, as distinguished from ordinary star clusters, fall into two classes having entirely different characteristics, namely, the galactic nebulae and the extragalactic nebulae. Galactic nebulae are found within the galactic system and also in the exterior systems. Two types of nebulosity are found in the galactic system, the diffuse nebulae and the planetary nebulae.

Diffuse nebulae are of irregular form, and often of large angular dimensions. Some of them, like the Great Nebula in Orion, are faintly luminous. This great nebula is the brightest of the bright diffuse nebulae. The galactic nebulae are concentrated toward our own Milky Way Galaxy, unless they are members of other systems; they are clouds of gas and dust in the star fields.

Extragalactic nebulae are systems exterior to our own. These nebulae seem to avoid the region of the Milky Way, because they are generally obscured in these directions by the dark nebulae of our system, which congregate there.

The Great Nebula in Andromeda is an extragalactic spiral galaxy, whereas the Great Nebula in Orion is a vast, gaseous, galactic nebula—greenish and of irregular form.

Therefore, the nebula of Orion is within our own Galaxy and is a diffuse nebula. Since it is younger than Andromeda it is still in a gaseous state, whereas the latter is a spiral nebula. The fact that the planet Hatonn belongs to one of the star-suns of the galactic system of Andromeda indicates the greater age of this galaxy. The Universal Temple of Records is also located on Hatonn and only a world of great spiritual advancement could be so honored.

The negative space intelligences from Orion are not coming directly from the nebula itself, but are coming from planets of star-suns in the vicinity of Orion. The word "Orion" is used by space visitors to indicate the general area from which the evil influences originate.

Further confirmation of the Bible interpretation is found in mythology. Orion is the Mighty Hunter, the strong one. His aspect is so imposing in the sky, that in all peoples' legends he represents something great or giant.

In Greek mythology it was the vainglorious giant hunter Orion who boasted that no animal could be his match. His bragging excited the ire of Juno, who sent a scorpion to sting him mortally on his foot. In the sky, Orion is supposed to counter the attack of Taurus, the Bull (Venus). Also, according to the Greeks, the Pleiades were the Seven Daughters of the titan Atlas who were changed to doves when pursued by the giant Orion and finally were placed in the heavens. Before him (Orion) flee the Pleiades or the Singing Stars.

To the ancient Egyptians in the V Dynasty, the constellation of Orion was Sahu, hunting through the heavens for gods and men to rip apart and boil for food. The Hebrews knew it as Kesil, the Foolish or Self-Confident, or as Gibbor, the Giant, identified with Nimrod and tied to the heavens for impiety.

In the modern Arabic Orion is al-Babadur, the Strong, and al-Shuja, the Snake. In China the constellation is now Shen, to mix. Among the Buriats of Siberia Orion represents three wapiti being chased by the demon-hunter, Erlik-Khan, overlord of the underworld, and his three dogs. One of the wapiti has been wounded and is bleeding (red Betelgeuse). When the hunt ends, the world will cease to be.

A Peruvian story says this constellation is a criminal held in the heavens by two condors. In North Africa, the stars in Orion emerge from a muddy well, and Rigel, the last star to rise above the horizon, is the foot in the mud. To the Greeks, in addition to being the Mighty Hunter, Orion was called the Giant, the Warrior, the Cock's Foot, and the Double Ax.

From the time of Ovid and Hyginus, we have the story of how Orion was named. Hyrieus, Orion's father, had been childless, but he was a good man. One day he was visited by three strangers who were Zeus, Poseidon, and Hermes, in disguise, and he showed them unstinting hospitality. Granted a boon, he asked for a son, whereupon the three gods took an ox-hide and urinated on it. Hyrieus buried the hide according to instructions and, at the end of ten lunar months, Orion, or Urion after the fluid that made him, was born from the Earth.

The stranger-gods, the hero born of the liquid of the gods, the supernatural birth from the Earth: these are more serious matters than this almost flippant Roman myth makes them. Zeus was the sky god and could be symbolic of many planets in space, including the Earth. Poseidon was the god of the sea and is symbolic of Atlantis (Poseid) and Lemuria (Pan). Hermes was the winged god and messenger of other gods. The fact that the gods urinated in order to create Urion (later called Orion) shows that the waste of Earth and other planets (Zeus), and of Atlantis and Lemuria (Poseidon), and of angelic orders (Hermes), was used to populate originally the Orion worlds.

The "waste" were those souls who no longer could advance in these other areas. Remember, space friends have said: "To the slop we throw out we never return." The "slop" or "waste" was discharged or secreted into the Orion area—and the arriving souls had to begin the lessons of life over again. Only through countless experiences under the Orion vibrations could they discover the

Great Path. It is these souls we are dealing with when we speak of *The Intruders.*

The hide with the urine on it was buried in the ground. This means that the "waste" representing souls of the cast out ones was placed on Orion worlds—from this "waste" came forth the inhabited planets of the star-suns in the vicinity of the Orion nebula. These souls migrated to Orion, but in contrast with *The Migrants* who arrived on Earth, their abomination period was *before* the migration, and not *after* it.

In other versions of the Orion story, he is a son of Poseidon. This would indicate also that individuals from Atlantis (Poseid) migrated to Orion. It is believed that the good people escaped from Atlantis by spacecraft and went to the planet Mars while the evil destroyers lost their physical equipment in the sinking of the Lost Continent and migrated to Orion in spiritual form.

Myths of Orion's death vary. Does his death signify his being "bound"? He was bold enough to challenge Artemis to a contest in throwing the discus; or he tried to rape one of her maidens and so was slain by an arrow of the goddess. Or, she caused a scorpion to sting him, which is why Orion's constellation sets as Scorpio rises into the sky.

Since Artemis, in Greek religion, was known as a virgin goddess of nature, does this mean that Orion challenged nature? It is possible, for the discus is an ancient symbol of interplanetary Saucers. Perhaps Orion, like the doomed Lucifer, tried to exalt his throne above all others. Instead of hydrogen power utilized by Lucifer, Orion tried to subdue the Universe with spacecraft (discus), but in this contest nature (Artemis) won out. Or he tried to subdue (rape) one of nature's attributes (Artemis' maiden) and so was bound (slain) by a power or active (arrow) of nature (Artemis). Does this mean that Orion also tried to be the all-powerful one through the mastery of the "terrible wind"?

Scorpio is the Flying Eagle, and as already shown, is connected with Ezekiel's vision, St. John's Revelation, and the Tracks On The Desert. Is it any wonder that Orion sets as Scorpio rises into the sky?

Still another myth says that Artemis loved him so that she forgot her duties. Once, as Orion was swimming or wading far out in the sea, Apollo shone so strongly about him that he was a dark blur on the water. Then Apollo challenged Artemis to hit the vague mark. The unerring huntress immediately slew, unwittingly, the giant.

Does this mean that because of the experimentation of the Orion peoples, nature was perverted or "forgot her duties"? Apollo, symbolic of spacemen of the positive forces, "shone so strongly" about Orion that he was a "dark blur". Did the good forces (Apollo) gain complete control over the misused natural forces and thereby cause Orion to be slain (bound)?

The ancient inhabitants of Mesopotamia and India knew that Orion's early rising portended storms. Even today, this section of Creation is a stormy section—one that seeks to conquer, to subdue.

The Babylonian Talmud states: "If it were not for the heat of Orion the world could not exist because of the cold of the Pleiades; and if it were not for the cold of the Pleiades the world could not exist because of the heat of Orion."

This means that without positive and negative polarity there could be no creation. Without the evil (negative) Orion, the good (positive) Pleiades, would have no incentive to progress. 'The negative forces keep the positive forces in continuous spiral movement, otherwise there would be no advancement in the Cosmos. In fact, there would be no Cosmos!

Space intelligences have said: "Orion is the Great Hunter of the Universe. It is gorgeous in the skies and men of Venus know it very, very well. It is somewhat erratic, and like a Great Hunter it is always after its prey—especially Taurus the Bull. Orion is surrounded by small round ball bodies (Type 2 "fireballs"?); these are always in action between the Sun of our Solar System and Orion. No one on Earth has seen them yet. There are fighting worlds in Orion. They are always ready for action and looking for trouble. Orion disturbs other planets and keeps them from operating in the correct manner. Also, Orion is not too highly evolved scientifically because they use the old-style craft. However, they are masters at projection. Orion interferes and holds back. People of Orion are not our kind of people, they do not belong to our Confederation. They interrupt and are unruly. At present time there is a small group of people on Earth working for Orion. These people are sometimes small in stature with strange, oriental type eyes. Their faces are thin and they possess weak bodies. They come among you to disperse all things not in keeping with their own ideas; they upset our plans. They run amuck and we avoid them. They prey on the unsuspecting; they are talkative; they astound intellects with their words of magnificence. While their wisdom may have merit, it is materialistic, and not of pure aspiration toward the Father. We have our own men who watch over these pirates of Creation. They have their own Council and the Orion Confederation; but they know little through their own ingenuity for they are the Universal parasites! Disturbers, negative elements; soon they will be eradicated. Watch out for controlled persons in your midst. Our men will spot them and you will be informed of them. They come often in disguise, but men of the Confederation are never deceived. We know them! The Orion people are *The Intruders* in your world and they come from planets belonging to countless star-suns engulfed by the nebula of Orion. If the Orion men fail in their mission of disturbance, they return not to Orion, but to Sirius. This is their cycle of return. They must learn the Great Path—they will learn, but in the meantime, we will not have them disturb our preparations and plans for the Earth planet. We try to help them and suggest work to aid them, but they are a stubborn race. They cannot enter your atmosphere usually by spacecraft, but they can and do reach the Earth world by projecting their intelligence into weak Earthly bodies which they completely control for short periods of time in order to perform their disturbances. Watch for them; their numbers increase as the "sorrows" of Earth increase. They will persist, but they will not succeed—but we will succeed, for our mission is of the Father's authority and His will shall prevail. Worry not about these Orion influences; they cannot harm those who serve the Infinite Father. Pity them, love them, pray for them, for they know not what they do!"

The strange disappearance of two men on November 11, 1953, once again touched off the controversial issue of whether or not human beings are being snatched off the Earth by weird interplanetary flying machines. Many feared that the inexplicable levitations into the sky by invisible and unknown forces, sometimes accompanied by electrical or magnetic phenomena which science is powerless to explain, were caused by the visiting Flying Saucers.

Space friends are true friends! They are not subjecting captured men to vivisection or horrible death in monstrous spacecraft chambers of horror. With the power at their command they wouldn't be wasting their time with a mere handful of earthians. What then, are they doing? Certain people are disappearing; of that there is no doubt. Some are levitated into the sky, even in the presence of witnesses. Others never return from plane rides, and the wreckage is never found. Commercial and military planes crash and no bodies are discovered. What happens to the missing occupants?

On November 18, 1953, the Los Angeles Mirror reported that two missing electricians may have been *kidnapped* by interplanetary invaders in a Flying Saucer. The two Saucer enthusiasts were Karl Hunrath and Wilbur J. Wilkinson. They had taken off in a rented airplane from Gardena Airport on November 11th with a three-hour gas supply. Despite widespread search, no trace of the plane or its occupants has been seen. The rumor that the plane was found dismantled on the top of a California mountain with no sign of the two men is unfounded. Officials claim that nothing has turned up in the case as yet.

Wilkinson's wife told reporters that Karl Hunrath was an avid believer in Flying Saucers. She also told them that the two men believed the end of the world was nearing and that strange little men from the planet Mars or "Masar" were ready to invade us. Mrs. Wilkinson evidently misunderstood much of what Hunrath and her husband were doing and saying. First of all, the world is not going to end, and the "little men" are not from Mars or "Masar" but are from our own satellite, the Moon. The space visitors have proven this already by their actions.

Hunrath claimed to know the whereabouts of a Flying Saucer that had recently landed. Wilkinson's den was lined with Flying Saucer pictures, weird signs and formulas, which Mrs. Wilkinson said were supposed to be the new interplanetary language. "Of course, I don't quite go for all the Flying Saucer talk, but Karl convinced Wilbur they actually existed," said Mrs. Wilkinson. She then said, "Karl had tape recordings of conversations with men from other planets who landed here in Saucers." She showed reporters messages tacked on the wall of the den which were supposedly received by radio from the interplanetary visitors. One was from Regga of the planet Masar."

Karl Hunrath called up several of his acquaintances in Los Angeles the day before his disappearance. He informed them that he was going to take a trip. He said: "Others have left the Earth to go to other planets, so do not be surprised if I leave soon." The Flying Saucer pictures in the den had been taken by George Adamski, and the "weird signs and formulas" were received by our group working in Northern Arizona, starting in early August, 1952. The tape recordings that Hunrath had were taken during receptions of the Arizona research group.

In *Clips, Quotes and Comments*, B-10, May 15, 1954, a bi-weekly release of the Borderland Sciences Research Associates, correspondence of Mr. Harold T. Wilkins is quoted. Mr. Wilkins wrote: "It happens that I have spent years of research into petroglyphs and prehistoric symbols, in Central, South, and North America, and my tentative conclusions were that some of the Wilkinson glyphs suggested or resembled, not Maya or Aztec symbols, but forms found in the North Brazilian jungles, the Matto Grosso, and one in the unknown prehistoric civilization in La Plata Island, off Ecuador; another in California; and the ancient water sign of cataclysm. Also, another recalled the Mu-an sign of coition or the double uterus. How can the question be resolved when even the Los Angeles postal authorities do not know where Hunrath's family has gone? I know not how came Karl Hunrath or Wilbur Wilkinson to have all this very peculiar and recondite knowledge which cannot be picked up in a day, or even in a year . . ."

The symbols are not reworked Aztec figures, and Hunrath received them from our group for study purposes. That is why they were found in his and Wilkinson's den. These symbols are given in this book under *The Solex-Mal*, in the section called: *Other Tongues*. Much of this symbolism is characteristic of the ancient scroll writing of the Atlanteans and of the ancient pictographic writing of Lemuria. Atlantis and Mu used modified forms of the original Solex-Mal. Symbols of this type exist in South America, especially in the Matto Grosso because the ruins of great antiquity there were originally colonies of the Lost Continents. Colonel Fawcett, the famous English explorer died while attempting to locate these fabulous lost cities of the ancient "white" Indians of Brazil.

The Wilkinsons have three children and moved to Los Angeles from Racine, Wisconsin on June 28, 1953. Hunrath had been in correspondence with Wilbur and convinced him that he should come to the west coast because of important Saucer developments. Wilkinson was then employed by Hoffman Radio Corp., where he was quickly promoted to head of the inspection department.

Wilbur, who was thirty-eight, had his den and home full of all sorts of electronic equipment, radios, turn-tables, and tape recorders. Mrs. Wilkinson told reporters that her husband wasn't too interested in Saucers except when Hunrath was around. She said, "Karl was the one who talked us into coming to California because he said he could actually show a Saucer to Wilbur." She later told them: "I just can't help but think that Flying Saucers really had something to do with their disappearance."

I knew Karl Hunrath personally, but I never met Wilkinson. It was in the Winter of 1952 that I first met Karl at George Adamski's on Mt. Palomar. He claimed he had just arrived from the east where he had been working at Oster Mfg. Co. in Wisconsin. During the next few months he visited many Saucer researchers including: Frank Scully, Gene Dorsey, George Van Tassel, Gerald Heard, Mr. "R" of radio contact fame, and he was my house guest in Prescott, Arizona for a week. It was during his stay in my home that I gave him copies of our findings.

He was a strange man who would change his mind and ideas from one moment to the next. You couldn't help but like him, but at times a feeling would come over you that made you wish there were a million miles between yourself and Mr. Hunrath. Everyone who came in contact with him had the same experience. Was he controlled by Orion forces?

He visited Saucer researchers as a friend, then systematically began to spread rumors about them and their work which had no basis in fact. He came to California unknown and soon was stirring up dissension wherever he went. Was it his purpose to cause trouble in the "hot-bed" of controversy existing among the California Saucer enthusiasts? Was it part of a plan formulated by negative forces? Why was Hunrath a brilliant scientist one moment and a not too bright electrician the next?

Theories as to the present whereabouts of Hunrath and Wilkinson are plentiful. Some believe that he has gone to Mars or some other planetary "haven"—and there are many of Karl's "followers" in Los Angeles who will tell you that this is positively so! Several experienced pilots believe Karl cracked-up on the side of Big Bear—a rugged, mountainous area of California. The plane didn't carry much fuel, and Big Bear is deceiving to those who have not flown over it before. Hunrath hadn't flown in a long time, and he had never flown near Big Bear before. The down-draft and illusive qualities of the mountain could have doomed the small plane. However, the wreckage should have been discovered when the snow melted in the Summer of 1954. Some people think the two men went to Mexico, but they didn't have enough fuel for the trip. It has also been reported that Karl is in England and will reappear shortly, and also that he has been seen recently in Los Angeles with his hair dyed! He has been called a spaceman, a man possessed of evil spirits, an angel, a member of the F.B.I., and a Russian spy. What he really was no one knows—but we can guess.

What really happened to the two missing then and where are they now? It is not believed that space visitors had anything to do with their disappearance. Karl and Wilbur are not on Mars or any other extraterrestrial body; they are on Earth whether dead or alive. Here is an ad that appeared in the personal section of the Los Angeles Times on April 13, 1954. "Worried telepathists: This does it for you. Please prove my well being by writing of contacts you may recall." *Karl*, Box R-240, L. A. Times.

Biometrically, Hunrath does not show up as "unusual", but what samples were tested? Handwriting, etc. of Hunrath when he was himself, or when he was under control? This would make a vast difference in biometer results.

Before Hunrath arrived in California he had become acquainted with another so-called "genius" from Ohio. This man called Karl one night saying he had just returned from Japan where he had been working with Dr. Nagata on electromagnetic experiments. He asked Karl if he could come up to see him since he had heard that Karl was interested in magnetic research. The man came and he stayed four days and nights! When he left, Karl had become an avid Saucer enthusiast. Karl said he thought the man was a "spaceman" because he answered his questions before they were asked and displayed telepathic powers. This man also is very brilliant at times, and then again, at other times, he apparently can't even add two and two! This same man had an article printed in an Ohio newspaper stating that the Saucers were from Saturn and were here to invade and conquer the Earth! This is the pattern of *The Intruder*—to disrupt, cause dissension, strife, trouble, interfere!

In Florida there is a minister who claims the world is about to end, but he will sell any interested party a piece of land in the vicinity of Orion for a few dollars. How does he expect to get the buyers from the doomed Earth to Orion? And if the Earth is going to end, why does he want to accumulate the ready cash? Again, the word "Orion" gives him away. He is under negative control!

In *The Saucers Speak!* a Wyoming evangelist is quoted as saying that God's throne and God, himself, are located in the Orion nebula. Once again, the word tells the story. He preaches that the Flying Saucers are piloted by fork-tailed devils—another *Intruder!*

In Michigan a group of sincere researchers came in contact with a young man born in 1935 who claimed to be from another planet. He said he was born on Earth, but incarnated here from elsewhere. He was small in stature and possessed a weak, thin body. He drew intricate details of strange machines for scientists and claimed the information came from his mentor, a certain Kagmon from outer space. The machines utilized crystals, cosmic rays, and light was supposed to be changed into energy by the Kagmonian Process.

This young man had a brilliant mind—a little too brilliant for one of his years. At other times he was moody, sullen, and crude. Once again, the pattern of *The Intruders* is revealed. An astrologer who read his chart, said: "He has a very remarkable pattern, I might even say more complex than any I have seen in quite some time." Biometrically, this subject's devices are shown to be incomplete, and there remains much to be worked out.

This young man was in his glory when he could subjugate others to his whims and fancies. Once he said: "We have no emotion for earthlings." An intuitive psychic mentally received the word, "infringement" three times when she first met this man. This is only one of many cases of "Orion control" over Earth beings.

The space friends have said that they would keep out all the negative forces, but they also said a "square star-body" was coming to Earth. As time goes on, the anti-Christ or negative forces will become more powerful. This is a sure sign of the Second Corning.

At the present time, only projected intelligence into weak Earth minds is permitted. And even this would not be so if the victim refused to be used and put under "control".

The "square star-body" has been observed in recent months! On November 7, 1953, a man in Ohio was out in his greenhouse when suddenly he heard a strange "whirling" sound. At the same time the greenhouse lights dimmed. He ran outside and saw a thirty-foot long barrel-shaped object rush overhead and apparently land in the woods back of his house.

The man called for a state patrolman and they both saw the object through the trees as it had landed in a clearing. They went into the house to call for more help and when they returned, the strange craft was gone. Later, the man found that his wrist watch was magnetized and he had to replace all of the greenhouse lights.

The next day he walked to the clearing where the craft had landed and discovered several small footprints in the Earth. Other witnesses, also saw the footprints. The unusual thing about them was the fact that the right footprint was longer than the left!

Scientists from Washington, D. C. looked over the site shortly after the landing took place. The story was on radio, but minus the details, of course. Whether the object was barrel-shaped or not is not known, but it left a *square* impression on the ground! This same man claims he was taken to another world later in this craft, and his wife says he disappeared for a short while recently. He is a heavy drinker and, therefore, an excellent subject for Orion control. Maybe he did go to another planet—but which one?

When this man says he wants nothing more to do with his space visitors, does it mean his rational mind at times fights the control?

On Wednesday, May 5, 1954, at 9:30 p.m., Herbert Flick of Phoenix, Arizona saw what looked like a "flying boxcar" go over the valley. Flick said the object was *square*, with a light on each corner. "It went toward the South Mountains at a high rate of speed," he said, "then abruptly turned, came back and passed over me." He estimated the object was a least at an altitude of two-thousand five-hundred feet. He watched it for about eight minutes, then it disappeared, heading east. At one time he noticed the square craft neared him, slowed down, and circled as if observing something.

Mr. Flick says the object he saw was very large, it appeared to be piloted, and was black. It must have been traveling at about four-hundred fifty miles per hour. The object was not a radiosonde suspended from a balloon, nor was it an airplane or helicopter.

On June 19, 1954, a weird light so bright it was difficult to look at, moved slowly across the sky over Port Huron, Michigan. Selfridge Air Force Base officials and police had no explanation for the glow, which witnesses said looked *square*, and sometimes, barrel-shaped. The object passed high in the sky and moved very slowly. It appeared at 5:00 a.m., and disappeared to the west at 6:30 a.m. The brightness of the light was compared by police to the glow of an acetylene torch. Hundreds of residents viewed the craft, and police phone lines were busy for hours handling calls from worried citizens.

A man and his wife in Iowa saw a *square*, brilliant object pass overhead from west to east. They claim it was very high and was moving slowly.

Oahspe speaks of "arrow ships" and "fire ships" and "crescent ships". It also mentions Orion ships in 49.18: "Thus Ah'shong, well skilled in the course and behavior of worlds, gathered together his millions of angels, trained in arduous enterprise and furtherance of Jehovih's will. Quickly they framed and equipped an *Orian* (Orion) port-au-gon, and illuminated it with fire-lights and bolts. A half a million miles, even on the outskirts of Anakaron, and they stood close above the earth, almost so near that the sweeping moon would touch the down-hanging curtains of etherean fire. And here they halted, that both mortals and angels belonging to the earth might behold and fear . . ."

The "Serpent People" of ancient legend are believed to have been Orion intelligences projected earthward. Is the fabulous "Rainbow City" under the Antarctic regions a central location for such projections? "Serpent People", "Anti-Christs", or *Intruders*— they all represent the same thing: negative polarity.

In ancient times man ran away from demons, devils, witches and monsters; today he still runs away from that which he calls the *unknown*. Many people remember the H. G. Wells' book, *War Of The Worlds*, or the masterpiece by another Welles named Orson about an invasion from Mars that frightened a good many radio listeners a little over a decade ago. However, there is no reason to be frightened about space "kidnapers", for the levitations are not always due to Saucer phenomena. Some of the disappearances have to do with other dimensions of time. When the Saucers pick up some-one from the Earth they are only picking up their own!

Farmers have been working in their fields, when suddenly they start to go straight up into the air. The only thing ever seen in connection with such levitation is a blinding flash of light that appears directly overhead and moves away swiftly.

On Glastenbury Mountain, near Bennington, Vermont, five persons vanished without a trace. Near Schaffausen, Germany, four men disappeared in a single day. Three of the levitations were witnessed by others, and all missing persons ascended straight up with great rapidity.

At Pillitsfer, Livonia, there were eight human ascensions in two hours. Near Perhawar, India, there were six ascensions, all witnessed by large groups of people, over a period of six months.

One of the most astounding levitations was that of the sixty-ton coastal schooner Maida in the Bay of Bengal several years ago. The ship was almost completely lifted out of the water, held there for a minute, and then allowed to fall back into the water with a great splash. There were many witnesses to this happening, and the day was clear and calm.

Every year there are literally thousands and thousands of human disappearances, and each year thousands remain unsolved. No trace of them is ever found. Many people who disappear, such as criminals, wanderers, dissatisfied husbands, etc., are recognized later even though they may be living under different names in far-away places. The bodies of murder victims are usually always found. So, thousands of human beings are going somewhere.

Recently, someone said: "The purpose of the kidnapping is to obtain human specimens for laboratory experimentation; the final object being the conquest of the Earth and the subjugation or destruction of all humanity."

If the Saucer people are intelligent enough to come to us across the great space frontier I doubt very much if it would take hundreds of years to make their surveys. Levitations have been going on for centuries. It has been argued that the kidnappings are necessary because conditions are quite different on other worlds and therefore space visitors must study our atmosphere, our germ life, and, of course, they must study *us*.

It would not take very long to accomplish such a task, and besides, the Saucer intelligences have said that living conditions are not very much different on other worlds than on our own. True, there are differences, just as there are on our own Earth; but they are not as great as present-day science believes. When we think of laboratory analysis we think of our own standards according to our understanding at this time. Vivisection is not necessary for study according to space visitors. They have greater developments for the study of everything; they do not destroy the created beings of the Infinite Father. They never kill! Even the thought of killing is abhorrent to them.

Therefore, the Orion forces are not kidnapping people from Earth. Their only power is through "projected intelligence" and their square star-bodies may be observed more and more in the future, but they can do no harm to those who refuse to be influenced by them. Levitations and other disappearances are due to time factors and space friends picking up their own people to take them home again.

Recently, astronomers discovered that two stars were born in the Orion Nebula. These young stellar twins are symbolic omens of things to come from that section of Cosmos; but the Infinite Father is with us and Orion shall be "bound" again as he was in the past.

We need not concern ourselves with *The Intruders*, "for they are the spirits of devils, working miracles, which go forth unto the kings of the earth and of the whole world, to gather them to the battle of that great day of God Almighty." (Revelation 16:14). Isaiah 41:29 says: "Behold, they are all vanity; their works are nothing: their molten images are wind and confusion." These are *The Intruders!*

CHAPTER 7

THE GUESSERS

To give a numerical estimate I would say that rather more than a million stars in the Milky Way possess planets on which you might live without undue discomfort. If you were suddenly transported to one of them you would no doubt find many important changes, but the changes would not be as remarkable as the similarities. I think that all our present guesses are likely to prove but a very pale shadow of the real thing." From *The Nature of the Universe*, by Fred Hoyle, English astronomer.

Scientists of today claim that the Earth's neighborhood of nearby planets is rather slummy. Of course, they still like to think that the planet Earth is the center of the Universe: here the Creator placed his greatest creation, Man! The other worlds are "slummy", created only for man's amusement and entertainment.

They are dreaming (and what dreams!) of a satellite space station that will dominate the world. Every two hours it would circle the Earth, and as the Earth turns below it, every part of its surface would come into view. This station would be useful for launching atom-armed guided missiles. Once a great supply of such missiles had been put on the station, potential aggressors below would be forced to keep the global peace. However, it doesn't seem likely that the first government placing a space station in our skies will be working for "global peace". It will control the entire world for its own benefit. Besides, "peace is not for the strong"; we will never have peace through "force".

The space station would have little military value, say some scientists like Dr. Milton Rosen of the Naval Research Laboratory in Washington, D. C. Equipping it to make observations would be exceedingly difficult, and any missiles it might drop would be lucky to hit the right country. Space travel will have to wait until the scientists have made some basic discovery equal in novelty to Faraday's discovery of electro-magnetism. They say a beam of high speed particles pushed at close to the so-called speed of light by nuclear energy might do the trick. No one yet has the foggiest idea about how to do it. Men like Dr. Rosen realize what is necessary before space travel is a reality on Earth. "A basic discovery equal in novelty to Faraday's discovery of electro-magnetism" would be the utilization of the Fourth Great Primary Force, or the RMF. The Earth is under what we might call a "Divine Quarantine". A rocket or nuclear driven space ship will go from the Earth to the Moon, but it will never go through the cleavage layer of the Earth's Resonating Electro-Magnetic Field. This cleavage layer is called "chinvat" in *Oahspe*. It divides the Earth's rotating field (which contains the Earth and the Moon) from the ether, or outer spaces. We will not be able to leave the RMF of the Earth until we have discovered the secret of magnetic propulsion, and we aren't going to discover that until we accept higher metaphysical principles. In other words, man on Earth simply can't go to other worlds until he advances spiritually—his own ignorance of the eternal verities has him "quarantined".

Dr. Wehrner von Braun, Germany's rocket expert in World War II, says: "What the United States needs is a daring, inspiring program (probably the same thing he told Hitler) that has a real chance of controlling the world. Atom bombs carried by air-planes are nearly worn out as war preventers. Guided missiles are important weapons, but the Russians are working on them too. A satellite station would put the U. S. far ahead in the *race for power*. Even a small satellite could be made to shine at dusk. It could inflate a plastic balloon which would gleam as brightly in the sunlight as a first-magnitude star. This 'American Star', rising in the west, should make a powerful impression on the peoples of Asia. A special commission should be set up to study the whole matter, of course. The public will not be told the decision of such a commission. To announce even its yes or no would reveal the summation of many military secrets. If the decision is yes, the first news for the public may be an 'American Star', rising in the west and sweeping swiftly across the sky."

This happened before when the first news the American public had regarding Atomic Bombs was after the first one had been exploded over Japan, ushering in the "Atomic Age" that was born in New Mexico. The people were not consulted on this matter, either. There was a chance that a chain reaction might have been set off and the entire world destroyed. The chance was a slim one, but nevertheless, a definite chance. Should so much power and authority to decide these grave matters rest in the hands of a few? Who is making these decisions? Are the same "black magicians" who destroyed other great civilizations back in life today? Are they the "mad scientists" of our time?

Men steeped in militarism, dedicated to war and its results, are the men who control atomic power! Few military men can be "Doves of Peace" when their very occupation depends on war. Without war there is no longer any need for the military, the manufacturer of ammunition, tanks, weapons, guided missiles, aircraft, etc. War certainly is not the joy of grieving mothers, widowed wives, or orphaned children. Every nation on Earth is controlled by men who are lovers of themselves only, full of vanity and pride, seekers of material wealth and glory, not performing their duties in a humble fashion as servants of the people, but indulging in madness that would bring complete destruction to all civilization on Earth. But this will not be allowed to happen!

Benjamin Franklin once said: "Gentlemen, we give you a Republic; now try and keep it." The question is: Have we kept it?

The militarists and the international bankers cry out: "Peace is for the strong! Unite, build bigger bombs, better missiles, make monsters of hate out of the young men, kill and destroy . . ." The voice from the pulpit cries out: "To live by the sword is to die by the sword!" The measure to use in determining whether any nation is truly Christian or not is whether that nation follows the Christ.

"But I say unto you, That ye resist not evil: but whosoever shall smite thee on thy right cheek, turn to him the other also." (St. Matthew 5:39).

"He that killeth with the sword must be killed with the sword." (Revelation 13:10).

Did America "turn the other cheek"? We rained terror and desolation upon the heads of our enemies resulting in the worst holocaust in the history of mankind. The strong will not rule in the New Age.

"Blessed are the meek: for they shall inherit the earth." (St. Matthew 5:5).

History proves that every nation and empire that ever existed fell when it thought it would surely be eternal because of its particular brand of strength. The Third Reich was to last one-thousand years—it lasted less than two decades. People of the world must open their blinded eyes: we are not on the road to peace! Those who wish to enslave us belong to the "hidden empire" and control us without our knowledge. They give us "darkness for light". Theirs is the path of destruction and annihilation.

America does not need a space station and she does not need to control the world. America needs God! The impression we need to make on the peoples of Asia is the impression of brotherly love, not that we possess bigger and better weapons!

Why haven't the "powers that be" announced what they know about the Flying Saucers? If they acknowledge extraterrestrial origin, it would mean that they must acknowledge extraterrestrial allegiance as well. There would be extraterrestrial interference with established government, and no world power would welcome such a situation. If Universal truth came to the people of Earth, their schemes and plans for mankind would crumble. No longer could they exploit the masses. They would be caught "with their pants down"; their veil of "security" would be lifted and the picture would not be a pretty one that appeared to the eyes of the people.

Who among us likes to feed the pigs? Or give to selfish people representing powerful selfish interests, even though their representatives come riding in Cadillacs and dressed in striped pants with top hat and carnation? Space intelligences see through all selfishness; smell it as we smell intoxication corning down the street. They prefer to deal with men who have a bare minimum of previous obligation to this or that cause and a maximum of obligation to all the Universe. Who will fulfill these obligations faithfully and efficiently?

Firecrackers are appropriate for children; revolvers and machineguns for so-called responsible men; but atomic powers require atomic men for their good and long continued use. New and greater powers generate new and greater responsibilities which require wisdom, intelligence, and character commensurate with them.

There is a *"race for power"*—who will get to the moon first? What half of the world will enslave man's thoughts in the future? Does it matter to the people whether they are dominated from the Earth or the Moon? The fact remains that they are not given information; they are not consulted on important issues that might mean life or death; and they are led to war like steers to slaughter. Does America wish to be a "Columbus" to the unknown worlds? To lead peoples to their conquest? To add another name to those of the forty-eight states that comprise the Union? Take possession of the other worlds in the name of the United States? To colonize them? To cultivate them? To people them? To transport thither all the prodigies of art, of science, and industry; and to constitute them a republic, if they are not already one? I fear for the natives of these unknown worlds considering our own history. The so-called "primitive people" of our own planet have undergone brutality at the hands of their earthly brothers. Their lands have been stolen outright; their ways of life destroyed. Would people of other planets be treated even as kindly? Man's inhumanity to man—when will it cease?

The idea of extending our own violence into outer space is at this moment circulating all over the planet Earth. The same pulp magazines that are influenced by creative space intelligences print monstrous tales inspired by the opposite, or negative forces. Scientific articles published in leading journals add to the power of confusion. If man on Earth can conquer space, then he will extend his miseries to the Universe. Humanity, now having sufficiently corrupted this planet wishes to spread its poisons to larger areas. The vast astronomical distances which are God's "quarantine" regulations must somehow be overcome.

A wild dream that planet after planet, system after system, and in the end, galaxy after galaxy can be forced to come under the dominion of the planet Earth. The destruction or enslavement of other men in the Universe: this is the "noble" goal. First they say other worlds are uninhabited "balls of gas"; yet, they plan to travel to such "worthless" worlds. What good would it do to go there in the first place if this were true?

If men on Earth make it to Mars, there will undoubtedly be a West Mars and an East Mars. The American and British Zones and the Russian Sector, of course! What a dither the United Nations would be in! Who is going to own which planet? Will Russia try to take Jupiter by force?

In *Collier's* magazine for March 22, 1953, there was an article called: *Who Owns The Universe?* by Oscar Schachter, Deputy Director, Legal Department, United Nations. He said: "Now that scientists have shown that man can conquer space and that new worlds lie within his reach, the question of 'owning' the moon and the planets no longer seems to be so much of a joke. Today, the question is not at all far-fetched and, in fact, it may well have important consequences for all of us.

"Will governments claim 'ownership' (or, more correctly sovereignty) of the moon and other celestial bodies, just as claims today are being made to the barren wastes of the Antarctic? Will there be national rivalry to plant the 'Stars and Stripes', the 'Union Jack' and the 'Hammer and Sickle' far off in space, so that the governments can then assert exclusive control and keep others away? A conflict may arise when the first rocket ships reach the moon and other celestial bodies. The old story of territorial rivalry; but this time extended into the heavens themselves.

"Although we have been talking about outer space, we have said nothing about where outer space begins; or to put it in another way, how far up does the territory of a country extend? Whenever a country could prevent or interfere with the movement of a rocket ship or space station it would have the legal right to do so. Would this not, in effect, simply be a rule that 'might makes right'? And would it not place rocket ships and space stations at the mercy of those national states which would be able to interfere with their free passage? Beyond the airspace we would have to apply a system similar to that followed on the high seas."

The above quotation is ludicrous in the extreme! In answer to the question: "To what tribunal would questions of space law be referred?" Mr. Schachter says: "A dispute in space that involved two or more governments could be submitted to the International Court of Justice at the Hague, just as international disputes are today."

What a surprise is in store for those who would put their "brand" on the Universe—a much higher authority exists in outer space!

On Sunday, September 27, 1953, the Los Angeles Examiner ran an article called: *Mars . . . Target For Tomorrow.* It said, in part: "Man is almost ready to leave his home of a million years . . . the Earth . . . and venture restlessly to other worlds . . . into space, to the Moon . . . and then to Mars."

First of all, the Earth hasn't been "home" to man for a short million years—millions would be more like it. More *guessing* without a shred of evidence to back it up. Yes, man "ventures restlessly" to conquer all space, to spread his disease, his war, his greed, to other worlds. Dr. von Braun, creator of the German V-2, and now director of the United States Army's guided missiles development project, says: "Man *wasn't* built to leave the Earth!" He is quite right; man wasn't built to leave the Earth in space ships that will "blast off" for this or that celestial body. Everything man creates on Earth is created through force. He hammers, he tears, he rivets, he pounds; now he's going to "blast off" to other worlds. He thinks by the use of brute force he's going to be Lord of Creation. When he learns to use natural forces and not fight them he will have found the key to space travel, indeed, a "key" to many things. The rock on which many scientists have wrecked their ships is materialism. In their studies they have eliminated forces and their workings, saying: "A force is the result of atomic movements." This is true; all forces are—except the Force which *first* starts atomic movement.

In 1950, a book was published called: *The Conquest Of Space*, by Chesley Bonestell and Willy Ley. Ley also wrote, *Bombs and Bombing*, and *Shells and Shooting*. Therefore, he should be an expert on "Conquest Of Space".

Ley says: "The high temperature of the moon-day increases the velocity of the hydrogen molecule to above the moon's escape velocity."

If this hydrogen escapes into space, where does it go? Since the escape velocity from the moon is the same for a space ship or for hydrogen, if a ship which reaches the "dividing line" or neutral point between the Earth and the Moon falls Moonward after crossing that line, and the Moon's gravitational force takes over, the same would apply to the hydrogen atoms escaping from the Moon, and they would be drawn to the Earth. Or, do they fall back and orbit as a band around the moon?

Ley says the modern astronomer, or rather his helper from the field of physics, also knows why the Moon is airless, in fact he can prove that it was "always" without air. The realization that the Moon must have lost its atmosphere quickly (although it presumably had a gaseous envelop for some time during the early days of its career) led to Simon Newcomb's famous statement that the Moon is a world without weather on which nothing ever happens. Newcomb may not have meant it literally, and it is not literally true. There is a strange kind of "weather" on the Moon, caused by the same factors which removed the weather we know, the weather caused by air and moisture.

How could the Moon have "always" been with-out air if it at one time during its career had air and moisture? *The Guessers* are so contradictory.

Ley says the temperature range on the Moon, from lunar midday to lunar midnight, amounts to almost four-hundred degrees Fahrenheit. Rocks exposed to such temperature changes at regular two-week intervals will crack. Their *crystalline structure* will give way under repeated expansion and contraction and the surface will flake off. Incidentally, the brightness of the Moon and a few other factors, support the assumption that the Sun's light is reflected by pulverized basalt or similar rocks.

If their assumption is correct, that the Sun's light is reflected from the Moon, by basalt or similar crystalline rocks, then the natural disintegration of those rocks will release tremendous quantities of hydrogen and oxygen. This also proves that the Moon has an atmosphere! Any mineralogist will confirm the fact that all crystalline structure contains hydrogen and, or oxygen.

Ley says sunrise over the large crater of Plato is just like sunrise over any other crater. But as the dividing line between darkness and light, the terminator, advances, the floor of Plato grows darker. At high noon it looks like an inkspot. What happens in the crater of Plato? Evaporation of moisture forming a light-absorbing mist? Or just melting ice? Or crystals with freakish optical qualities?

Professor William H. Pickering thinks he saw a snowstorm on Mount Pico. And he repeatedly observed grayish spots moving around inside the crater. Cloud formations betraying the presence of moisture? Or vegetation springing up and being killed off by the heat of the Sun in a rapid cycle?

Once again, here is an obvious contradiction.

How can you have thermal erosion and not have an atmosphere?

Ley says the first era of astronomy was naked-eye observation, the second era is telescopic observation, and the third era will be spaceship exploration. Astronomy, he says, confirms first-era knowledge by optical instruments, but it is less definite in its conclusions regarding the questions poised by the telescope— mostly concerning the surface conditions of planets. This is an admission that they know very little. Ley says several times: "We will know such and such when we get there." Until then, Mr. Ley, you are a *guesser*.

Ley says: "Oh, we are sure about a number of things. Take Venus, for example. It is almost a second Earth as far as size goes. Its diameter is only two-hundred miles less than that of Earth. The mass is eighty per cent of that of our rather massive home planet. The albedo is fifty-nine per cent, the highest albedo in the Solar System. Venus most decidedly has an atmosphere. The Venus year is 224.7 of our days long, a fact easily explained by the tighter orbit and higher orbital velocity. Venus' orbit is the most clearly circular one in the whole Solar System and the disk of Venus the most nearly perfect circle; it does not show any traces of an equatorial bulge."

That short paragraph contains the sum total of the definite knowledge science has about the planet which approaches us more closely than any other! You are "sure" about some things, Mr. Ley? A *guesser* is never "sure" of anything.

Now let's take a look at the instruments used for modern astronomical observation. There are four of these; all based on variations on the principle of the human eye. (1) Telescope; (2) camera; (3) thermocouple; (4) spectroscope.

The spectroscope is an instrument that measures the wavelengths of the chemical elements when they are heated to a gaseous state and observed through a set of prisms.

Many scientists have used spectroscopic analysis as proof of the other planets being unable to support life. To what degree can spectroscopic analysis be relied upon?

The following examples are given to show the contradictory nature of findings:

According to Belopolsky, Venus rotates in about twenty-four hours, as determined by the spectroscope. However, according to Dr. Slipher, Venus rotates in about two-hundred twenty-four days, as determined by the spectroscope.

According to observations too numerous to mention, the seeming motions of stars, occulted by the Moon, show that the Moon has an atmosphere. According to the spectroscope, there is no atmosphere on the Moon.

The ring of light around Venus, during the transits of 1874 and 1882, indicated that Venus has atmosphere. Most astronomers say that Venus has an atmosphere of extreme density, obscuring the features of the planet. According to spectrum analysis, by Sir William Huggins, Venus has no atmosphere.

Spectroscopic examinations of Mars, by Dr. Campbell, Director of Lick Observatory, showed that there is no oxygen, and that there is no water vapor on Mars. Spectroscopic examination of Mars by Huggins shows abundance of oxygen and water vapor— the same as the planet Earth.

Most astronomers agree, however, that there is water on Mars and that it has an atmosphere. Yet they have had no success in using the spectroscope and only a few vacuum thermocouple readings have produced heat measurements. Astronomers are even in disagreement with each other on the topography of Mars even though it is the most easily viewed of all planets from the Earth. Guesses and more guesses!

Charles Fort, who showed up the spectroscope for what is really is, said: "When anything new appears, for which there is no convention, the bewilderment of the astronomers is made apparent, and the worthlessness of spectroscopy in astronomy is shown to all except those who do not want to be shown."

Ley says: "The hard work in spectroscopy is the proper application of the principle. At first, most of the hard work consisted of finding out by experiment which element, what lines, and where; and what the gases of the atmosphere through which light passed did to the lines originally contained, and so forth. And now the hard work consists mostly in untangling lines. Only a very few elements produce just a few lines; most of them cause whole sets. And one of the lines of element A is only too likely to obscure a line of element B, which in turn and in wonderful collaboration with element A, may blot out the lines of element C and D."

Since there are many elements in our atmosphere, how are we to be sure that the spectroscope is giving us a true picture? Might not the hydrogen we see on the Sun be in our own atmosphere?

Those who say that astronomy, physics and mathematics are "true and pure" science need to investigate the situation more thoroughly. An English astronomer, John Robinson, is not afraid to come to grips with the most modern theories and searchingly analyze them. For example, he strikes a blow to the theory that the planet Venus may be a dust-bowl instead of a cloud-enshrouded planet. The Dust Bowl theory is based on the spectroscopic examination of the upper atmosphere of Venus which reveals no water-vapor and quantities of carbon-monoxide at that level. Robinson points out that at seventy miles above the surface of the Earth the atmosphere contains no oxygen or water vapor at all, and that the atmosphere is almost one-hundred per cent hydrogen, an entirely unbreathable and highly inflammable gas. The Earth nevertheless teems with life despite the fact that there is no oxygen and water-vapor in the outer four-hundred miles of its atmosphere. All oxygen, water-vapor, and hence life exist only within a few miles of the surface. Robinson says: "It is the bottom layers of atmosphere rather than the top ones which decide the habitability of a planet. Living creatures live and breathe in the lowermost layers of atmosphere next to the solid surface. It is the composition of these strata that counts and not the composition of those ten or a hundred miles up." Robinson's book, *The Universe We Live In*, should be read by everyone for it proves that science is not "pure" anything except *guesswork*.

Dr. William A. Baum of the Mount Wilson and Palomar Observatories and Dr. A. D. Code of the Washburn Observatory, Madison, Wisconsin, recently announced that Jupiter's atmosphere is made up largely of hydrogen and helium, not methane and ammonia as was previously thought. However, these scientists believe because of the discovery of hydrogen and helium on Jupiter, the heavier gases, such as nitrogen and oxygen that make up the Earth's atmosphere are nearly absent on Jupiter. But Robinson has shown us that at seventy miles above the surface of the Earth there is neither nitrogen nor oxygen and the atmosphere is nearly pure hydrogen. Therefore, Jupiter is similar to the Earth and we can expect to find living creatures close to the planet's surface as we do here.

Once the "true and pure" science said methane, now they say hydrogen. *True and pure?* By whose criteria?

James Rainwater and Val Fitch of Columbia University say that the nucleus of the atom is some fifteen to twenty per cent smaller in diameter and about twice as dense as had been supposed. Since a fifteen per cent reduction of the diameter of a sphere reduces its volume almost by half, the nuclear particles must be crammed into about half the space they had been thought to occupy. The "true" science of physics admits to one-hundred per cent error!

University of California and Australian astronomers now believe the Universe is *double* the formerly accepted size. Another one-hundred per cent error! However, such inconsistencies are phenomena of all transitions from the old to the new. And shortly "all things shall be made new."

The Guessers dedicated to experimentation in nuclear energy are not bringing us "peace in our time", but are trying to pass off their mass murders as war. Their boast is that this year they can kill more people in one second than all the rest of Earth's scientists put together in one year, or all the years of Earth's history. Atomic war has no remedy—that is why *The Harvesters* are here!

On March 10, 1922, at the Franklin Institute, Philadelphia, Pennsylvania, Prof. Francis William Aston warned mankind in a lecture against what he called "tinkering with the angry atoms". Aston was the famous British Nobel-prize-winning chemist. His words on that occasion have a strange prophetic ring: "Should the research worker of the future discover some means of releasing this energy from hydrogen in a form which could be employed the human race will have at its command powers beyond the dreams of scientific fiction, but the remote possibility must always be considered that the energy, once liberated, will be completely uncontrollable and by its violence detonate a neighboring substance. If this happens, all of the hydrogen on Earth might be transformed into helium at once, and this most successful experiment might be published to the rest of the Universe in the form of a new 'star' of extraordinary brilliance, as the Earth blew up in one vast explosion."

Other well-known scientists have said that here is a power to return the Earth to its lifeless state of billions of years ago. Dr. Albert Einstein said: "The hydrogen bomb appears on the public horizon as a probably attainable goal (now reality). If successful, radioactive poisoning of the atmosphere, and hence annihilation of any life on Earth, has been brought within the range of technical possibilities." This has also been explained by such eminent physicists as Dr. Bethe, Dr. Leo Szilard, Dr. Edward Teller, and others.

Radioactive material is carried by winds, taking it thousands of miles, carrying death to distant places. Dr. David Bradley says: "I have emerged with the firm conviction that if life as we know it is to continue, man must understand and deal with the menacing aspects of atomic energy. It is perfectly clear that nature had no intention that any of her children should be monkeying around with radioactive elements, else she would have provided us with some sixth sense to protect us from running headlong into dangerous amounts of radiation. No, she evidently expected us to take our daily dose of cosmic and Earth's radiation as we take the cuts and bruises of ordinary living. The idea of getting them out in the form of concentrated extracts was man's."

In *The Hell Bomb*, William L. Laurence says: "No matter how one looks at it, the advent of the H-Bomb constitutes the greatest threat to the survival of the human race since the Black Death. Peace, step by step, appears to be the only alternative to possible catastrophe."

A message received months ago at Giant Rock, California, said: "The increase in the explosive power of nuclear devices has reached a critical limit. Every explosion brings about interruption of the lines of force maintaining equilibrium of your planet. Every explosion charges your breathable atmosphere with radioactive particles that will not lose their penetrating qualities for several thousand years."

Government scientists are discovering that atomic explosions at sea make eating tuna and other large ocean fish very dangerous. Also, atomic detonations are mussing up the radioactive dating of the recent past. The Type 1 "fireball" has nullified much of the deadly radiation in our atmosphere, but there is still enough to cause strange changes around the world. Although hydrogen detonation will never be allowed, atomic war would mean the world would emerge from its darkness and terror and in the gray light the wretched survivors would look upon the battered wreckage of a civilization that has crumbled to ruin in a matter of a very short time—self destruction that wise men had warned the world against since the days of Nagasaki and Hiroshima.

Those who are "experts" and "authorities" of guesswork hold the fate of the Earth in their hands. But assistance has come from outer space, and no longer will they be allowed to function as the self-appointed guardians of mankind.

In Proverbs 24:2, we read: "For their heart studieth destruction and their lips talk of mischief." These are *The Guessers!*

CHAPTER 8

THE REMNANT

"His lightnings enlightened the world: the earth saw, and trembled." (Psalms 97: 4).

The "lightnings" of the Creator have been observed for thousands of years and at last, in the Aquarian Age, Man is beginning to respond to their message.

Theological dogma has enslaved mankind as it pictures "heaven" as a place where those who have been true to church tenets will be led by the hand of the Master into shaded groves and there left for eternity to rest and meditate on the harp-playing "angels" singing praises unto the Father.

Needless to say, this is not the case when we consider the reality of "heaven". However, it is natural for man to picture the after-life in this manner, for he constantly hopes to be rid of the materialistic pursuit of lucre and fame. Love for money there is, but only as a means of his attaining freedom to do what he wants when he wants it. But man is never satisfied with "inactivity"; men who retire almost invariably get active again in some way. And when we think of an eternity of "idleness", it becomes ridiculous to say the least.

To picture the "many mansions" our Infinite Father has prepared for us as rest homes where men lie about in a state of morbid drowsiness or lethargy, is both childish and an insult to our Creator. People who really think, will never entertain such thoughts for a moment.

The Aquarian Age then, is not going to see a decline of inventive activity or pursuit; the Master is not going to abolish everything except a picnic-society that drives the Father to distraction with all-sung hymns!

The Father's "mansions" are bee-hives of activity, where each individual is working out his destiny and serving his fellowman to the best of his ability. Our "heavenly" reward in the Golden Times will be the opportunity for more and more expressive labor in order to better serve ourselves and others. Harp-playing forever? I'm afraid not. That would soon become "hell", as anyone knows who has been forced to practice music lessons day in and day out. Man needs intense activity and the opportunity to expand his consciousness. Working at something you despise in order to eat, of course, is something else; and living to work, or working to live will cease as such. Every person has something wonderful to contribute to society, and many times in our present setup these persons never get a chance to present their talents to the world because of the faulty economic practices of today.

The New Age will see a great theological upheaval. Dr. Harry Emerson Fosdick said: "A religious reformation is afoot, and at heart it is the endeavor to recover for our modern life the religion of Jesus as against the vast, intricate, largely inadequate and often positively false religion about Jesus. Christianity today has largely left the religion which He preached, taught and lived, and has substituted another kind of religion altogether. If Jesus should come back to earth now, hear the mythologies built up around him, see the creedalism, denominationalism, sacramentalism, carried on in His name, he would certainly say, 'If this is Christianity, I am not a Christian.'"

In 1945, a minister in Wisconsin: "For years I have seen it coming: a new world system. I have watched as one by one my visions became visible in the affairs of the world. A complete turn about; a whole new setup. There will be a new world religion modeled upon a basic formula, and people will respond willingly, for it will be a soul religion as well as an intellectual one. The dry and parched souls of the people will be drawn into the peace and freedom, and blossom as the rose. No one shall hurt his neighbor, but man will feel deeply that he is his brother's keeper. The new religion will fill the need of every living soul, and as a result of the freedom from fear of the unknown, health will come to all as a divine heritage and man will adore his Creator. But before the new Earth is established and in working order 'all hell will break loose'.

Thousands of people will drop in their tracks. America will not escape, as she must pay for her sins too. There shall be 'wailing and gnashing of teeth'. Most of this will be caused by the die-hards, those who cling to the old order of things. The young will take it in their stride as will those who have the vision of the new heaven and Earth in their hearts. The 'me and mine' complex will be destroyed. Those who cling to the old methods and beliefs will go down with the old order. Now is the uncovering period. All the deceit and trickery and selfishness of human kind will be aired, as it has been enacted through the ages. Be surprised at nothing, for *evil*, which is *live* spelled backward, must be uncovered to be destroyed. Within a few years the whole world will learn that a false economic system, invented and fostered by a few greed crazed lusters after gold has caused every war on the face of the globe. Now they will learn that breaking the laws of Mother Nature and Father Creator has made disease ridden bodies. Nothing has broken out in all its fury yet. This will come within the next decade (1955). After that mankind will be on the upward grade and the whole world will reflect it."

What people on Earth will survive to inherit the New Age? The world population will be reduced greatly. Where there are now thousands there will be tens. But it is not tragic if one loses his physical equipment on Earth. Certain souls have evolved to the place where the old Earth can no longer teach them anything, therefore, either they or the Earth must graduate to a higher level. Shortly, the entire Earth will be made new in the new vibratory rate and the advanced souls, or *The Remnant*, will inherit the kingdom of God on Earth. The other souls, who refused to give up the old order of things, will be taken out of flesh life and will be re-settled on other worlds that can give them the lessons they need. So only the good and beautiful is to come to all men; there is no retrogression, for all are advancing toward the Father.

The Holy Bible speaks of *The Remnant* many times, and *The Prophets* were those who led and guided "those who were to remain" in ages past.

"Lift up thy prayer for the remnant that are left." (II Kings 19:4).

"Except the Lord of hosts had left unto us a very small remnant, we should have been as Sodom, and we should have been like unto Gomorrah." (Isaiah 1:9).

"And it shall come to pass in that day, that the Lord shall set his hand again the second time to re-cover the remnant of his people, which shall be left." (Isaiah 11:11).

"... the remnant shall be very small and feeble." (Isaiah 16:14).

"And now for a little space grace hath been shewed from the Lord our God, to leave us a remnant to escape, and to give us a nail in his holy place, that our God may lighten our eyes, and give us a little reviving in our bondage." (Ezra 9:8).

"And the slain shall fall in the midst of you, and ye shall know that I am the Lord. Yet will I leave a remnant, that ye may have some that shall escape the sword among the nations, when ye shall be scattered through the countries." (Ezekiel 6:7-8).

"I will surely assemble, O Jacob, all of thee; I will surely gather the remnant of Israel; I will put them together as the sheep of Bozrah, as the flock in the midst of their fold: they shall make great noise by reason of the multitude of men." (Micah 2:12).

"And I will gather the remnant of my flock out of all countries whither I have driven them, and will bring them again to their folds; and they shall be fruitful and increase." (Jeremiah 23:3).

"Even so then at this present time also there is a remnant according to the election of grace." (Romans 11:5).

"And the same hour was there a great earthquake, and the tenth part of the city fell, and in the earthquake were slain of men seven thousand: and the remnant were affrighted, and gave glory to the God of heaven." (Revelation 11:13).

Even when a nation as a whole deserted the faith of their fathers in ancient times, there always remained a "remnant" whose faithfulness prevailed. The outstanding example of this is, of course, the "righteous remnant" who returned from the exile.

Space intelligences said that they were separating "black from white".

"And before him shall be gathered all nations: and he shall separate them one from another, as a shepherd divideth his sheep from the goats: And he shall set the sheep on his right hand, but the goats on the left. Then shall the King say unto them on his right hand, Come, ye blessed of my Father, inherit the kingdom prepared for you from the foundation of the world." (St. Matthew 25:32-34).

"For many are called, but few are chosen." (St. Matthew 22:14).

The Remnant constitutes the "sheep", the "white", the "wheat". For them the days will be shortened, but there shall be great tribulation on Earth, as it is written.

Only the "beginning of sorrows" is here now. Reports from Canada say that two very strange things are taking place there. The *gauges* on automobiles are going wild. When they are taken in for repairs to a garage nothing seems to be wrong with them. When they are back out on the highway they go "wild" once more.

The other happening is even stranger. Radios that are shut completely off have been turning themselves on for no apparent reason. This is the beginning of the "Great Telling" space friends have told about in the past.

Perhaps the rash of weird phone calls of late is also connected with this phenomena. The phone will ring, and when answered it is discovered that no one is on the line. The line is open, but no one speaks! Space visitors are checking "frequencies", pulling "tests" for the big event of speaking to the world through all devices capable of reception. On the day of the "Great Telling" millions of citizens of the civilized parts of the world will know beyond the shadow of a doubt the fact that space visitors are here and they will know why they are here.

Every week I receive several letters that tell of strange happenings. A lady in Kentucky wrote: "My phone rang; I answered it. There was absolute silence so I hung up. Ten minutes later the phone rang again. And once again I answered it. Silence. Ten minutes later the phone rang again. Silence. By this time I was getting angry, so I quietly but firmly said, 'I don't know who you are, nor why you are doing this, but please, please stop it. It is not pleasant to be annoyed in this manner. Please stop it.' I started to hang up when a very soft spoken voice in perfect English said, 'Please be calm, we are checking on those whose auras are the right color.' Since that most unusual phone call I have observed three Saucers."

Telephone engineers have told me that very strange things are happening to telephones since they have had many complaints from telephone users, especially in the mid-west. Television and radio engineers have experienced weird happenings while on duty. Tape recorded programs have been mysteriously erased or garbled and they have heard unknown code coming out of the air from apparently nowhere. These engineers are not given to vivid imaginations since their profession calls for men of a practical and methodical mind.

The following cases are excerpts from letters I have received:

A lady in London, England wrote: "Lately at night time I have been hearing strange notes and rhythms which have been quite outside ordinary wireless experience. I worked in wireless stations and know Morse code exceptionally well, but this is not any code we know; it is very different."

A lady in Cincinnati, Ohio, wrote: "One day in the latter part of May, 1954, I was awakened about three in the morning. I heard the sound of code in my room. It was similar to Morse code, pitched rather low, and seemed to be just in my room. I listened to it for about ten minutes and fell asleep with it still going. There was a sense of peace connected with it, and I felt there was nothing to fear. I knew it was strange for code to be heard without a receiver but somehow it didn't bother me. In June, I heard it again for a few minutes."

A housewife in Medford, Oregon wrote: "One night the strangest noise suddenly came over our radio which was off at the time. I asked my husband what it was. I wish now that I had turned the set on, because we may have heard voices, but the sound was so loud and I was so surprised I couldn't think of anything. The sound was similar to Morse code but had a musical note to it. Later we learned that two Saucers had been observed in the area at the same time we received the signals on our radio."

A woman in New Castle, Pennsylvania wrote: "Several times lately our television set has gone absolutely crazy. We heard strange code-like sounds and even voices. We called our neighbors but they were receiving nothing like that on their sets. We have a brand new GE model and it's in perfect condition—we know, because we've had it checked."

A lady in Los Angeles, *California* wrote: "My husband and I have an old television set in our den. This set has been out of order for weeks. On the night of August 31, 1954, I went to bed in the front bedroom about 12:30, my husband turned in shortly thereafter. About one in the morning he called me and asked if

I had turned on the TV set. I told him I hadn't turned it on, and besides, it wasn't working. He said the set was making a strange, buzzing sound, and he could see the tubes from the back of the set and they were all on, even the viewing tube which hasn't been working for weeks! My husband turned up the volume to see if he could hear anything and a beautiful voice came out strong and loud, saying: 'Strange waters shall gush forth out of the rocks.' My husband turned off the volume and I asked him what the man's voice was. He believed it was some minister talking. I asked him how the set got on, and why did it work at all. We checked it and found the set was only a little bit warm, so it wasn't on for long. Our television set had turned itself on some way! The next morning we checked the TV programs in the paper to see what had been on the channel the night before. We had been tuned to Channel 5-KTLA-TV. We learned that this channel is off the air entirely after 11:30 every night and the voice came on after one in the morning. It certainly was unusual for a TV set that is out of order to suddenly turn itself on, and produce a voice from a channel that has been off the air for over an hour and a half! The set is still in the den, and still doesn't work."

Recently four people tried to contact space visitors by telepathy in Los Angeles, California. They asked for a signal of some kind after they thought they were getting a reception. They wanted to know for sure whether it was really coming from space friends or if it was from their own minds. Suddenly a TV set that hadn't been on for over four hours started showing a "blip" similar to radar blips. This moved around on the TV screen. They pulled the plug out of the wall and moved the set into the middle of the room, but the blip still kept coming in! No power of any kind was being received by the set; as far as anyone in the room was concerned it was a dead set.

A lady in Ingleside, Illinois wrote: "During June, 1954, my TV set suddenly operated automatically. For some unexplained reason, a picture became visible, just as plain as could be, with the set switch off. However, there was only a picture, no sound. A picture of people remained clear and undistorted for about forty-five minutes. I switched the set off and on, but it had no effect other than to include sound. I called my next door neighbor to view this unusual happening, and he was equally startled. Later, my TV set operated normally."

The mystery of KLEE-TV hit the headlines in the Spring of 1954. At 3:30 p.m., British Summer Time, September 14, 1953, Charles W. Bratley, of London, picked up the call letters KLEE-TV on his television set. Later that month, and several times since, they have been seen by engineers at Atlantic Electronics, Ltd., Lancaster, England. The call letters KLEE-TV have not been transmitted since July, 1950, when the Houston, Texas station changed its letters to KPRC-TV. A check of the world's television stations confirms the fact that there is not now and never has been another KLEE-TV. Paul Huhndorff, chief engineer of KPRC-TV, to whom the Britishers sent their report, has no explanation. He says that members of the old *KLEE-TV* staff have identified the pictures of the signals as looking like the standard call-letter slide they used. Engineer Huhndorff offered three theories. The first two he discounts as being nearly impossible. The third is that some intelligence in outer space has received the signal and has transmitted it in the hope of communicating with the planet Earth.

Everyone remembers the *strange* case of the face on the TV-screen, and the same phenomenon happened again on September 12, 1954 in Indianapolis, India. John and Virginia Mackey said the image appeared to be that of George R. Shots, Mrs. Mackey's grandfather who died April 28, 1954 at the age of seventy-four. Mrs. Mackey said she first saw the face while watching a network show. When the image became more intense, whether the set was tuned to an Indianapolis station or to a blank channel, police were called. A parade of officers saw the face for themselves. Mrs. Marie Johnson, Mrs. Mackey's mother, also identified the face as that of her father, as did a number of other relatives.

There have been countless reports of strange things happening to anything that will act as a receiver. On October 3, 1952, Van Tassel at Giant Rock, California, received the following: "I greet you in love and peace. I am Ashtar. Those individual beings from Schare now on your planet are being instructed to transmit certain carrier frequencies that will cause a variety of conditions to be apparent in your many types of electronic receivers."

Besides the above happenings, many strange things have been falling from the sky. Charles Fort world be in his glory if he were alive today! Ashes come from the sky; ice bombs; large chunks of foul-smelling jelly; molten metal; white, filmy substance like cotton candy; and fragments of this and that. Added to this is the great mystery of the pockmarked wind-shields. Reports on the latter have come in from Canada, England, France, and from many parts of the United States. Tar-like substance, or ash-like material, has been found on cars and some of it is magnetic. On the evening of April 22, 1954, radio station WIND in Chicago reported that a strange blue mist had settled on a car, and while its occupants watched intently, the glass in the automobile shattered to pieces. Other witnesses said a blue dust sediment imbedded in their glass after shattering took place. In England, observers saw weird, yellow flames strike their windshields. This is one of the phenomena of the New Age; more will be seen in the future and the "glass" sickness will spread to objects made of metal. What would happen to civilization if steel was so affected? The answer is obvious.

These new vibrations are not only changing things in the physical world, but they are responsible for the change in man's thinking—and they will change him spiritually, as well.

Many years ago a woman in Santa Fe, New Mexico, had an unusual experience where she saw seven beings sitting in council around a table. These beings said: "We shall communicate with your planet Earth soon. There are those spiritually minded enough to hear our communications and listen." This sounds like the Council of the Seven Lights mentioned by Van Tassel, or the Council-Circle 7 mentioned in *The Saucers Speak!*

Many more startling discoveries will be announced in the near future. A leading aviation company is reliably reported to be conducting experiments in interplanetary radio communication at the present time, and the government continues its investigation through Project NQ-707. We have experienced some mighty peculiar things in the past few years and in the months ahead these things will become even more peculiar!

Aquarius has its ominous side too, for astrologers equate it with cold, rainstorms, floods, and dark. We know that for some time the world has been experiencing a fantastic number of disasters from tidal waves to dust storms. But these catastrophic events have been prophesied for centuries and the New Age under the dominant influence of Uranus will first see all old conditions upset, for Uranus is the disrupter or smasher. What we are prone to call death and destruction is usually the prelude to something better and finer—what is the death of the old year, but the birth of the new one?

We would expect space visitation in the new Air Age. Man on Earth will sail through interstellar space himself in the new world of the future. He will know Truth, for the Light of Aquarius will not permit falsity to exist in any form.

When Ganymedes (Aquarius) is raised to heaven (or above the horizon of the North Pole) Virgo or Astraea, who is Lucifer, descends head downward below the horizon of the South Pole, or the pit; which pit, or the pole, is also the Great Dragon or the Flood. From this we can see that in the New Age (Aquarius) all falsity and evil (Lucifer) will be done away with on Earth and submerged forever (the pit).

There is a striking similarity between the pure water rushing forth from the jar of Aquarius and the words of St. John in Revelation: "He shewed me a pure river of water of life, clear as crystal, proceeding out of the throne of God and of the Lamb." And remember the words spoken over the TV set that wasn't supposed to work: "Strange waters shall gush forth out of the rocks."

Set your heart upon God and not upon things, upon Cause and not upon manifestation, upon Principle and not upon form. As the old landmarks disappear one by one beneath the rising tide of the new life, go boldly on, knowing that the best is yet to be, and that "Eye hath not seen, nor ear heard, neither hath it entered into the heart of man that things that God hath prepared for them that love Him. Greet the unknown with a cheer".

Remember the following quotations from *The Saucers Speak!*

"By your year of 1956 there must be a new Saras."

"Show us when you are ready to venture."

"Watch all nature for signs of catastrophe. These signs, such as tornados, earthquakes, floods, and so on will come to Saras soon and will get worse as time goes on."

"Some will not see it, except from elsewhere—from outside."

"More detonations soon, more disasters on Saras."

"The cosmic dust cloud will come. And it will darken the Sun and Moon. Strange things will happen in your world. Great meteors shall be seen in the skies."

"Never fear for the aged, they can help again when they are brought to life."

In Iowa, a research group received the following by radiotelegraphy: "We find few now ready."

Many of the above statements have come to pass already, and others will shortly come to pass. *The Remnant* will be small, for "few are now ready". Show the space visitors if you are "ready to venture"; if you belong to those who shall remain, you will see chaos from "elsewhere—from outside."

The following message was received by Van Tassel:

"The Bible again explains to Earth people our purpose here. In St. Matthew 24:39-42, it reads: 'And knew not until the flood came, and took them all away; so shall also the coming of the Son of man be. Then shall two be in the field; the one shall be taken, and the other left. Watch therefore: for ye know not what hour your Lord doth come.' We have registered in our records the names and locations of those who have lived with right intent. These are the ones who shall be taken up in our ships while the Earth goes through cataclysmic upheavals. Those who have contributed to and lived by destruction shall be left to the agonies of the effects they have helped to cause."

Later, *The Remnant*, will be returned to the surface of Earth where they will be the new race in a new world.

In Colville, Washington, an elderly lady received the following:

"By a seeming miracle shall men's eyes be opened to the wonders of a world now unperceived by them. Not a miracle but a perfectly natural action of an ever existent law will bring this phenomenon to pass. As hath been told thee aforetimes, there be a change rapidly metamorphosing much of the material world through the introduction of Cosmic Energy into the very atomic structure of all material objects. When ye consider all material forms (whether animate or what ye do term inanimate) as the result of a certain specified rate of vibratory action, it will be the easier for thee to comprehend the action of a vastly accelerated rate of vibration upon all manner of objective manifestations. At the appointed time, this influx of Cosmic Energy, vibrating at an inconceivably increased speed, will cause changes marvelous to behold. Lo, the wonders of the now invisible realms of enchanting beauty will be revealed to Man, if so be he hath previously attuned himself to his own highest concept of beauty. Of material beauty there shall be no end, but far greater than any mere physical demonstration shall be the revelation of that spiritual fullness of life which alone can satisfy Man's inmost yearning for true and lasting happiness."

The Cosmic Energy now bombarding the Earth and her inhabitants will actually change man's thinking. Recent findings by Dr. Seymour Kety and his associates at the National Institute of Mental and Nervous Diseases indicate that the physical brain is not a "thinking" machine, but at best can be compared to a radio set! Dr. Kety's conclusions are based on studies of blood circulation through the brain. These studies carried out at the Institute showed the following results:

(1) The average-size human brain requires about three-fourths of a quart of blood a minute; (2) It consumes about an ounce and a half of oxygen, brought to it by the red blood cells; (3) It uses only about a teaspoonful of sugar, the "fuel" of the body, per hour. The most surprising discovery in Dr. Kety's experiments is that these three requirements are the same, regardless of what the brain is doing. These findings are somewhat disturbing to various theories expounded in the past, one of which stated that intelligence varied with the richness of the brain's blood supply. The other theory propounded before the National Academy of Sciences, was that thinking required a definite amount of "fuel".

Therefore, if man's brain is nothing but a receiving and transmitting instrument similar to a radio set, he must be able to receive and interpret the "music of the spheres" or the Great Cosmic Intelligence that forever is permeating all space; man merely must "tune in" to it. Those who refuse to receive the new vibrations mentally, will lose their physical equipment on Earth and thereby give up their "radio sets" that will not accept the new lessons. They will go elsewhere and acquire new "sets" that will allow them to learn and progress as they must.

Other parts of the human body are affected by the new vibrations also. The pineal gland and the solar plexus becomes radioactive under the influence of the cosmic rays. The body is in continual touch with the whole existence. The skin is no border of the body as we sometimes imagine; there is continuous mutual meeting and mingling of the single human body and the whole of the cosmos which also includes other human bodies. In the human body there are said to be six-hundred million psychic centers. By psychic is meant the extensional apertures. Many more centers exist, of course, in the known cosmos. As the single human being comes in contact with the great influx of Cosmic Energy, he will realize that he possesses some very strange abilities and powers. The rays will actually stimulate the pineal gland and the third eye of the human will be opened once again.

Those individuals who refuse to accept the higher vibrations mentally, allowing for great spiritual growth and advancement, will experience a definite physiological reaction. In the study of the electrochemistry of the blood, the answer to what will take place is found.

The blood stream of man is composed of the serum and the cellular constituents, plus colloids. The countless millions of cells in the circulating blood must maintain their ability to remain free of all other elements in the stream. Research is revealing the importance of electro-chemistry. All blood cells carry a charge, the charge is of the same de-nomination. Like charges repel, and so the cells as well as the colloids repel each other resulting in the *existence* of electrical cushions capable of preventing the cells from touching one another. When thrombosis (clotting) occurs, it is precipitated by the discharge of cell or colloid charges which allows for the agglutination or formation of the clots.

Each human blood cell is surrounded by a Resonating Electro-Magnetic Field; if a person refuses to accept the new Universal lessons presented to him for his use, he sets up an action within his body that causes the RMF to collapse. Clotting occurs and he is said to have died of a "heart attack". The only reason heart attacks are on the increase is because of the new vibrations and man's inability to cope with them, accept them, and understand them. Therefore, no "god of wrath" destroys man; man eliminates himself by his thoughts!

What are some of the promises of the New World and its Remnant?

"Then cometh the end (of the Age), when he shall have delivered up the kingdom to God, even the Father; when he shall have put down all rule and all authority and power." (I Corinthians 15:24).

There shall be no governments or dictatorships or monarchies as such in the New Age; and death will be no more.

"The last enemy that shall be destroyed is death." (I Corinthians 15:26).

"And God shall wipe away all tears from their eyes; and there shall be no more death, neither sorrow, nor crying, neither shall there be any more pain: for the former things are passed away. Behold, I make all things new." (Revelation 21:4-5).

"That in the dispensation of the fullness of times he might gather together in one all things in Christ, both which are in heaven, and which are on earth; even in him: In whom also we have obtained an inheritance." (Ephesians 1:10-11).

"There is neither Jew nor Greek, there is neither bond nor free, there is neither male nor female: for ye are all one in Christ Jesus." (Galatians 3:28).

"Ye are of God, little children, and have overcome them: because greater is he that is in you, than he that is in the world." (I John 4:4).

The Remnant can truly say: "Behold, what manner of love the Father hath bestowed upon us, that we should be called the sons of God: therefore the world knoweth us not, because it knew him not. Beloved, now are we the sons of God, and it cloth not yet appear what we shall be: but we know that, when he shall appear, we shall be like him; for we shall see him as he is. And every man that hath this hope in him purifieth himself, even as he is pure." (I John 3:1-3).

"And many of them that sleep in the dust of the earth shall awake, some to everlasting life, and some to shame and everlasting contempt." (Daniel (12.2). *The Remnant* shall know "everlasting life", but *The Outcasts* shall not exist in the New World.

In Daniel 12:3, we read:

"And they that be wise (teachers) shall shine as the brightness of the firmament; and they that turn many to righteousness as the stars for ever and ever." These are *The Remnant!*

EPILOGUE

The book you have just read and the thoughts contained therein are but a "pale shadow" of things to come. Time is running out, but there will be no "end", there will only be a "beginning". Terrestrial Man seems incapable at this moment of making "One World", but he will soon face the more profound challenge to create "One City of the Universe".

Man will go on into ever expanding *grandeur*, for even when the whole celestial Universe has been mapped, studied and charted, there will be Universes beyond to tempt human imagination.

In all great adventures of ideas the only prayer which we can address to God is: "Grant us patience." And, "Seek ye the Lord while he may be found, call ye upon him while he is near." (Isaiah 55:6).

"So shall my word be that goeth forth out of my mouth: it shall not return unto me void, but it shall accomplish that which I please, and it shall prosper in the thing whereto I sent it. For ye shall go out with joy, and led forth with peace: the mountains and the hills shall break forth before you into singing, and all the trees of the field shall clap their hands." (Isaiah 55:11-12).

Remember the words of the Master in St. Mark 13:37: "And what I say unto you I say unto all, *Watch!*"

AIN SOPH AUR

BIBLIOGRAPHY

The following works are recommended to those interested in the Saucer phenomena for they are considered authentic and contain excellent source material.

Arnold, Kenneth and Palmer, Ray, *The Coming Of The Saucers*, Amherst, Wisconsin, 1952.

Bethurum, Truman, *Aboard A Flying Saucer*, Los Angeles, Calif., 1954.

Fry, Daniel W., *The White Sands Incident*, Los Angeles, Calif., 1954.

Heard, Gerald, *Is Another World Watching?* New York, N. Y., 1951.

Keyhoe, Maj. Donald E., *The Flying Saucers Are Real*, New York, N. Y., 1950.

Keyhoe, Maj. Donald E., *Flying Saucers From Outer Space*, New York, N. Y., 1953.

Layne, Meade, *The Ether Ship Mystery And Its Solution*, San Diego, Calif.

Layne, Meade, *The Coming of The Guardians*, San Diego, Calif., 1954.

Leslie, Desmond and Adamski, George, *Flying Saucers Have Landed*, London, England, 1953.

Pelly, W. D., *Star Guests*, Noblesville, Indiana, 1950.

Van Tassel, George W., *I Rode A Flying Saucer*, Los Angeles, Calif., 1952.

Wilkins, Harold T., *Flying Saucers On The Attack*, New York, N. Y., 1954.

Williamson, George H. Bailey, Alfred C., *The Saucers Speak!* Los Angeles, Calif., 1954.

306 Morse code at night in bedroom.
309 The QUARK ALLIANCE?
313:1 Cosmic rays cause the body to become
    radioactive
* Invisible suns 54:4 op TRJN HRS!

31:1 Des/Les...Orthodox Science, Orthodox Theology
32:2 The [pupa] of science.
35:2 Destruction of microcosmic worlds by atomic
    explosions
35:4 ...landing their craft on a pin head
48:3 <u>The Astronomer Herschels cool inhabited sun</u> ? ✱
49:1   "   "   "   ↓   "   "
51:3 Hanging prominences which appear from nowhere
52:4 Pitch black in outer space
56:4 (Saucers can't travel in a STATIC field)
57T BUT THOUGHT IS A STATIC !?
57:2 Saucers torn apart by their own RMF field
    by poor construction?
58 STATIC Δ ELECTRONIC DEMONS LRH?
  " MIND is the only intelligence.
97:1 OUTLINE OF A <u>FISH</u>
142:2 To yoke heads of creatures to make them
    work together
161 THE COSMIC UTILITY AND GALACTIC COUNCIL
    WORKERS.
161-62 PARENTS OF THEIR OWN CHOICE
166:1 Radio Reception by INDUCTION / VOICE COIL
    INDUCTION — Radio turned off — YELLOW BRICK
    ROAD ? (262B) SHORTWAVE
215:2 A CRYSTAL BEING / 221 Sentient Fireball
216 Why then don't we see more green fireballs
    after Chernobyl?
226:1 Copper as precious as gold
231:3 THE WORLD GETTING WARMER (1953)
249:2 WORLD HUMUS SHRINKING BECAUSE OF
    2000 yr cycles of cosmic eruptions
  " 3 DISAPPEARANCE OF SOIL BACTERIA CAUSING THIS
  " 4 INFO ON HUMUS DESTRUCTION TOP SECRET !
250:1 Earth becoming sterile due to cosmic
    bombardment?
251:5 The land of the new age is in the west
253-4 Two more moons circling earth !?
    artificial objects
254 Herschel's lights on moon !
260T The Wanderers are the Illuminatis !
262 The Mission not UFOs (ET 101)!
265 The shameful son who sleepeth in harvest
264:2 ...humanity now almost in process of
    unconscious <u>segregation</u>
288 Man is quarantined here until....
289:1 The Black Magicians are back !
303 EVIL backwards = LIVE
  " Those who do not make it will be
    asked to leave
                                    ET 101 !

Lightning Source UK Ltd.
Milton Keynes UK

172558UK00001B/11/P

9 781437 520248

WORD chet III (RMF) = Resonant Magnetic Field
315 (The Lyall Watson weido page) !